To Jean,

In appreciation of her interest and support, and in fond memory of good western terms together.

Don D. Walker

Clio's Cowboys

CLIO'S COWBOYS

Studies in the Historiography of the Cattle Trade

by
DON D. WALKER

UNIVERSITY OF NEBRASKA PRESS
Lincoln and London

Library of Congress Cataloging in Publication Data

Walker, Don D   1917–
  Clio's cowboys.

  Includes bibliographical references and index.
  1. Cowboys—The West—Historiography —Addresses, essays, lectures. 2. Cattle trade—The West—Historiography —Addresses, essays, lectures. 3. Ranch life—The West—Historiography —Addresses, essays, lectures. 4. The West—Historiography —Addresses, essays, lectures. 5. Cowboys—The West—History —Addresses, essays, lectures. 6. Cattle trade—The West—History —Addresses, essays, lectures. 7. Ranch life—The West—History —Addresses, essays, lectures. I. Title.
F596.W26   978   80–24725
ISBN 0–8032–4713–3

To Marjorie

Contents

Foreword

WITH so many seemingly important aspects of history to write about, why choose the historiography of cows, cowboys, and cattlemen? The answer must be in part autobiographical. The scholar starts with a commitment to his own world, and my world was a late small piece of that great empire called the cattle kingdom. Boyhood memories became warmly attached to cows and stockmen. I can still feel the soreness after riding all day *behind* the saddle of a maternal uncle while he looked for his forest-grazing Herefords. I can see the hundreds of whitefaces nuzzling the hay and beet pulp in my father's feedyard. And I can see and taste the treasure chest of golden oranges which my father brought home after taking those cattle to a California market.

From cows to books about cows was as natural as moving from girls to love stories. Before I became "sophisticated" and acquired "high taste," I read *The Lone Cowboy* and *Chip of the Flying U*. And long before the professional years began, I was gathering a modest, shirt-tail library of cow books. Philip Ashton Rollins once told a bookseller that he wanted "every damn book that says cow in it." My own collecting was necessarily less inclusive but nevertheless earnest. From reading to writing was also natural. After the first inspired efforts at being a Hemingway, an Eliot, or a Joyce, I reined myself in and began to write fiction and history within my own true range. Thus the presence of cows and cowboys.

However, something further happened as the years and the thoughts accumulated. Distances grew; perspectives altered. The cow as a fascinating object remained—one could dig back and feel the emotional link—but she became also something to think about, a piece of a many-detailed, many-faceted universe of things and ideas that needed to be fitted together in meaning. Thus one became philosophical even about cows. Thus one became interested not only in the history of the cattle trade, but also in the history of the history of the cattle trade.

A number of the following studies have had earlier publication in somewhat different versions: "Prose and Poetry of the Cattle Industry: Fact and Image as the Centuries Changed" as "The Prose and Poetry of the Cattle Industry, 1895–1905," in *Pacific Historical Review* 45 (1976): 379–97; "Freedom and Individualism on the Range: Ideological Images of the Cowboy and Cattleman" as "Freedom and Individualism: The Historian's Conception of the Cowboy and the Cattleman," in *"Soul-Butter and Hog Wash" and Other Essays on the American West* (Provo: Charles Redd Monographs in Western History, 1978), pp. 69–81; "Theory of the Cowboy Novel: Some Ranchhouse Meditations on Its History and Prospects" as "Criticism of the Cowboy Novel: Retrospect and Reflections," in *Western American Literature* 11 (1977): 275–96; and "The Fence Line between Cowboy History and Cowboy Fiction: Frontier in Dispute or Meeting Ground of Human Understanding?" as "On the Supposed Frontier between History and Fiction," in *Crossing Frontiers,* edited by Dick Harrison (Edmonton: University of Alberta Press, 1978), pp. 11–29. My thanks to the editors of these journals and books for their first confidence in accepting these studies and now for their kind permission for a further publication.

To many good friends and helpers I owe a debt of lasting gratitude: particularly among these the cowboys and cattlemen I have known and ridden with, the librarians who have found in their own kind of thickets the sometimes unbranded research materials, and the teachers and scholars who have shown me the way the mind and the pen should work. Finally, my appreciation to Marjorie, who has ridden with me the whole way, through the dust and golden grass and heady summits of a long and exciting venture. And to Mr. Tubby, who always followed faithfully.

Introduction

WHEN the first domestic cow walked into the American West we perhaps do not know with historical exactness, but we can suppose that she probably walked in one of the herds of Father Eusebio Francisco Kino in the last years of the seventeenth century. When the first historian with a special interest in cows rode into the American West, we perhaps do not know with any greater certainty, but we can again mark the important beginning. We can say that, whatever the other small stirrings of historical interest, Joseph Geitling McCoy rode point. His book, *Historic Sketches of the Cattle Trade of the West and Southwest,* called by J. Frank Dobie "the granddaddy of all range histories," will thus serve to mark the beginning in the West of a historiography of the cattle trade.

From the publication of McCoy's work in 1874 to the present, a seemingly endless string of memoirs, biographies, and histories has moved from the presses to the library shelves. Ramon Adams's *The Rampaging Herd: A Bibliography of Books and Pamphlets on Men and Events in the Cattle Industry* lists more than 2,600 items, and many more have appeared since that bibliography was first published in 1959. Following *Historic Sketches* with almost scriptural importance came the ranching sketches of Theodore Roosevelt, the novels of Owen Wister and Andy Adams, the National Live Stock Association's *Prose and Poetry of the Live Stock Industry,* and in a later decade the classic studies of Edward Everett Dale, Ernest Osgood, Louis Pelzer, and Walter Prescott Webb. Yet while the history of cows has thus seemed to flourish for more than a century, the history of cow history has been neglected. Except for book reviews, bibliographical notes, brief critical summaries of sources, and occasional biographical tributes to the trail bosses of the profession, there has been little critical study of the historiography of ranch and range. Yet the craft of history, even as it is applied to cows, cowboys, and cattlemen, needs an account of and accounting to itself.

Historiographical criticism involves many sorts of problems, but for purposes of introductory discussion we can separate them into two general kinds: those which are narrowly historiographical in the sense that they are limited to questions of kinds and quality of evidence and to questions of inferences and conclusions possible from this evidence; and those which might be called literary (or even esthetic) since they involve matters of structure and style as evidence takes on meaning and meaning is embodied in imaginative forms.[1] Such separation is of course arbitrary; it is a pragmatic tactic for dealing with different aspects of a complex matter. Ultimately, as these studies will suggest, all critical concerns are joined in a sense of the close relationship, if not unity, of history and literature. If the first kind of problem seems scientific and the second artistic, we again must be pragmatically cautious. For ultimately no absolute distinctions between history as science and history as art seem possible. At least such distinctions are not the high goal of these studies.

A criticism concerned with the first kind of problem is likely to be criticism in the narrower sense of that term; that is, it is likely to be judgmental. Its controlling question might well be: how good is this piece of history? The answer will usually be determined by assessing the completeness of the evidence, the quality of the evidence, the interpretation of the evidence, and the historian's responsibility to the evidence, that is, the extent to which the historical conclusions have been persuasively but empirically reached rather than subjectively imposed.

A survey of cattle trade historiography in this critical mode might well assert that Ralph P. Bieber's facts are more factual than were Joseph G. McCoy's facts. The thorough use of sources, the corroboration by multiple sources, the cautious pull of inference are convincing. Fact is separated from mere opinion. This survey might also assert that Andy Adams's account, in *The Log of a Cowboy,* of pulling steers from a bog is as historically truthful as any other account. Here the proof is not in the sources. One is persuaded instead by the internal evidence that Adams himself was an eyewitness who remembered honestly and matter-of-factly. And this survey might well further conclude that Robert R. Dykstra's version of Dodge City is more historically valid than was Stanley Vestal's. In this instance the conclusion is backed by the thoroughness of documented evidence and what might be called the professionalism of the historian. While obviously focused by the mind of a particular historical scholar, the version is nevertheless more objective, less personal in style and thesis.

A criticism concerned with the second kind of problem is less concerned with judging specific historical texts, although obviously it must use such texts, than with critically exploring the whole literary and philosophical methodology by which the historical facts are selected and composed into the narrative and expository structures of history. It does not begin with a conviction that this text is good history or that text is bad history, but with an intellectual curiosity about the nature of history itself. It means asking new questions; it means asking old questions again, as a new present and a different gathering of materials shift the ground of our accustomed certainties. Such critical examination and reexamination is, of course, vital to any scholarly discipline that tries to escape the dead hand of tradition and the sterile comforts of official forms and conventions.

The essays that follow are generally in this second mode of criticism. They are concerned primarily with the philosophical nature and literary methodology of cattle trade historiography, not with the validity of specific historical conclusions. At the points where such validity seems at issue, the concern is first of all with the ideological and rhetorical elements which have entered, perhaps without the historian's full awareness, into historical argument. For example, it can be suggested that Edward Everett Dale, perhaps the dean of twentieth-century cattle trade historians, whatever his professional interest in "the real conditions of ranch life" and true conceptions of the range cattle industry, was at heart a romantic historian. If his romantic sensibility and values did not always openly show as they did in Francis Parkman and even in the essays of his teacher, Frederick Jackson Turner, they nevertheless shaped and toned his range histories in important ways. But this is not to say that as a consequence Dale was a lesser historian. It is simply to take into account some of the important elements active in what I believe should be called the creative process of historiography. We are trying to understand history and historians, not make corrections of historical fact.

These studies proceed from a number of important assumptions, all of which I trust are openly evident in the studies themselves. However, two of them should perhaps be introduced in some explicit fullness if the reader is to venture into the essays, as the writer hopes, with at most a small burden of doubts and uncertainties.

First, the following studies assume that the historiography of the cattle trade is not a special kind of historiography, in spite of the fact that it may seem to deal exclusively with such special subjects as cows, cowboys, and cattlemen. It may indeed have its special problems, for example, a scarcity of primary sources, a thinness of social texture in which human relationships can be traced, a strong ideological pressure toward the romantic and the mythic; but at the point of philosophy and method it nevertheless shares the concerns common to all historiography. This means that the historiography of the cattle trade must be considered within the context of western historiography, which in turn must be considered within the context of American historiography. This means indeed that ultimately there are no local, regional, or national boundaries to historical thought and method. It means, to dramatize the point, that ideally each cow and cowboy should be viewed as the concrete center of a whole historical universe. Practically, of course, this may be impossible; the hard particular facts, like a cow chip or a rusty spur, may not be luminous with larger meanings. Nevertheless, one hopes that the historian and the historiographical critic will bring to the task of understanding the hard and perhaps dull material a mind—one is tempted to say a vision—with this range of awareness.

It becomes necessary to emphasize—indeed dramatize—this point because cattle trade historiography has seemed in many, if not most, instances intellectually ingenuous and unphilosophical. It has seemed to go on for the most part rounding up cow facts, untroubled by the intellectual crises of our time. Yet these crises, though thought up in eastern and European universities, disturb the scholarly calm across the grasslands. As long as the historian seems to proceed on the assumption that history results when each cow is located in past time and space, as long as he seems to write history without consciously reexamining and reaffirming this assumption, we have reason to ask for critical studies. Even naïve realism need not be used naïvely.

But if it seems appropriate to call for philosophical consideration of cattle trade history, it also seems appropriate to ask for a pragmatic caution about the metaphysical and epistemological bogs into which the high-minded historian may ride. It is not that cows, cowboys, and cattlemen are trivial, fragile, or unresponsive as historical objects—they need and will bear the same intensive understanding that we may traditionally give to kings, mistresses, and wine lists—it is simply that historiography is after all a practical craft, to be appreciated as it manages to get on with its story, not as it provides absolute answers to eternal questions. Philosophers of history must deal with such ultimate questions as the reality of past time and the possibility of objective knowledge, but historians—even when they are philosophical—must make do with tentative and partial answers.

Second, the following studies assume that the literary problems of historiography are as important and as difficult as the preliminary problems of sources and evidence. They assume that while an approach to the latter problems can perhaps be roughly modeled on the methods of inductive science, the approach to literary problems cannot. Whatever the historical evidence—and it will be argued in some of these studies that even the most rigorously factual evidence may not be luminous with historical meaning unless validated by empathetic understanding as well as by inductive logic—an imagination arranges as well as represents this evidence, thus giving form to the verbal structure called a work of history.

One immediate consequence of this assumption is to bring the literary genres in comparative relationship to history. Whatever the ultimate differences between the imaginations of the historian and the novelist, as we see these imaginations functioning in history and fiction, there are nevertheless important similarities, if not identities. Thus to insist, as many western historians have traditionally insisted, on a radical distinction between history and fiction is to reduce our sense of the true complexity of both history and fiction. It is to blind ourselves to legitimate and enriching possiblities in forms. And the literary problems of historiography are, of course, not solved by the act of dissociating them from imaginative literature.

The traditional position of many historians and historically oriented literary critics has been one of insisting, to put the distinction in other terms, on a separation of truth (history) from falsehood (fiction). That which purports to be history and bears the conventional signs of authenticity is regarded as true. These signs include such matters as accuracy of detail (the right range plants on subregional ranges, the right brand of coffee beans on the chuck wagon, etc.), a seeming closeness by way of eyewitness testimony, and a convincing western empathy revealed in diction, tone, and values. That which purports to be fiction but neverthe-less bears the same signs of authenticity is regarded as historical and therefore true.

The result is that history is sometimes reduced to a random or personal configuration of so-called facts and that little if any attention is given to the shaping, perhaps distorting effects of style and rhetoric. A case in point is the traditional assessment of Sam P. Ridings's *The Chisholm Trail: A History of the World's Greatest Cattle Trail, Together with a Description of the Persons, A Narrative of the Events, and Reminiscences Associated with the Same.* J. Frank Dobie called it "a noble book, rich in anecdote and character."[2] Ramon Adams included it without critical comment in *The Rampaging Herd,* but in *Burs under the Saddle: A Second Look at Books and Histories of the West* he pointed to a small cluster of errors, for example, the use of legend instead of fact when dealing with Billy the Kid and the frequent misspelling of proper names, for in-stance, *John* G. McCoy for *Joseph* G. McCoy.[3] Recently William S. Reese has called Ridings's history "the best book on the Chisholm Trail."[4]

What exactly in Ridings's book warranted Dobie's adjective *noble* is not clear. One supposes that the book has its share of vitality, that feature being for Dobie "the primary requisite of all prose writing." One supposes further that the book meets Dobie's other criteria: "readability, fidelity to range life and historical information."[5] But what can the student of historiography make of these criteria and the judgments that supposedly follow from

them? Every historian, one supposes, hopes to write prose that is
quick if not pulsing with vitality. That alone may make him
readable. But he also aspires to be faithful to his subject and thus
to give truthful information about it. But here his real difficulties
begin. It is obviously not enough to pledge with Stetson over the
heart to be vital, faithful, and factual. For to be factual may
diminish one's stylistic vitality, or at least seem to, and to be vital,
unless the vitality grows from roots in the historical material itself,
may be to impose a personal excitement and energy disturbing to
objective faithfulness and fact. The ranching prose of Theodore
Roosevelt, for example, has a distinct vitality; however this vitality
is more often a personal exuberance than a condition of fact.

   The Chisholm Trail continues to be a useful case in point.
Perhaps implicit in Adams's brief critical notes is the notion that
Ridings's historiographical weaknesses could have been re-
medied by getting the true facts on Billy the Kid and by spelling
some important names correctly. Or if this seems to trivialize
Adams's concern, that the overall factualness of Ridings's book is
the central, if not exclusive issue. However, a reading of the book
reveals other personal features of style and idea which, however
vital they may be, are not clearly compatible with a fidelity to the
historical world as object. There is, for example, a strong streak of
Texas chauvinism; Texas is "one of the greatest, if not the
greatest State, of the Union of States," with a beauty "unsurpassed"
and with cattle in the old days with horns "so large that in this day
they are beyond conception." There is, for example, a tendency to
indulge in historical elegy, to linger nostalgically over "the scenes
of childhood in the west" that "will never be seen again." And
there is at the point of the Indians a use of the quaint historical
drama of a weaker race "being crowded out by force and by the
intrusion of a superior race. Such has been the course of the
world, both before and since we have had recorded history."

   The literary result of a radical separation of history and ?
fiction has been not only a simplistic notion of history but also a
naïve conception of fiction. From one critical position the separation is perhaps at most academic. If the critic works with texts like
Edward Dorn's *Gunslinger* or Michael Ondaatje's *The Collected
Works of Billy the Kid,* he starts with the assumption that whatever
his writer's concern with time, the writer's base of reality is as far

removed from history as is the Garden of Eden. But literary texts from *The Virginian* and *The Log of a Cowboy* to the fiction of Eugene Manlove Rhodes and A. B. Guthrie make up a different kind of roundup. Indeed, one might even call it a mixed herd, knowing that it is not always easy to cut it into appropriate bunches, say, fictionalized history, historical fiction, or pure fiction using history. Yet whatever the varietal differences, the books in this roundup share a sense of relationship to history.

For the historian or the historically oriented literary critic, the classic maverick has been and remains *The Virginian*. Recently published or republished comments illustrate the critical result of dealing with a novel without apparently taking into account its special nature as novel. Dobie observed of Wister's novel that the hero is a cowboy without cows, that he does not even smell of cows. Nevertheless, Dobie acknowledged, the work does "authentically" realize "the code of the range" and does make "absorbing reading."[6] Reese comments: "Whether totally accurate or not, it is absorbing reading."[7]

These are, to say the least, curious observations, particularly when one remembers that they are after all directed toward a novel. *Authentically* and *totally accurate* are a historian's terms; they have little if any value in the vocabulary of literary criticism. Obviously *The Virginian* must have truth in it if it is to merit our praise, but being truthful in a novel is not the same thing as being authentic and accurate. As readers we believe in Wister's hero not because he associates with cows and therefore smells of them, not because what he does exactly matches what someone has done in history, but because he becomes for us an imaginatively realized person. One supposes that the reader is absorbed in Wister's story because he (the reader) believes in the imagined persons and experiences the novelist is delineating.

One can suggest further that we are persuaded of the truth of J. Evetts Haley's *Charles Goodnight*, indeed are absorbed in the reading of it, not just because it is accurate in the sense that its information can be historically documented, but also because the biographer has imagined his subject in a way not unlike the way of the novelist.

These introductory critical observations are of course offered not to provide exhaustive and final answers to questions, but roughly to lay out the trail to be followed, to sketch some boundaries, and to establish, as already indicated, some guiding assumptions. Adapting an appropriate metaphor, the introduction must be that part of a book which serves as point. A sense of completion, of ultimate clarification (if the long trail takes us there), must await the passing of chapters in their time and course.

So much, one might say, for introduction. We are to move in a certain direction, and all will become clear at the end. What is conclusion will appear as conclusion. What the book proves, if it proves anything, will be proved when the final period has been struck.

Unfortunately a rhetorical structure is rarely so rightly designed. What is conclusion is rarely that which becomes clear at the end. And that which is emergent, that which the argument presumably induces, has usually been pointing the point all along.

Thus one rightly makes explicit that which is neither assumption nor conclusion in a strictly logical sense. Perhaps we should call this habit of mind or philosophical style, if the latter is not too pretentious, the writer's way of seeing and feeling which gives him a predilection to tones, themes, and values not because these are overtly central to the book's substance and argument but because the writer, out of his own set of intellectual circumstances, has come to think this way.

Two convictions in particular need mention here, for both work their way into the various discussions to follow. Neither is, I believe, merely idiosyncratic; neither is, I believe, incompatible with scholarly discourse. To admit them is to betray no higher degree of subjectivity. And to recognize them may help the reader to find that common context of thought and feeling which the writer hopes to share with him.

The first of these convictions is that abstractions, while necessary to metaphysics, theology, and the sciences generally, tend to be death to history, literature, and the criticism which deals with them. But obviously this radical "abstraction" at once needs qualification and explanation. No generalized discussion can proceed without the help of focusing and organizing ideas. The raw discrete data in any field cannot make sense unless strung together, to use William James's phrase, on some general principle. Indeed meaningful relationships among particulars will not become apparent unless they are approached by means of tentative abstractions, finders Chauncey Wright called them. But to say that abstractions thus have pragmatic usefulness, indeed necessity, is quite different from supposing that abstractions have a kind of final meaning and value in themselves. The abstractions are a means of dealing with the concreteness of the world, but it is that concreteness which constitutes the primary reality. Between Being, as used by the ontologist or theologian, and John Chisum, as used by the biographer or historian, is the full distance between the most highly abstract and the most personally concrete. The historian and the novelist, in my judgment, have no business aspiring toward Being. While obviously they cannot put together history or fiction with only a collection of concrete John Chisums, they must stay as closely as possible to the particular cows, cowboys, and cattlemen. Whatever abstractions they may tentatively construct and use must finally be validated by these same cows, cowboys, and cattlemen.

There is, to repeat, nothing idiosyncratic in this position. Philosophy itself, particularly in the forms of pragmatism and existentialism, has over a century made us skeptical of metaphysical abstractions. The existential description of man as being part possibility and part facticity is of course an anthropological abstraction, but we accept it, if we accept it, not because it has a kind of grandeur and logical cogency but because it conforms to our own sense of concrete existence. Even phenomonology, which ultimately may be transcendental and thus aimed toward high, nonempirical abstractions, begins with a rigorous examination of perception. While it is doubtful that the historian can proceed phenomenologically, ge can agree that our knowledge of the world, including its historical past, must begin as close as possible to a pure concrete perception of how things actually were.

The central anthropological consequence of this turning away from abstractions is a concern for the historical or literary person. One cannot say merely a concern for the individual, for the individual has tended to become an empty abstraction itself, an idea of the particular human being as standardized as the model of an exchangeable part. The concept of person is of course an abstraction too, but it is an anthropological abstraction closely grounded in the radical, irreducible uniqueness of human existance. It is, in short, flavored, if not constituted, by concreteness.

The second conviction, then, is that the person counts immeasurably in history and literature. This does not suppose that every person of a time and place can be taken into account in a historical or imaginative reconstruction, but it does suppose that unless a historical time has been reached by an understanding at the level of persons existing in that time, the reconstruction is incomplete and ill-founded. This means, for the studies that follow, a persistent search for the historical or imaginative person in the cattle trade. For as much as any other type in our national culture, the cowboy—and the cattleman too—has become an empty abstraction. Even when old photographs give him a face beneath the dirty Stetson, he is still a cowboy, a frontier social type, supposedly given as are the cattle he drives to certain patterns of feeling and behavior. What he was or is as a person we do not know. Nor do we seem to care that we do not know. Cowboys, like cows, seem to become significant only in numbers, as a group or class or breed.

Again there is nothing idiosyncratic in this position. What makes it new and controversial, if it is controversial, is its presence in a discussion of the cattle trade. In general anthropology, whether in personalistic philosophy and psychology, existentialism (including psychology and theology), or renewed biographical approaches in history, the person holds our attention and value. The cowboy, at least the standardized version of him, may say, as we think he may have said, that he does not give a "good goddamn" what history makes him out to be or to have been. But even an understanding of that attitude, if indeed it ever stirred in any head beneath any Stetson on any range, would be well worth the scholar's effort.

History through a Cow's Horn: Joseph G. McCoy and His *Historic Sketches of the Cattle Trade*

> When I get onto the subject of the history of live stock, I am very apt to consume too much time, and talk too much.
>
> Joseph G. McCoy

In May 1874 *Historic Sketches of the Cattle Trade of the West and Southwest,* by the pioneer western cattle shipper Joseph G. McCoy,[1] was published in Kansas City, Missouri. More than a century later, this "granddaddy of all range histories," as J. Frank Dobie called it,[2] remains of enduring importance.[3] Indeed, in the historiography of the cattle trade, it retains, like the other titles in the select group of "big four" cattle books,[4] something of the aura of Scripture.

Yet even as historians have valued McCoy's book for its pioneering, firsthand authenticity, they have recognized its historical errors. The important edition would prove to be not the 1874 original, with its errors of fact and printing, its curious illustrations, but the closely edited version of 1940. With a lengthy introduction and more than four hundred footnotes, Ralph P. Bieber sought to add further historical worth to what he regarded as "an invaluable contribution to the literature of the cattle drives."[5] Ramon Adams, in his bibliography of the cattle industry, judged the Bieber edition "easily the best" "because of the valuable footnotes."[6] Likewise Joe B. Frantz and Julian E. Choate, in their study of the cowboy, insist that the Bieber edition far outstrips all the others, "including the original." "The combination of McCoy and Bieber," they conclude, "results in a story of prime quality and significance."[7] Most western historians, I dare say, agree with these assessments.

The nature of these judgments, however, raises some important historiographical questions. If we are asking to know the nature and value of McCoy's work, do we get our answers by appreciating the scholarly emendations of the editor? Can we honestly say that the combination of Bieber's notes and McCoy's original text results in a *story* of any kind, let alone one whose quality and significance can be so summarily judged? One can speak of McCoy's story, and one can perhaps speak of Bieber's story, if *story* is an appropriate term for the heavily expository account of cattle driving developed in his introduction. But there results no historiographical synthesis, no fusion of new fact and old structure. Bieber's notes, however meticulous they may be, do not really function as parts of McCoy's story. McCoy was writing history one way; Bieber is writing it another way. Indeed, one cannot easily call to mind another work of western history in which the original historian and the later editor have worked upon their material in such radically different rhetorical modes. Thus while Bieber adds substantially to our knowledge of McCoy and cattle driving, he tells us little about the book McCoy wrote.

It is time, I believe, to consider *Historic Sketches* in a different critical perspective. We cannot measure McCoy's historical achievement until we know more clearly what it was he was doing when he wrote his book. We cannot really correct his historiographical errors until we know the full consequences of his sometimes highly personal conceptions of what had happened in the cattle trade and the highly idiosyncratic historical style in which he articulated these conceptions. Insofar as history consists in a sequence of factual assertions, its revision can perhaps be rightly made through a parallel series of factual emendations. Thus in note 200 Bieber can correct McCoy's inaccurate explanation of the origin of *maverick*. Thus in note 215 he can indicate there is no evidence that cattle were shipped from Sedalia, Missouri, in 1866. History, however, does not consist merely in a sequence of factual statements. It also involves larger structures, generalized conceptions, and generalized images. And it is not enough to suppose that since these conceptions and images have been inductively validated, if not inductively derived, all we need in the way of proof is a testing of the specific evidence from which the induction supposedly has arisen. Even the most dogmatic historical empiricist must see complex historiographical problems in moving from the facts of the sources to the conceptions and images of the history.

A case in point is what we can call the historical image of the cowboy. How shall we judge the image of the cowboy which emerges in *Historic Sketches*? We know that McCoy had abundant opportunity to observe the cowboy on the trail and in the cattle towns, but can we suppose that he possessed an objective, matter-of-fact way of seeing and further, if he had this way of seeing, that he had a prose style which would faithfully convey this objective perception?

We can illustrate the central problem in the following way. If three different cattlemen closely observe the same Hereford bull, they will presumably report the same general conformation. Even though one of the observers may prefer the Angus as his own production breed, he is not likely to see the Hereford bull in significant subjective distortion of color and build. Furthermore, if these cattlemen report their observations in a full and objective manner, secondhand observers, seeing the bull through these reports, should develop images of approximate congruity. The uniformity here will of course not be due entirely to the fullness and objectivity of the reports. A Martian given the same accounts may develop images badly distorted, if even recognizable when seen by the eyes of the cattlemen themselves.[8] In part the uniformity of the bull image comes from the epistemological fact that even secondhand observers are likely to use, in their shaping of the evidence, directional ideas, preconceived patterns of meaning. Speaking simply, we can say that everyone involved in this transaction of words knows, roughly at least, what a Hereford bull looks like.

A cowboy, however, is another matter. If we say that everyone knows what a cowboy looks like, we can mean little more than that everyone expects a Stetson hat and high-heeled boots. A simple standard image of this kind reveals almost nothing about concrete persons who may be cowboys. And it tells us nothing important about historical cowboys. Thus historical observers of cowboys were not looking at bulls with standard conformations; they were seeing men who, however much they might resemble each other in hats, chaps, boots, and spurs, were concrete per-

sons. What these persons thought and felt, and consequently
what they did, could not be simply assumed as one assumes that
Hereford bulls eat grass. The observer could at best give an
impression, an interpretative impression which might be deeply
insightful or might be shallow and blind, but in any case might
leave an image blurred, ambiguous, and thus open to a variety of
readings.

McCoy, to repeat, had abundant opportunity to observe the
cowboy. However, to suppose that he thus left us an image of him
as firm as the figure of the Hereford bull to the cattlemen is to
forget the difficulties inherent in observing human beings and to
ignore the critical problems in reading his (McCoy's) text. The
historians who uniformly praise *Historic Sketches* as an important
piece of cattle trade history show little uniformity in their ways of
seeing McCoy's image of the cowboy. Fred Shannon found
McCoy telling "in vivid style" incidents concerning "the unheroic
cowboy."[9] Ramon Adams observed that McCoy "seemed to have
little use for the cowboy and throughout his book speaks of him
disparagingly."[10] Frantz and Choate, on the other hand, conclude
with this high tribute: "From the larger view of the cowboy at
work and the cowboy at play, McCoy has absolute honesty and
dependability." He was preeminent among the "truth-tellers."[11]

Did these historians see the same image in McCoy's pages?
Were their readings biased, or is McCoy's image so unsteady, so
abstract, so multifaceted that such varied judgments were not
only possible but likely? From the further point of view of historiographical criticism, the problems raised by these interpreta-
tions and judgments should perhaps be obvious. One easily supposes that the historian who has "little use" for a subject, who
writes "disparagingly" of that subject, is not likely to be a good
historian of that subject. Thus one supposes that Adams's general
judgment of McCoy is based on grounds other than McCoy's
depiction of the cowboy. In the contemporary intellectual climate, we are likely to suppose that the cowboy "unheroic" is more
historical than the cowboy heroic, but the nature and limits of
stylistic vividness in historical prose remain uncertain. Certainly,
as we shall see, McCoy's depiction of the cowboy is sometimes
colorful, but is colorfulness what the historian properly hopes is
vividness? And may not a high degree of colorfulness sometimes

subvert the concept of the unheroic, with the rhetoric, if not the facts, thus becoming heroic? Finally, what shall we make of the claim of "absolute honesty and dependability"? By what signs in *Historic Sketches* are we to know that we can depend on the historical authenticity of the cowboy we find there? And *absolute honesty* is so generous a phrase that it would perhaps be more appropriate in a handbook of eulogies and nominating speeches than in the dictionary of historical biography. Even Geoffrey of Monmouth, whom some regard as one of the great falsifiers in the history of history, can perhaps be called honest.

It should be obvious when we are dealing with the historical objects in McCoy's *Sketches* that we are not dealing with them by way of images as firm and clear as those we may have of a Hereford bull. Assessing McCoy's facts may be one acceptable level of historical criticism, but even that level, in this historiographical instance, involves problems that some historians seem unwilling to acknowledge. For what indeed constitutes historical factualness? When McCoy writes that a place along the Kansas Pacific Railway called Abilene was selected in 1867 as his cattle shipping point, we are clearly in the presence of a verifiable fact. When he writes that about thirty-five thousand head of cattle were driven to Abilene in 1867, we seem to have what can be called an approximate fact, some guessing, some rounding off obviously going into the figure he is using.[12] But when he writes that Southwestern cattlemen possessed "a strong inate [*sic*] sense of right and wrong," he is giving us not a fact but an ideological assumption.[13] And when he characterizes the vice president of a railway company as "a burly biped of teutonic extraction" and the treasurer as "a soulless, conscienceless money lover," obviously he is using epithets of doubtful factualness. Even if we could corroborate that the treasurer loved money—which he probably did—we could not possibly document his soullessness as fact. In writing this part of his history, McCoy has moved from the rhetoric of factual information to the rhetoric of polemical attack.

Even a casual reading of *Historic Sketches* shows that much of it is indeed attack and self-justification. The "crude" illustrations in the first edition which Bieber omitted from his edition as having "little or no historic value" may not historically supplement the text, but they are nevertheless closely related to the rhetoric of the text. Their caricaturing manner is indeed the manner of much of the prose itself.

A critical understanding of *Historic Sketches* thus requires far more than an assessment of McCoy's factual information. It requires a consideration of his style, his point of view, the kinds of rhetorical forms and structures, for these are functioning features of the history itself. Indeed, the ultimate historical meaning of even the hardest of seemingly discrete facts may perhaps be manifest only through the historian's form and style.

I

Many readers of *Historic Sketches* are no doubt surprised to discover that its author was still a young man, some years short of forty and several years short of the mid-point in a long life that would reach a decade and a half into the twentieth century. The sense of an older writer comes in part from the retrospective quality of the book and the consequent experience of seeming to look back at developments as if they stretched out over a time much longer than the relatively few years that contained them. The sense comes also from the manner of the telling, from the crustiness if not crankiness of the historian, from those special personal features which Dobie identified, in a curious cocktail of terms, as vinegar, fire, and phlegm. It is the literary manner, one might easily guess, of a somewhat embittered old man.

At the time of writing *Historic Sketches,* the relatively young man was no doubt more than a little embittered. In less than a decade his ambitious plans had pushed again and again at frustrating frontier realities: the intransigence of railroad management, the ups and downs of the cattle market, in sum, the sheer unwillingness of new historical circumstances to yield to a man's will. In this world of hooves and grass highways, it might seem fitting to let the railroads symbolize these circumstances, ironically necessary and invited yet so impersonally blind to the older ways of frontier enterprise. Indeed it is tempting to define McCoy primarily at odds with the railroads. Certainly here was a central antagonism of his life. There were the difficulties at the founding of Abilene, later litigational involvements with the Kansas Pacific, and even thirty years after the first herds reached Abilene he only reluctantly proposed that the railroads be allowed representation in the National Live Stock Association. Perhaps, as a delegate from Missouri observed, McCoy had "repented" on railroads, but his own characteristic statement at the time left him at best with a halfway change of heart. "I am not the enemy of railroads," he said; "neither do I sit up Saturday nights and Sundays to especially love them."[14]

If, however, we are seeking the man who wrote *Historic Sketches*, we must look more deeply through the features of his personal style. He was not just an idealistic young westerner fighting the economic power of industrial capitalism. He will not do as a Populist hero. He was an idealist, to be sure, but an idealist of a special sort: a man often pitting an exaggerated sense of himself against other men and historic events, thus always vulnerable to failure, thus always ready to judge with a personal intensity that was sometimes vindictive, yet nevertheless able at times to transmute these judgments into vivid satire.

This is admittedly a biographical construct pieced together from a small pile of facts and a larger stock of inferences. It is in one sense a fiction, not because it is untrue—we have here no way of determining absolute truthfulness or untruthfulness—but because it holds together, if it holds together, through imaginative insight, not by way of an accumulation of documented facts. We must take this way because the biographical sketches, earnest and factual though they may be, tell us almost nothing about McCoy the historian.[15]

II

Nearly half a century after the publication of his book on the cattle trade, McCoy, now identified as "Founder of the Abilene Cattle Trail," wrote an article entitled "Historic and Biographic Sketch." The subject was the cattle trade of Kansas and his personal involvement in it. For the most part it is the early book in brief. Reading it in relation to that book, one realizes that the larger work could rightly have been given a slightly different title: *Historic and Biographic Sketches of the Cattle Trade.* For whatever the

book's fullness of seemingly objective detail about the business of
trailing and selling cattle, it is in important ways an autobiography
of Joseph G. McCoy.[16] If it does not recount his life completely
from birth to maturity, it does articulate a personal development of
history, personal not only because McCoy was the inside observer
but also because he was the protagonist. Observing himself amidst
the multiplicity of the nineteenth century, Henry Adams in *The
Education of Henry Adams* adopted the third person point of view.
His own historical person could be, as the historian put it, a manikin
with whom events and forces could be focused and measured. It
could all be so highly impersonal. If there was personal disappointment in what historically happened, that disappointment
would not show: it would be masked in literary objectivity, in the
detachment and irony of the biographical style. Writing about
himself in the cattle trade, McCoy too used the third person. But
there was no attempt at being impersonal, no sophisticated effort
to mask his frustrations, anger, and disappointments. On the contrary, the third person allowed a personal enlargement, seemingly
without the egotism that would have followed the asserting *I*.
Whatever the size of the historical Henry Adams, the Adams of *The
Education* seems small. Helplessly he awaits the buffeting of history. Whatever the size of the historical Joseph G. McCoy, the
McCoy of the *Sketches* seems large. He does not wait for history;
confidently he commands it.[17]

Only a writer with McCoy's personal vision of history would
have established a setting and occasion so grandly dramatic for his
destined appearance. The Civil War had effectively stopped the
increasing beef migrations from Texas; a flood of cattle, to use the
traditional metaphor, was dammed within the state. Then in 1866,
the war over, drives began to Missouri; but for a number of reasons, the ventures proved both hazardous and economically dis-
appointing, even disastrous. "Over the business of cattle ranching," wrote McCoy in the *Historic Sketches*, "a deep gloom settled,
crushing to earth the hopes of many whose herds numbered mul-
tiplied thousands. . . . But it is said that the darkest hour is that one
just before the break of day. And so it was in this case. Just how and
from whence came that brighter hour, that dawn of day, will form
the theme of a future chapter."[18]

It was time to bring the protagonist onto the stage of history. The man for the occasion was the youngest of three brothers from Illinois. McCoy characterized him in the following manner: "Ambitious, energetic, quick to scent out and untiring to follow a speculation, fully possessed with an earnest desire to do something that would alike benefit humanity as well as himself; something that, when life's rugged battles were over, could be pointed to as an evidence that he had lived to some good purpose and that the world, or a portion thereof, was benefitted by his having lived. This young man conceived the idea of opening up an outlet for Texas cattle."[19] The idea became, the historian wrote further of himself, "an inspiration almost irresistible, rising superior to all other aspirations of his life, and to which he gave unremitting attention and labor for years."[20]

In the shaping of his plan or, perhaps one should say, in the realization of his dream, there was, the historian acknowledged, an important conversation with a leading drover from Texas, Colonel J. J. Meyers.[21] A practical consideration of the matter would, one supposes, have assumed a consultation with the men most desperately in need of moving their cattle to market. As historian, however, McCoy was never so matter of fact and pragmatic.[22] The sense of personal destiny seems always to have been in mind. "From the hour of that informal interview between the Texan drover and the Illinoisan," McCoy wrote, "the project, such as was soon developed at Abilene, became a fixed fact or purpose in the mind of its projector. There are moments in ones [*sic*] existence when a decision, or a purpose arrived at, shapes future actions and events—even changes the whole tenor of ones life and labor. . . . The decisions and determinations formed at that interview, fixed the life and labor of the Illinoisan."[23]

To turn the idea into a reality, the young Illinoisan needed first the cooperation of the railroads. And thus began a series of confrontations between the undaunted man with a mission and the beings of power who seemed to see themselves blindly as the centers of the western universe.[24] The personal outrage of the idealist erupted in savage comedy. "Entering the elegant office of the President [of the Missouri Pacific] and finding that dignitary arrayed in much 'store clothes,' quietly smoking a cigar while

looking over some business papers, the Illinois 'Bovine Puncher,'
dressed in a style that greatly contrasted with the official's garb—
rough, stogy, unblacked boots, a slouch hat, seedy coat, soiled
shirt, and unmentionables that had seen better days twelve
months previous," timidly states his business. The railroad official, "tipping his cigar up at right angles with his nose, and striking
the attitude of indescribable greatness, when stooping to notice
an infinitesimal object, and with an air bordering on immensity,"
replies in scorn and rejection, even ordering the Illinoisan from
the room. Remembering the shock, the historian wrote: "If the
heavens had fallen, the Illinoisan would not have been more
surprised and nonplussed than he was by the answer and conduct
of this very pompous railroad official." Leaving the office, he
wonders "what could have been the inscrutable purpose of the
Jehovah in creating and suffering such a great being to remain on
earth, instead of appointing him to manage the universe."[25]

It is not necessary here to develop the historian's full involvement in the building of Abilene and the cattle trade of
Kansas. We are seeking a sense of the man, a pattern of his
self-image, on the assumption that through his self-image he saw
his larger historical world. Obviously, in the instance of Joseph G.
McCoy, style and structure of history arise (again one is tempted
to use the stronger verb *erupt*) out of personal visions and enthusiasms, not out of studied adherence to professional principles
and methods.[26]

One further episode is, however, highly relevant to this
profile. It again pits McCoy as protagonist against the railway
company. During the season of 1869, the Illinoisan had worked
particularly hard to increase the shipment of cattle. "Indeed," he
wrote, "it would be difficult for a man to exert himself more, or
devote nearer all his time, night and day, to work and business
than he did; often two hour's sleep would suffice him; and scarce
a week passed in which he did not spend one or more nights
without sleep; so determined was he to repair his damaged fortunes, and to make the Abilene enterprise a complete success. For
it was," he repeated, "the undertaking of his life, and upon its
success or failure he felt that not only his fortune depended, but
his manhood, and the respect of his relatives and friends. . . . Its
success was nearer and dearer to him than life itself, and no more

cruelly withering, and heart-crushing day ever dawned in his history, than that upon which, by a combination of adverse circumstances, coupled with bad faith, he lost the shipping yards and cattle business of Abilene."[27] The circumstances and the bad faith the historian revealed in self-conscious detail. At the close of the shipping season, McCoy invested every dollar he could get in a herd of nine hundred head, planning to winter them on hay before fattening them on grass the following summer. To pay feed bills, he depended on a payment of more than five thousand dollars from the railroad for cars bedded and loaded. However, when he entered the general offices in St. Louis, the heavens fell again. "To his dismay," the historian wrote, "the Vice President, a burly biped of teutonic extraction, and the Treasurer, a soulless, conscienceless money lover, after scratching their pates and looking dubiously at each other, as if hesitating between acting out their honest convictions by paying the amount due, or repudiating the contract, piped out in dishonest tones, that they did not know of any contract existing wherein the Railway company had agreed to pay for having cattle loaded at Abilene."[28] Still hoping to obtain justice, McCoy then prepared a circular setting forth the basis of his claim. Copies were mailed to the directors and to the president of the company, and to the latter the Illinoisan took his case personally. Again he was turned away. "On entering the President's room," the historian wrote, "that *petite* functionary was found alone, apparently meditating upon what a queer thing it was to be a president of a railway and yet be so small a man. Arising, with a bland smile, he greeted the Illinoisan in a friendly manner, inviting him to be seated and make known his desires." McCoy stated his case; the president remembered some arrangement or contract; but at this point "the immense corporeal proportions of the Teutonic vice-president hove in view at the door-way." The little president suddenly remembered the circular and flew into a rage. "The interview ended by the President telling the Illinoisan to 'go and sue the Railway Company as soon as he chose,' in a voice indicating that to sue a corporation over which he presided with all his might and weight would be something, no insignificant mortal like a cattle man would dare have the temerity to do."[29] Returning to Kansas, McCoy then struggled to keep ahead of his creditors. "Whole weeks," he wrote, "were spent by him without adequate rest or sleep. An iron man could not have scarce withstood such constant strain and labor, much less a man of flesh and blood." His creditors closed in; many of his good-time friends deserted him. Finally, "with only a single ten dollar note, he withdrew from business, compelled by adversity and sickness, induced by overwork and anxiety, causing complete nervous exhaustion. The entire succeeding summer he was nearer a dead than a live man."[30]

However, in this account of his historic struggle, if he lost physically and financially, he gained in moral purpose and human insight. "A firm consciousness of rectitude of purpose," McCoy philosophized, "and an inward sense of honorable manhood will raise a real man above any and all adverse circumstances, and lead him to pity, while he despises the weak and heartless creatures who snap and snarl beneath his feet." "The experience of the year 1870," he added, "will long be remembered by the Illinoisan as affording a full insight into the hollowness of human nature, and the frivolous flunkyism of the majority of mankind."[31]

Obviously one cannot assert confidently that this is objective history and biography. One can confirm from other evidence that McCoy did indeed get into financial trouble, that he did have a long legal skirmish with the railroad, but the inner dimension of his personal history, what we might call the confessional side, cannot be corroborated with empirical evidence. However, we are not here obligated to achieve such biographical certainty. The self-image in the history may not faithfully match the mirror-image which theoretically the biographer with an abundance of accounts, a multitude of firsthand intimates and observers can construct, yet it is nevertheless out of this self-image that the history was taking shape and meaning. If we would know the history, we therefore must know the historian's persona within the book, for it is that persona which is giving perspective, style, and tone to the account of the cattle trade.

Obviously some facts of the cattle trade will speak for themselves; that is, they will seem self-evidently factual, to be trusted because of their matter-of-fact nature, not because of the testimony offered to prove them.[32] However, "facts" which are interpretive observations will be only as factual as the observer was steady, disinterested, and nonjudgmental. Needless to say, McCoy was rarely that sort of observer, particularly with regards to people. If he could see a stretch of grassland with a biologist's detachment, he could rarely see friends and foes in anything even remotely resembling scientific objectivity. After all, as his history recounted, life had taught him the hollowness of human nature and the flunkyism of the majority of mankind. Acquired from experiences in Abilene or merely hardened by his failures there, such preconceptions became a set of personal lenses through which he saw historical men and events.

III

The historiographical consequences of this way of seeing are many, but in a brief study perhaps they can be rightly limited to three: what might be called history by epithet; history structured as heroic biography and heroic moral drama, the big-hearted men versus the scoundrels; and the colorful, sometimes oratorical style. These consequences are of course closely interrelated, style being both cause and effect, structure being both shaper of style and stylistic shape. Further, as a consequence of these consequences, for the reader and critic, particularly for the historian inclined to use *Historic Sketches* as a primary source, there comes a conditioned skepticism about much in McCoy's book that is seemingly objective and factual. This does not mean, however, that our stake in the book has been wholly devalued. If there is a seeming loss of fact, there is a gain in literary complexity. If we are more interested in understanding a special vision of history, less in knowing the hard details of cows and cowmen in Abilene, the subjectivity is our gain. Certainly the book should not now seem like an unreal shadow in an old cow pen.

    In a strict sense history by epithet is not history at all, for whatever the inescapable presence of the historian, history assumes some effort to achieve distance, to let the historical men and events claim their own reality. McCoy, however, in the anger and high judgment of his personal vision, had little if any distance. What he had to report about those men who were in a sense the enemies or the villains of history was in the nature of a savage personal attack. These villains are, of course, primarily those who oppose in one way or another the advancement of the cattle trade. When James M. Dougherty is confronted by a Missouri mob, McCoy observes that never had Dougherty seen "such bipeds as constituted that band of self-appointed guardian angels." Attempting to drive cattle to Sedalia, Missouri, R. D. Hunter loses his herd to "a coon-capped biped, calling himself the sheriff of Vernon county." When the Kansas legislature passes the "Texas Cattle Prohibitory Law," the historian attributes the action to "certain old broken down political bummers and played-out adventurers." "Utterly unscrutable as to means employed," he goes on, "destitute of honorable manhood and incapable of doing a legitimate business in an honest manner; full of low cunning and despicable motives, these ghouls resorted to every device their fertile brain could conceive to defeat the efforts of the parties who were at work in Abilene." When the governor of Kansas supports the Abilene enterprise, he brings down upon his head "the bitter maledictions of certain pot-house politicians." In 1868, when the governor of Illinois calls a convention of experts to deal with the Spanish fever, the delegates are, McCoy fiercely notes, "a collection of quondam quacks, and impractical theorists, and imbecile ignoramuses." Some of them are "esculapians of the most deadly type—others mere political bummers—sent to that convention by their respective Governors to relieve the community, for a short time, at least, of a pestilential crew." Even the livestock men themselves do not escape the threat of the historian's savage labels. If they do not organize or form associations and thus seek to remedy "the many evils, abuses and extortions which have been heaped upon them in the past," the historian warned, "then are they degenerate dung-hills, and unfit to bear the proud distinction to which as a class they aspire."[33]

McCoy's anthropology—if this is not too philosophically sophisticated a term for a man of bold simplicities—was uncomplicated by the ambiguities of human nature. There were the hollow men, as we perhaps can call them, the frivolous flunkies, the scoundrels of donkey stupidity and avarice. These he thought he had discovered in the ventures and misadventures of the years before writing his book. In spite of such discoveries, however, he was not a pessimist. On the contrary, insofar as he revealed assumptions about the moral genesis of man, he was an optimist. That is, he seemed to believe in the innate goodness of some men while there is no evidence that he believed in the innate evil of others, however worthless they might seem to be. In short, in McCoy's history there are good men and there are bad men. If some men in McCoy's world perhaps lived in the gray moral region between goodness and badness, he chose to ignore them, or, as is more likely the case, his rather superficial analysis of human nature allowed him to sort all men into simple moral groups where his narrow set of labels could seemingly apply. The biographical result of boldly asserting simple virtues or faults is a kind of heroic emphasis; the historical figures become not so much individualized persons as they become larger-than-life cartoon characters.

The largest class of good men in McCoy's history are, as one might expect, the Texas ranchmen and drovers. They possessed, he wrote, a "strong natural sense," "a strong, innate sense of right and wrong"; "most of them are honorable men, and regard their verbal contract as inviolable, sacred, and not to be broken under any circumstances whatever." "Sanguine and speculative," he summarized, "impulsively generous in free sentiment; warm and cordial in their friendships; hot and hasty in anger; with a strong inate [*sic*] sense of right and wrong; with a keen sense for the ridiculous and a general intention to do that that is right and honorable in their dealings; they are, as would naturally be supposed, when the manner of their life is considered, a hardy, self-reliant, free and independent class, acknowledging no superior master in the wide universe."[34]

Repeated here for emphasis are McCoy's claims of an innate sense of right and wrong, for such claims indicate the very center of what might be called the big-heart school of range biography. R. D. Hunter has "a big heart, throbbing with the warmest pulsations of sympathy." Willis McCutcheon is "a true big hearted man." The heart of T. F. Hersey is always found "in the right place and full of warm blood for his friends." The heart of W. W. Sugg is "true." E. H. Gaylard has "a big, true heart full of sympathy for the unfortunate." J. M. Day is "kind hearted." John T.

Alexander is "warm-hearted." George N. Altman has "many
good qualities of heart." And L. M. Hunter is "a man with many
good qualities of head and heart."[35] Gathered from the biographical sketches of McCoy's book and piled here in summary,
these assertions have the uncritical, repeated simplicity of a
stereotype. One might suppose the ingenuous hand of a
primitivistic mythmaker. But McCoy was a cattleman writing
about cattlemen; supposedly he knew them as few other men did.
There is no reason therefore to take his statements as anything
other than statements of his own kind of truth. The proof of the
truth, as we shall see in another study, was like the moral
superiority of cattle over sheep taken for granted.[36]
    With the good heart go related attributes. Major Seth Mabry
is "chivalric" and "courteous." Upon the countenance of W. W.
Sugg "truth and honesty" sit "enthroned supreme." J. M. Day is
"honorable" and "straightforward." John T. Alexander "ap-
preciates true manhood, is upright, honorable, and highminded
in his business transactions." J. B. Hunter is "a genuine upright,
self-made man." Major Jay S. Smith manifests "a high sense of
honor and manhood." Colonel Oliver W. Wheeler is a "generous,
chivalrous gentleman, whose impulses are ever true and good."
George R. Barse is "a whole-souled, good-tempered man." R. C.
White is "a kind, courteous, true man," and George Groves possesses "unquestioned integrity of character."[37]
    In a minor way McCoy's heroic way of biographic definition
is epitomized in his sketch of H. M. Childress. "A convivial, jolly
fellow, always full of fun and frolic, with a heart as large as that of
an ox. He will walk boldly into death's jaws to relieve or avenge a
friend; has a nerve of iron, cool and collected under
fire . . . . Generous, scrupulously honorable and honest, chivalric
and impulsive; in his heart he wishes every one well, and is never
so happy himself as when he can make his friends happy, by
performing generous acts of kindness."[38]
    In a major way the heroic emphasis can be seen in McCoy's
portrait of Charles Goodnight.

By nature he [Goodnight] is gifted with a genius fitting him to command,
even in a land of sovereigns. His life, although cast upon the wildest
frontiers and subjected to the rudest circumstances, has been such that
he had not lost the higher, nobler, tenderer feelings and sensibilities of

an exalted manhood. The secret of his gratifying success is his diligent, persistent application to, and study of his business until he was a complete master thereof, both in theory and practice, coupled with an upright life and an unswerving integrity of character. He has no superiors in the great new west, and his success has been as deserved as great.[39]

Whether biographical notes or major sketches, these characterizations have little to do with the customary ways of historical re-creation. McCoy was an on-the-scene observer, but he does not tell us what he saw. There is never a concrete touch by which we might distinguish one cowman from another. There is rarely if ever a narrative of reality-confirming action. Childress, we are told, will walk boldly into death's jaws, but we do not see him walking. We are left with the historian's high opinion. Obviously if a man is from Texas and raises cows, his high moral stature can be assumed.

These are the good men of the cattle trade. The scoundrels and the fools remain nameless, but their portraits are more extended, less filled with the clichés of the standard biographic sketch of tribute and praise. Indeed, to come alive with his special kind of force, McCoy's prose needed the energy of anger and outrage, a sense of personal affront from the stupid knaves who would keep the history of Abilene from going in the direction he (McCoy) had decided it should go.

The historic gallery of scoundrels and fools includes satiric portraits of several self-important men. None are stockmen; all are meddlers in the proper course of human events. There is the great merchant of Abilene, with two-thirds of his small supply of brains going to self-esteem. There are the scientific experts trying to solve the mystery of the Spanish fever. "Their bulky disquisitions clothed in high-sounding words when shorn of their verbiage and compressed into intrinsic truth and practical common sense, would remind matter of fact cattle men of the fabled mountains bringing forth the mouse." And there is the editor. His portrait, more fully presented here, will perhaps represent McCoy's fiercely sustained judgment in this gallery of historic knaves and fools.[40]

Early in Abilene's history certain interests began pushing to make Abilene a town instead of a cattle market. This meant forcing the cattle trade to other western outlets; it meant a con-

sequent loss of business. It was, as McCoy put it, "Abilene's suicidal folly." Desiring to publish a weekly newspaper, these interests
had "procured a biped," as McCoy named him, "of the genus
editor; although but a feeble and doubtful specimen," who during the summer of 1872 "busied himself with making excuses for
the decline of Abilene's business and pretending that the cattle
trade was of no benefit." "As to talent," the historian wrote of him,

even average ability, he had little or none. Low cunning, shrewd wire-
pulling, and cheeky presumption, coupled with loathsome flunkyism,
and vindictive, unscrupulous hatred of all whom he could not manipu-
late, constituted his make up and capital. A closer inspection of the
personal appearances of the editor, caused the gravest discussion and
doubts in the minds of the villagers, whether he was a real human, or only
an extremely well developed specimen of the ape family. The disposition
and degree of manhood, or rather lack of manhood, that he soon developed, fixed the conviction that if at some time in the distant future,
some enterprising phrenological Darwin should chance to exhume his
cranium, it would be regarded as a rare specimen and as conclusive proof
of the soundness of the "Darwinian Theory," an undeniable connecting
link between the animal and human race. However, as the cranial formation would show but little brains before the ears, and still less above the
eyes, but an enormous development behind the ears, where the bump of
self-esteem and ambitious proclivities to seek office are supposed to be
located; it would doubtless be classed as of doubtful origin or classification and labelled "a what is it."[41]

Given the literary proclivities revealed in these sketches and
satiric portraits, it is hard to suppose, whatever the historian's
intentions to convey practical and correct information, that he
easily resisted his own pressures to move into a colorful and even
oratorical style. Again and again his rhetoric soars; again and
again it transforms the perhaps homely object into an image of
lively color; and by intention or accident it occasionally juxtaposes
the grand and the common, with pleasantly comic results.

Again it is the ups and downs of the cattle trade that provide
the personal dynamics of McCoy's prose, evoking that sometimes
curious mix of local experience, biblical allusion, and official
literary tradition. When the prospects of driving cattle northward
first opened, "we can readily believe," he wrote, "that the bright
visions of great profits and sudden wealth that had shimmered
before the imagination of the drover, leading him on as the subtle

mirage of the desert does the famishing traveler—nerving him to greater hardships, and buoying him up in many a wild, stormy night, whilst he kept silent vigil over his herd—were shocked, if not blasted, by the unexpected reception given him in Southern Kansas and Missouri by a determined, organized, armed mob, more lawless, insolent and imperious than a band of wild savages." After the opening of Abilene had been advertised by letters and papers, "all Texas was reading and talking of the new star of hope that had arisen in the north to light and buoy up the hitherto dark and desponding heart of the ranch man." For John T. Alexander a few years of cattle shipping in connection with disastrous business transactions had epic results. "A fortune of colossal proportions," wrote McCoy, "riven to shreds, as is the oak by the lightning's hot bolt. Scattered as if by a cyclone, as are the fragments of a rock riven ocean steamer." Even the economic fact of bank interest could arouse the historian's ascending metaphoric power. "It is an insatiable leech industriously sucking life-blood both day and night, whether the day is sacred or secular, sunny or stormy, or whether the markets are good or bad it matters not; 'the cry is give! give! continually.' " Or, to add a final example in another literary mode, the pleasures of outdoor life could stir the historian to a special poetic fervor. "There are," he wrote,

many comforts enjoyed in camp life, out on the great plains in the summer season, not the least among which is the delightsome breeze which so gently sweeps over the land, bringing health, vigor, and "the balm of a thousand flowers" upon its wings. The freedom and abandon which naturally abounds, coupled with the jovial hilarity inevitable to robust health, to which may be added the often recurring sharp appetite for the feasts of game often provided by the skill of some semi-nimrod herder, all conspire to render camp life upon the broad plains a joy forever.[42]

Cattleman Theodore Roosevelt would have agreed wholeheartedly.

To see the picturesqueness of McCoy's imagery, we can focus appropriately upon the figure of the cowboy. Whatever the mundane simplicities of his life and work as a disinterested observer might have seen him, the cowboy of the *Sketches* is a wildly colorful literary cartoon. A brief composite version will illustrate. One begins with a noncowboy, an antithetic image of the northern man unaccustomed to handling Texas cattle. "A Northern man," the historian wrote,

will often rush into the corral wherein is a single bullock. He will have scarcely got cleverly in the corral before the bullock, with arched back, downset head, extended nostrils, and glaring, fiery eyes, darts toward his supposed adversary, who, suddenly taking in the dangerous situation, but too late to retreat by the way of his entree, rushes post haste to the nearest fence, which is usually so high he cannot spring to the top of it; but reaching the top with his finger tips, draws his body as high as possible, and clinging to his hold with frantic grip, yells lustily for help. In the meantime the bullock, failing to pin the body of the man to the wall, puts in vicious strokes with his horns at the dangling coat-tails and posterior of the thoroughly alarmed man. When the frightened fellow is relieved from his perilous attitude, he finds, on casual examination, his coat-tails in shreds, and the seat of his unmentionables ripped in a shocking manner, much resembling a railroad map of a western commercial metropolis.

We do not see the cowboy in a similar predicament, but we suppose his experience and skills would lead to a different outcome. McCoy's cowboy, however, is never the figure of mundane skills and work. The historian's prose will not allow him that ordinary existence. On the trail, "when the night is inky dark and the lurid lightning flashes its zig-zag course athwart the heavens, and the coarse thunder jars the earth, the winds moan fresh and lively over the prairie, the electric balls dance from tip to tip of the cattle's horns—then the position of the cow-boy on duty is trying far more than romantic."[43] Can the cowboy introduced on this literary stage to handle a stampede be other than romantic, that is, if his own heroism is to match that of the heavens and earth?

Reaching the cattle town, the cowboy cuts loose or, as McCoy put it, "he can go free and have a jolly time." And he is never more jolly than when dancing.

The cow-boy enters the dance with a peculiar zest, not stopping to divest himself of his sombrero, spurs, or pistols, but just as he dismounts off of his cow-pony, so he goes into the dance. A more odd, not to say comical sight, is not often seen than the dancing cow-boy; with the front of his sombrero lifted at an angle of fully forty-five degrees; his huge spurs jingling at every step or motion; his revolvers flapping up and down like a retreating sheep's tail; his eyes lit up with excitement, liquor and lust; he plunges in and "hoes it down" at a terrible rate, in the most approved yet awkward country style; often swinging "his partner" clear off of the floor for an entire circle, then "balance all" with an occasional demoniacal yell, near akin to the war whoop of the savage Indian.[44]

One need only add the bragging cowboy to see clearly how the historian's literary manner has lifted the cowboy above the flat level of information into the realms of legends and folklore. A cowboy from New Mexico is unacquainted with champagne but decides to try the "critter." After drinking one quart and getting ready to start a second, he suddenly feels the effects of the first. "Hesitating for a moment," McCoy wrote,

in which his eye was observed to tingle with a newly aroused wildfire he arose to his feet; then suddenly jumped about two feet into the air and brought his ponderous fist down on the table with the force of a trip-hammer, and screamed in tones near akin to the warhoop of a Comanche: "I'm a s——n of a b——ch from New Mexico, by G——d. I'm just off of the Chisholm trail—wild and woolly—and I don't care a d——n. I can whip any shorthorn in America, by G——d." All the while jumping up and down like a caged wild demon—his long uncombed hair hanging a profuse mass over his face whilst his eyes shot forth piercing tiger glances. Had he had his pistols, death's cold leaden pillets would have been distributed promiscuously.[45]

McCoy's comic mix of the grand and the commonplace should already be evident in the textual passages above, but two further instances may sharpen the critical note. As a consequence of Abilene's "suicidal folly" in turning away the cattle herds, the town became desolate and deserted. "Some of the best citizens," wrote the historian, "became entirely bankrupt from the stagnation of trade, while others, with cadaverous cheek and weird eye, watched any ominous ripple in the sunflower, to see if perchance, a homesteader was making his entrance into the dead village, bringing farm products which could only be bartered off at very low prices if sold at all." *Ominous,* backed by *cadaverous cheek* and *weird eye,* joined to a *ripple* in a field of sunflowers is one such ironic juxtaposition. An additional example, taken from a speech nearly a quarter of a century after publication of the book, indicates the endurance of McCoy's stylistic habits. As McCoy warmed to the climax of an address to the National Live Stock Association, he became particularly biblical. "Abraham, who first communed with the infinite God, who first received the revelations of God's goodwill toward mankind, he was a ranchman and had cowmen and cowboys. His only son followed in his father's footsteps and held his flocks on Judea's plains and valleys. And did you never note how cute that grandson, Jacob, was? How he not only figured Lamaan out of both of his daughters for wives, but got away with almost the entire herd of cattle by that streaked, speckled and spotted scheme at the watering troughs?"[46] The linguistic distance between *the revelations of God's goodwill toward mankind* and *that streaked, speckled and spotted scheme at the watering troughs* is the distance between the grand style and the vernacular. Move from one to the other or juxtapose them and the result will be comic.[47] Mark Twain, of course, knew this rhetorical truth well.

IV

In a concluding perspective shaped by these features, what shall we say finally about the importance of *Historic Sketches* as a contribution to the historiography of the cattle trade? Obviously it remains, as Dobie said, the granddaddy of all range histories, and granddaddies, whatever their stubborn pride and crankiness, are still to be honored. Obviously it remains a wonderfully rich deposit of nineteenth-century attitudes and terms: like other books of its time, it holds in its bag of ideas a curious transitional mix ranging from frontier primitivism to a polemic Darwinism; its prose is a literary relic of considerable charm.[48] Obviously, as Joseph G. McCoy was an important pioneer in the western cattle business, so is the book important which expresses and images him, even though it is filled with self-pleading and perversity, certainly with neither biographical completeness nor proportion. And obviously the book does, as its writer intended, provide information, some of it practical and correct, and most of it, as perhaps it should be, seen through the horn of a cow.[49]

But to hold up McCoy's book as one of the great truthtellers is to ignore its special features of structure and style.[50] Truth it does tell, but that truth, for the most part, is not the sort of truth one customarily expects from the historian.[51] McCoy was, to be sure, an eyewitness, but he was an eyewitness with little detachment and much inner anger, anger that could blind and distort his perceptions. As an account of trail driving, his work seems much less reliable than *The Log of a Cowboy,* and that work, according to its author's intentions, was fiction.[52] As a historical source on the cowboy, McCoy's book is almost empty of hard, individualized, concrete details, but filled with generalized sketches drawn in bold exaggerating lines and color. And whatever the author's opportunities to know and observe them in a firsthand manner, as a historical account of the cowmen themselves, the work is a gallery of standardized sketches, all of them stamped with the biographical encomiums of a range brotherhood. The men themselves, as one believes they must have existed, escape the historian.

A concluding case in point is the instance of Shanghai Pierce, the unforgettable Texas cattleman who ought perhaps to seem natural wearing any sort of frontier hyperbole. Pierce, like Goodnight, remains a challenge to biographers. Whatever the distinction of Chris Emmett's *Shanghai Pierce* and J. Evetts Haley's *Charles Goodnight,* it can be argued that both biographical subjects overwhelm their biographers. In these works biography is still in the heroic phase. McCoy's three-page sketch is even more strikingly in the heroic mode. With all of its errors of fact, some may argue that it nevertheless remains true to the spirit of old Shang, his energy, his shrewdness, his loud voice, and his love of a good story. Yet such truth is almost impossible to assess in any kind of rigorous biography or historiography. When McCoy writes, "And if they [Pierce's listeners] ever get within cannon shot of where he is, they hear his ear-splitting voice more piercing than a locomotive whistle—more noisy than a steam calliope. It is idle to try to dispute or debate with him, for he will overwhelm you with indescribable noise, however little sense it may convey,"[53] we are left with an interesting folk caricature. The historical person of Shanghai Pierce has escaped the historian's pages.

In the literature of the West, *Historic Sketches of the Cattle Trade* will undoubtedly remain an important work—but not a classic of rangeland historiography. And we shall perhaps come to value the book even more—when we know it for what it is, not for what we have too easily assumed it to be.

The Rancher as Writer: Theodore Roosevelt's Sketches of the Cattle Trade

In the first of his western books, Theodore Roosevelt observed of ranch life that "it is a phase of American life as fascinating as it is evanescent, and one well deserving an historian."[1] Although he was, by the time of writing the observation, both ranchman and writer of history, he did not become the historian of ranch life. His next western book, *Ranch Life and the Hunting Trail,* dealt, as its title indicates, with ranch life, but it was a firsthand report, a series of sketches, rather than a history. It revealed the ranching phase of American life as fascinating, and the robustness of the account was tempered by a sense of time's decay, but it did not attempt the breadth of scope, the range of time, the documented impersonal objectivity of history. It was nevertheless an invaluable contribution to history, a source excited by a sense of the importance of its observations yet disciplined by mature literary skills. However, a history of ranching in America would need to wait a later time and another committed historian.

The literary and historiographical importance of ranching was for Roosevelt a direct function of his own enthusiastic involvement in it. When he wrote that the "free, open-air life of the ranchman" is "the pleasantest and healthiest life in America," he was bearing a personal testimony. He could scarcely have presumed to speak for all ranchers although some, perhaps many, might have agreed. And when he added that this life "from its very nature" is "ephemeral," he was in a sense speaking personally too.[2] His own overriding sense of destiny allowed no permanency in any of the frontier social forms. It was not simply a matter of the coming of barbed wire or the tragic consequences of the winter of 1886. Even without such specific threats to the free and open range, the life of ranching in its wilderness setting was doomed. Valuing that life highly while knowing its passing, Roosevelt gave history a touch of poignancy. Had he not been so ebullient a personality or had his future not been caught up so positively in the happy tide of reform politics, there might have been the elegiac too.

The story of Roosevelt's ranching venture in the Bad Lands of Dakota has been told many times.[3] Except for some framing dates and experiences, some biographical facts bearing directly on his writing, that story will not be repeated here. The concern of this essay is with the ranching as it became a literary and historiographical artifact, not with the rancher himself, although how that energetic stockman, that matchless cowboy, as he would be called, can be fenced out of his own verbal ranges is problematic to say the least. The central concern of the discussion to follow can be indicated in the following focusing questions: What is the image of the rancher and cowboy in Roosevelt's writings? What ideological assumptions work to give the ranch and cowboy these particular shapes of meaning? What literary and historiographical styles and structures work to give texture and form to the finished artifact?

I

Exactly when Roosevelt became interested in cowboys and ranching we do not know. Although specific titles are unmentioned in his personal papers—there is apparently no notice, for example, of McCoy's *Historic Sketches*—one of his biographers makes the inference that "with his voracious reading habits" he "must have been thoroughly familiar" with the romantic literature inspired by the activities of the cattle trade. And an economic interest may have been aroused particularly by General James S. Brisbin's *The Beef Bonanza; or, How to Get Rich on the Plains,* first published in 1881.[4] Whatever the specific moment and motivation, Roosevelt was already in the cattle business when he went west to hunt buffalo in the fall of 1883. Although hardly a wealthy young man, he had invested ten thousand dollars of his own financial resources in the Teschmaker and Debillier Cattle Company.[5] Now, charmed by the landscape, the business prospects, and the sports opportunities, during the course of a long unrelenting hunt he decided to take up ranching seriously. With Sylvane Ferris and William Ferris in charge, he would bring four hundred head of cattle to the Maltese Cross Ranch on the Little Missouri. The next year he would enlarge his operation further, adding as a favorite setting the Elkhorn Ranch some forty miles northward down the river and adding as cowboys two backwoodsmen friends from Maine, William Sewall and Wilmot Dow.

In 1884 Roosevelt was just twenty-six. Well-educated, well-traveled, comfortable if not rich, and well-placed socially, he must have seemed in many ways an unlikely candidate for Bad Lands pioneer. Yet obviously and enthusiastically he found the experience to his liking. "I do not believe," he wrote in his autobiography,

there ever was any life more attractive to a vigorous young fellow than life on a cattle ranch in those days. It was a fine, healthy life, too; it taught a man self-reliance, hardihood, and the value of instant decision—in short, the virtues that ought to come from life in the open country. I enjoyed the life to the full. After the first year I built on the Elkhorn ranch a long, low ranch house of hewn logs, with a veranda, and with, in addition to the other rooms, a bedroom for myself, and a sitting-room with a big fireplace. I got out a rocking chair—I am very fond of rocking-chairs—and enough books to fill two or three shelves, and a rubber bathtub so that I could get a bath. And then I do not see how any one could have lived more comfortably.[6]

No doubt, even with all we now know about Roosevelt, this seems to describe a vacation, an easterner's frontier lark. However, the young ranchman saw himself in a serious, practical role. Ten years later, he recalled his cowboy experience in a letter to Brander Matthews: "I have worked hard in cow camps for weeks at a time, doing precisely such work as the cowpunchers . . . . I didn't play; I *worked* [Roosevelt's emphasis], while on my ranch."[7] Nevertheless, the work must have been fun, at least for Roosevelt, if not for the common hand. The letters of the ranching years carry a repeated lyric of what Roosevelt seemed to suppose was the cowboy's work ethic. To Henry Cabot Lodge he wrote: "I have had hard work, and a good deal of fun since I came out here. Tomorrow I start for the roundup; and I have just come in from taking a thousand head of cattle up on the trail. The weather was very bad and I had my hands full, working day and night, and being able to take off my clothes but once during the week I was out."[8] To Lodge he wrote again a month later: "We are working pretty hard. Yesterday I was in the saddle at 2 A.M., and except for two very hasty meals, after each of which I took a fresh horse, did not stop working till 8:15 P.M.; and was up at half past three this morning. The eight hour law does not apply to cowboys."[9] "The round up is now over," he wrote to his sister Anna. "I have been working like a beaver; it is now five weeks since I have had breakfast as late as four oclock any morning. You would hardly know my sunburned and wind roughened face. But I have really enjoyed it and am tough as a hickory knot."[10]

If the young cowboy saw the importance of self-reliance and hardihood in the roundup, the young rancher also saw the importance of association and cooperation in the larger sociology of the range.[11] The roundup may have been, as he once said, a perfect democracy, but the traditional forms of political relationships must have seemed more happily emergent in the stockmen's meetings. In the fall of 1885 he was chairman of the Little Missouri Stockmen's Association. After the September meeting, the editor of the Bad Lands *Cowboy* observed, "Under his [Roosevelt's] administration everything moves quickly forward . . . ." He was reelected. In April the following year he was selected a member of the committee to represent the Little Missouri Association at a meeting of the Montana Association in Miles City.[12] To Anna he wrote: "I took my position very well in the convention, and indeed these westerners have now pretty well accepted me as one of themselves, and as a representative stockman."[13]

Although Roosevelt maintained his ranching connections until the century was almost gone, he needed only a few years to learn that there was no beef bonanza. The fall shipment of 1886 brought ten dollars a head less than the costs of production and shipment. The terrible winter of 1886–87, even if it was perhaps less destructive to Roosevelt's herds than to others, left the rancher with appalling losses—in optimism as well as in beef.

Coming at a time of increasing interest in eastern politics, it marked the end of his romance with the range. During the next ten years the rancher returned to Dakota in the fall not to be a cowboy but to be a hunter, to use the ranch as he had always used it as a base camp for a western safari.[14]

II

If Roosevelt was in his own judgment a reasonably good cowboy and a "representative stockman," he nevertheless brought to cowboying and ranching an unusual personal feature which probably set him apart as much as did the glasses he wore. To Lodge he wrote in 1886, "Really, I enjoy this life; with books, guns and horses . . . ."[15] It is the books that made the special difference. Earlier the same month he had written to his sister Corinne, "I have managed to combine an outdoors life, with a literary life also. Three out of four days I spend the morning and evening in the ranche house, where I have a sitting room all to myself, reading and working at various pieces I have now on hand. They may come to nothing whatever; but on the other hand they may succeed; at any rate I am doing some honest work, whatever the result is."[16]

Roosevelt's literary career had its substantial beginning with the publication in 1882 of *The Naval War of 1812.* The author was still in his early twenties. By April 1891 he could count eight books on the shelf. After listing them by title in a letter, he added in self-congratulation, "Rather a formidable list, are they not? The best books among them are *The Winning of the West,* and *Hunting Trips of a Ranchman.*"[17] Clearly, the West, its history and the contemporary experiences to be had there, had inspired a strong literary interest. Others of the early works and some of those yet to be written were concerned with things western. Indeed, the march of populations into the wilderness and the conquering role of the frontiersman in that march gave Roosevelt his central historical matter. This study, however, must have a yet more limited textual focus: the shelf shortens to a single book of sketches—*Ranch Life in the Far West,* portions of *Hunting Trips of a Ranchman* and *The Wilderness Hunter,* a long letter to John Hay, 9

August 1903, an article "In Cowboy-Land," *Century*, June 1893, and "In Cowboy Land," a chapter in the *Autobiography*.[18] Taken together, these writings constitute a modest anthology that might be titled *Roosevelt on Ranching*. Although they issued out of a literary experience of more than twenty years, they are consistent in their ideological assumptions and their literary method. These are particularly localized in *Ranch Life in the Far West*. And at the same time both are closely related to Roosevelt's broader western work, *The Winning of the West*, and to his most general theoretical notions about history and literature.

The bibliographical evidence suggests that Roosevelt was after all more hunter than cowboy-rancher. The life of ranching was valued finally not because it produced beef but because it occasioned hunting. One can nevertheless, using a selective focus upon those pieces which deal with the cowboy and the rancher in their worlds and in their work, argue the importance of Roosevelt's writings in the emerging literature of the cattle trade. But obviously this focus, lest it have a disjunctive narrowness, must give a sense of the larger context. Since the wilderness ranges of game and cattle were virtually the same, since the cowboy and the rancher were both varieties of the species *frontiersman*, since the need for manliness and self-reliance was common to trapper, hunter, and working horseman, one can never wholly separate ranching and hunting—at least as Roosevelt saw and experienced them.

III

Describing the sketches which would make up *Ranch Life in the Far West*, Roosevelt wrote to Richard Watson Gilder, editor of *Century*, that they "will (feebly) portray a most fascinating and most evanescent phase of American life; the wild industries, and scarcely wilder sports of the great lonely plains of the far west." It is, one might say, a very Rooseveltian statement. Even the parenthetical adverb shows the self-conscious reining-back of this most self-confident man. More importantly, it introduces a central historical thesis, a basic image of the cattle business, and a lyrical metaphor for the cowman's world.[19]

"I have been a part of all that I describe," Roosevelt further wrote to Gilder; "I have seen the things and done them; I have herded my own cattle, I have killed my own food; I have shot bears, captured horse thieves, and 'stood off' Indians. The descriptions are literally exact; few eastern men have seen the wild life for themselves."[20] Again it is a characteristic statement. The authority of the I-predication repeats with the sincerity of an oath. The I-was-there and I-saw-with-my-own eyes mean a literal exactness. The on-the-spot perspective and involvement guarantee a sort of personal omniscience. It was still, we must remember, the age of discovery. What the honest eye saw was true; what the camera plate held was reality.

The historical thesis is revealed in the term *evanescent,* coupled in rhetorical habit with the term *fascinating.* Roosevelt's earlier book, as previously noted, had already joined these adjectives as modifiers of the ranching phase of American life. And when he wrote Owen Wister in 1897 praising *Lin McLean,* he called that work "a historic document for one phase of the life of endeavor in our race's history which is as evanescent as it is fascinating."[21] The claim that ranching is merely a passing phase is, in form at least, clearly a historical proposition. It places ranching within the longer linear development of the race. It provides a causal background, and it points a direction into the future. Thus some would say that Roosevelt was a rancher with a sense of history.[22] Yet the thesis is at the same time a historical preconception, a running of a principle westward which had no immediate validation in the concrete evidence of the rancher's time and place. There is little evidence, so far as I know, that Roosevelt was knowledgeable about the history of ranching, either in the Dakota Territory or in other American areas where ranching had long been an industry, Florida and Texas, for example. He must have talked local history with established ranchers like Howard Eaton and Gregor Lang, but from these conversations he could hardly have inferred the grand principle of historical evanescence.[23] He would have been interested, one supposes, in the cowpen "ranching" of the western Carolinas, but there is no mention of it in *The Winning of the West.* Had he known more about the *rancheros* of Florida and Texas, he could have seen that their experience indicated persistence as well as change.

Evanescence would be exotically inappropriate to name the historical condition.

. *Evanescence* is, in fact, a strange term to find in historiographical usage. History deals with change, and some changes are rapid. But even if we suppose an accelerated rate, social forms and institutions do not disappear in a day or even a year, and when they are no longer around us as recognizable, functioning entities, we encounter their archeological leavings or know their vestigial presence. This is indeed the continuity we assume to be characteristic of history. We do, it is true, speak of some developments as ephemeral—to use another of Roosevelt's adjectives signifying the historical transiency of ranching—but the term is more aptly applied to the hoola hoop or the tent skirt than to the institution of ranching.

Evanescent is, furthermore, a seemingly curious word for such central usage in the rhetoric of an essentially conservative mind. Roosevelt can be described as a reform Republican, a progressive, even as a radical in the image of a fence-smashing bull moose, but all of this does not obscure his commitment to traditional principles and practices. His personal experience was weighted with the enduring rightness of home and country; his political vision was given its own particular clarity by the proven guidelines of courage and honesty. Yet the term *evanescent* has a biographical rightness, if not a historiographical one.

Intellectually Roosevelt was a convert to the evolutionism of his time. Whatever his personal moral modifications of a general development hypothesis, he seemed to take the long view that stretched history from a "beast-like man" in the remote past[24] to a cowboy-rancher in the dissolving present and implied a strong ongoing push into a distant but predictable future. Thus, one might argue, within a time-frame of many millennia, if not aeons, a frontier institution like ranching *was* ephemeral. Insofar as evolutionary history took its time sense from geology, it tended to squeeze the lastingness of human institutions to a brief, brief day under the sun. However, if Roosevelt theoretically accepted such a time-frame, he did not establish it rhetorically in the structure of his work. *The Winning of the West,* his major historical contribution, opens with the spread "during the past three centuries" of English-speaking peoples "over the world's waste spaces" and closes with the image of settler-folk pushing ever westward until the West will reach its natural limits.[25] The movement across the Atlantic has led to the further push into the prairies and far western mountains. The time-frame is relatively short, but the movement is ceaseless. The historiographical verbs and verbals suggest an unstoppable westering, with an unbroken "chain of causation" binding the destiny of the race and nation.[26]

Yet all of the changes brought on by this relentless westering do not dissolve the state of ranching into evanescence. A deduction from the metahistorical principle of evolution could give the historian development, and that development might lead toward extinction rather than toward a new institutional species. An induction from western history and from the contemporary evidence around him could give him a sense of frontier growth and modification. But neither would warrant the term *ephemeral.* The usage is thus perhaps more personal. Like Henry Adams, Roosevelt could conclude that all is change. And if that change threatened a form of life he loved, he could intensify that form's moment of value, he could mark its all too quickly passing, by calling it evanescent or ephemeral. But this would be to speak a personal lament, not to argue a historian's reasoned conclusion.

Roosevelt's special relationship to his material is further revealed in the term *fascinating.* Like *evanescent,* it is a strange word to find in historiographical usage. One thinks of a young boy (or girl for that matter) glued to his seat, oblivious of all else, as he watches the trail herd move through the colored canyons of the television screen. One thinks of even the most sophisticated adult spellbound as riders emerge out of the miles and miles of golden space on the movie screen. Both viewers are in a sense bewitched, fascinated by what they are seeing. However, the historian, whatever the intensity of his scholarly interest, can scarcely allow himself to be drawn into such an uncritical state. Whatever the need for sympathy and empathy in his craft, the historian cannot be fixed, even self-consumed by his subject.[27]

Was Roosevelt speaking loosely, or was he indeed fascinated by the ranching phase of American life? There can be no doubt, given the evidence of his books and letters, that he was attracted to ranching in a special, personal way. It was not a matter of business possibility although that was a factor in his motivation; it was not a

matter of disinterested historical judgment, a realization that
ranching, like religious communitarianism or homesteading, was
an important piece in the jigsaw puzzle of American expansion.
Whatever the biographical reasons, when Roosevelt called
ranching a fascinating phase in the race's history, he was again
making a personal observation. Few if any of his contemporaries
in the profession of history would have agreed that ranching is a
fascinating phase. Yet of course he was right when he said it deserved a historian. In the long view most historians must agree
that a development which fascinated a man like Roosevelt and has
fascinated thousands like him down into our own time must
finally be important in the cultural history of America and indeed
of the transatlantic West. If, writing his ranching sketches,
Roosevelt did not give us a distanced, critical history, he did give
us the sense of fascination. And that, as in the fiction of Wister
which he praised, would make his own writings "historic documents" in the story of American response to the cattleman's frontier.

The letter to Gilder further described ranching as a "wild"
industry of the "great lonely plains." The image evoked would be
fully sustained by the sketches to follow. Once again it was a personal conception. One suspects that had ranching not seemed
wild, Roosevelt would not have been fascinated by it. Had it been
an industry as tame as shoe manufacturing, he would have left it
to others or, like many enterprising and affluent Americans, let
his invested money "work" while he watched the sunsets from his
long front porch. Certainly ranching in the Bad Lands was carried on in a setting that could still be called wilderness. In the absence of fences, controlled pastures, close herding of any kind except during roundups, the cattle themselves were wild, compet-
ing with deer, antelope, and even buffalo for the sometimes limited forage. Yet others involved in ranching would have been less
likely to call the industry itself wild. In the historiography of
ranching before 1888, whatever the wild elements that surrounded it or loosened its economic context, the institution itself
was not regarded as wild. On the contrary, it was considered an
advancement—even if sometimes only an outpost—of civilization. Joseph G. McCoy, in his *Historic Sketches of the Cattle Trade,*
wrote of the wildness of the celebrating cowboys. Certainly he

recognized a degree of wildness in his town of Abilene. Nevertheless, it cannot be said that he thought of ranching as wild. Ranching, like the establishment of the trail and the marketing facilities, was simply an institutional stage in the cattle trade, a trade as fully civilized in its basic commitment to human order and control as any other. McCoy attached no value to wildness, at best tolerating it in the trail-driving cowboys. And a similar sense of ranching values can surely be attributed to General Brisbin and others.

Wildness invested with value suggests primitivism, and there can be no doubt that ranching, at least what seemed its wilder features, appealed to a primitivistic layer in Roosevelt's personality. It was not a case of a return to nature in the classic experience of finding again a primal goodness uncorrupted by civilization. Roosevelt was not in any sense a child of nature; he was instead a child of New York and Harvard. Unlike Leatherstocking, whom he must have admired and on whom at times his own ways seem to have been modeled, he read books, not the face of nature. Indeed, nature, in the benevolent, humanistic sense needed to support romantic primitivism, is missing from his thought. The frontier stockmen, like Boone and others before them, were not so much philosophers of nature as they were "pioneers of civilization."[28]

There was, nevertheless, a good deal of ambivalence about this civilization, a recognition that it was destined to spread over the land and wipe out the wilderness, that it would take social and political form in the "populous commonwealths,"[29] yet a lingering regret that its passing, whatever the rightness of settlement and cities, would mean the end of "what is perhaps the pleasantest, healthiest, and most exciting phase of American existence."[30] If this was not a belief in a return to nature, it was a preference for a primitive stage of existence, and it was a primitivistic judgment on the refined features of nineteenth-century civilization. "The great free ranches," he wrote, "with their barbarous, picturesque, and curiously fascinating surroundings, mark a primitive stage of existence as surely as do the great tracts of primeval forests."[31] "Ranching is an occupation," he had written a bit earlier, "like those of vigorous, primitive pastoral peoples, having little in common with the humdrum, workaday business world of the

nineteenth century; and the free ranchman in manner of life
shows more kinship to an Arab sheik than to a sleek city merchant
or tradesman."[32] The Far West "is no place," he observed, "for men
who lack the ruder, coarser virtues and physical qualities, no
matter how intellectual or how refined and delicate their sensibilities."[33] The cowboys, whom he admired and with whom he
sought to identify, have these ruder, coarser virtues; they are
unspoiled by the traits of civilization suggested by Roosevelt's
primitivistic gathering of pejorative terms: *humdrum, workaday,
sleek, refined,* and *delicate.* A few years after the publication of *Ranch
Life,* he commented with amusement on the revulsion to greasy
quilts in a logging story by Hamlin Garland. "They are distressing
to an overcivilized man," he wrote to Brander Matthews; "but for
my own pleasure this year when I was out on the antelope plains I
got into a country where I didn't take my clothes off for ten days. I
had two cow punchers along and the quilts and bedding, including
the pillows which they had, were quite as bad as those Garland
describes in his logging camp; yet they both felt they were off on a
holiday and having a lovely time."[34]

Roosevelt's account of wild ranching, with its occasional celebration of primitivistic rudeness, was however curiously softened
by touches that can only be called appreciations of the refine-
ments of civilization. The home ranch, as he characterized it in
the second of the sketches which made up *Ranch Life,* seems less a
primitive outpost than a vacation resort, perhaps an early version
of a dude ranch. Noting that many ranches provided a very limited fare, he contrasted the variety of his own larder. "We ourselves always keep up two or three cows, choosing such as are
naturally tame, and so we invariably have plenty of milk and, when
there is time for churning, a good deal of butter. We also keep
hens, which, in spite of the damaging inroads of hawks, bobcats,
and foxes, supply us with eggs, and in time of need, when our
rifles have failed to keep us in game, with stewed, roast, or fried
chicken also. From our garden we get potatoes, and unless
drought, frost, or grasshoppers interfere (which they do about
every second year), other vegetables as well." A more primitivistic
note concludes the observation: "For fresh meat we depend
chiefly upon our prowess as hunters."[35] Later he details the mid-
day dinner. "Whatever be the hour, it is the most substantial

meal of the day, and we feel that we have little fault to find with a table on whose clean cloth are spread platters of smoked elk meat, loaves of good bread, jugs and bowls of milk, saddles of venison or broiled antelope steaks, perhaps roast and fried prairie chicken, with eggs, butter, wild plums, and tea or coffee."[36] There were further amenities. On occasion the ranchman, seemingly well-fed, will have "a good deal of spare time on his hands, which, if he chooses, he can spend in reading and writing. If he cares for books," Roosevelt goes on, "there will be many a worn volume in the primitive little sitting-room, with its log walls and huge fireplace." Or after a hard day's work, he may prefer to "rock to and fro in the flickering firelight" or to "lie stretched at full length on the elk-hides and wolf-skins in front of the hearthstone, listening in drowsy silence to the roar and crackle of the blazing logs and to the moaning of the wind outside."[37]

In the closed contentment of the home ranch, the ranchman might seem to forget that his wild industry was situated on the great lonely plains. Or perhaps the realization that this great lonely world began just beyond the log walls made the fire-lit pleasure even more intense. Whatever the coziness of the domestic center, the image of vastness and loneliness pervades Roosevelt's account of his ranching world. The exploring stockmen thread their way "through the trackless wastes of plain, plateau, and riverbottom." The pioneer herds find their ways "among the great dreary solitudes." An outfit might be months "on its lonely journey, slowly making its way over melancholy, pathless plains, or down the valleys of lonely rivers." In winter, "when the sun is out the glare from the endless white stretches dazzles the eyes; and if the gray snow-clouds hang low and only let a pale, wan light struggle through, the lonely wastes become fairly appalling in their desolation."[38]

I have called this image Roosevelt's central metaphor for the ranchman's world, meaning that it organizes not only some abstract geographical features such as vastness and tracklessness, but also some subjective responses such as loneliness, dreariness, and the feeling of being appalled. Granted that such a metaphor had prevailed and would prevail from Washington Irving to Walter Prescott Webb, one must still ask, why this metaphor for the setting of one's so joyous freedom? The ranchman-writer admitted again to its fascination. "Nowhere, not even at sea," he wrote in *Hunting Trips,* "does a man feel more lonely than when riding over the far-reaching, seemingly never-ending plains; and when a man has lived a little while on or near them, their very vastness and loneliness and their melancholy monotony have a strong fascination for him."[39] In *The Wilderness Hunter,* he repeated the observation. "No man save the wilderness dweller knows the strong melancholy fascination of these long rides through lonely lands."[40]

In spite of such assertions of fascination, however, there remains the critical fact that nowhere in his sketches does the rancher render the experience of loneliness or melancholy. Whatever the trackless vastness and thus whatever the imagined possibilities of loneliness and melancholy, Roosevelt did not experience such loneliness, or if he did, the literary memory of it is so steady and stalwart that the emotional immediacy of the original experience has been seemingly forgotten. If the wilderness ever overwhelmed him, if he ever suffered from what Charles Neider has called ego exhaustion,[41] he did not show it personally in his sketches. There is thus a further rightness in calling this ranching world a metaphor, for its literary features seem not to have been discovered and shaped in the writer's own sense encounter. On the contrary, they seem to have come out of a literary tradition which imagines bigness and emptiness precisely because they are needed to challenge the persevering wilderness hero. That hero, in the person of Theodore Roosevelt, seems finally as much at home, as untroubled by disorientation and alienation, as Leatherstocking himself.

IV

A fresh reading of Roosevelt's ranching sketches, unguided by the intentions he declared in his letter to Gilder, further clarifies his achievements and his limitations as a contributor to the literature of the cattle trade. Writing, as his friend Wister put it, "while the iron was still hot, when the range was still a living thing and not a romantic memory,"[42] what could he offer? Not history, as we have already noted, but perhaps something important to history, the look and feel of events and places lived rather than merely read about. Critics of his own and later generations could scarcely fault him for the vigor, indeed the gusto, with which he told his story.[43] And whatever their contemporary prejudices, they could not be blind to the visual rightness of his prose at its best. If, as Henry Beers insisted, Roosevelt had little imagination, he had nevertheless an eager and often dependable eye.[44] Brander Matthews perhaps claimed too much for his friend, but in top form Roosevelt could, as Matthews said, "write about [things seen and done] so vividly and so sharply as to make his readers see them."[45]

Of the critical essays written about *Ranch Life and the Hunting Trail,* the best remains Wister's introduction to the Scribner's edition of 1926. In "The Young Roosevelt," Wister could write with an understanding possible only to someone like Roosevelt himself, someone educated in literary and historical traditions and at the same time experienced in the raw events of frontier life. Wister was on the right track in his characterization of Roosevelt's vision. In the long uncertain growth of a western literary criticism, we can be glad that Wister *saw* Roosevelt as he did, and we may wish that others had been able to *see* the cowboys and ranchers as Roosevelt did. Yet the seeing here also involves a sort of blindness. The claims of Wister, not to mention those of Matthews, need qualification. There is a paradox, a paradox which can perhaps be best understood if we examine Roosevelt's rendering of his ranch world and his manner of describing cowboys.

"Only a civilized and enlightened observer," wrote Wister in his introduction, "could adequately appreciate at sight such a life, such people, such scenery; to 'see' it needed both the gift and the experience to make comparisons. To *look* at it [Wister's emphasis] was by no means enough. Looking at it had produced merely caricature in the way of cartoons and melodrama."[46] The context here is western, but the critical position is Jamesian. More than anyone else Henry James had given special meaning to *seeing,* distinguishing it from mere looking and adding *appreciation* to suggest the enrichment of the novelistic vision. Perhaps James could not have appreciated a cowboy at sight, but he would nevertheless have agreed with his friend Wister that seeing a

cowboy involved a good bit more than being aware of his sombrero and chaps. It involved some perception of his inner and
moral nature. Whatever Roosevelt's differences with James—and
there were many, some of them rather strenuously put—Wister
could argue that Roosevelt had this perception. Certainly in a
limited sense of the word Roosevelt appreciated cowboys. Self-
reliant and fearless, yet capable of courtesy and the most whole-
souled hospitality, they were in many ways his personal heroes
and he lost few opportunities to identify with them. Yet it can be
argued that his description, however sympathetic it may seem to
be, is as much a cartoon as is McCoy's account of the dancing
cowboy of Abilene. Whatever the picturesqueness of the detail,
whatever the vigor of the narrative style, at the point of the
cowboy this is, as Beers said, a mind without subtlety.[47] His imagination, as both James and Wister might have defined that
novelist's gift, was superficial indeed.

One way to characterize Roosevelt's blindness is to say that
too often he could not see the particular for the general, the
person for the type. In the epistemology of history and literature,
the delicate equation between organizing conception and raw
phenomenal perception was overweighted with the former.
However fresh his material, he brought to it as writer a dominating burden of Cooper, Parkman, and a hundred other con-
tributors to a frontier tradition. The consequent unevenness of
Roosevelt's prose can be seen in a brief series of selected passages.
At one point in *Hunting Trips,* the following sentence narrates the
hunt: "Accordingly one of us sallied forth, but found that the
sacrifice was not to be consummated so easily, for the should-be
victims [deer] appeared to distinguish perfectly well between a
mere passer-by, whom they regarded with absolute indifference,
and any one who harbored sinister designs."[48] In all of Cooper is
there a bit of prose as stiff, as awkwardly abstract as this? Near the
conclusion of the same work, the style moves the reader closer to
the world out there beyond the writer's dominating consciousness: "The woods seemed vast and lonely, and their silence was
broken now and then by the strange noises always to be heard in
the great forests and which seem to mark the sad and everlasting
unrest of the wilderness."[49] Yet this too is self-consciously literary,
romantically vague and abstract. However, at occasional special

moments in Roosevelt's prose, the pressure of immediate experience asserted itself even in memory; the prose quickened, the detail became concrete, the traditional forms were pushed aside. "In the still nights we could hear the trees crack and jar from the strain of the biting frost; and in its winding bed the river lay fixed like a huge bent bar of blue steel." "We wound our way through a dense jungle where the gray, thorny buffalo bushes, spangled with brilliant red berry-clusters, choked the spaces between the thick-growing box-alders." "Little striped gophers scuttled away, or stood perfectly straight at the mouths of their burrows, looking like picket-pins." And one can find little fault with the sight and sound and rhythm of this account of an eagle attacking: "Instantly the great bird rushed down through the humming air, with closed wings; checked itself when some forty yards above the jack, hovered for a moment, and again fell like a bolt. Away went long-ears, running as only a frightened jack can; and after him the eagle, not with the arrowy rush of its descent from high air, but with eager, hurried flapping."[50]

If this was not perhaps seeing in the Jamesian sense, it was nevertheless using the eye honestly and letting it find its own appropriate sequence of images and words. Such instances in the rancher's prose have a high degree of visual integrity. But the seeing of cowboys was a more complicated matter. What he saw about cowboys he may have reported honestly; the trouble was that he saw much too little. There was perhaps, as Wister implied, no caricature and no melodrama, yet there was little seeing in the Jamesian sense. Roosevelt's literary imagination was content with the surface patterns of color and action. In his somewhat extravagant praise of his friend's observations, Wister was perhaps bringing some of his own imaginative insights to Roosevelt's sketches.

The roundup was the favorite scene. Roosevelt returned to it again and again. Indeed there was little else of cowboy work that he reported so fully. Here was action of the most vigorous sort; here was an event "full of excitement and adventure"; here was an exhibition of "pluck, self-reliance, hardihood, and dashing horsemanship."[51] Yet in the sketches there is a superficial fascination with mere movement; there is a young writer's fascination with the verbals of external action. Two passages from *The Wil-*

derness Hunter will illustrate: "The other men rode to the wagon to get a hasty dinner—lithe, sinewy fellows, with weather-roughened faces and fearless eyes; their broad felt hats flapped as they galloped, and their spurs and bridle chains jingled." "The dust rose in little whirling clouds, and through it dashed bolting cattle and galloping cowboys, hither and thither, while the air was filled with the shouts and laughter of the men, and the bellowing of the herd." To these let us add a sentence from *Ranch Life* telling of the commotion caused by a just-branded bull: "Down goes his head, and he bolts at the nearest man, who makes out of the way at top speed, amidst roars of laughter from all his companions; while the men holding down calves swear savagely as they dodge charging mavericks, trampling horses, and taut lariats with frantic, plunging little beasts at the farther ends."[52] Granted that Roosevelt's ranching pieces are sketches and thus perhaps by design lacking in any sustained probing of particular cowboys, particular skills and motivations, one nevertheless misses a way of seeing that even the sketch allows, an awareness that cowboys are persons as well as types, the evidence that seeing cowboys, even in brief, fleeting episodes, means discovering a name, a dusty smile, a grimace of pain, a token of something inside the weathered skin beneath the grand abstractions of manliness and hardihood. One concludes that however much he thought he identified with cowboys, Roosevelt kept his distance or continued to wear his social blinders.

Another way to characterize Roosevelt's blindness is to say that he had no Lin McLean. Whatever the ultimate shortcomings of McLean as a fully-appreciated literary cowboy, he did enable Wister imaginatively to close the gap between Harvard and the cow-raising hinterlands. Lin was a person. More important he was a vernacular person. His way of thinking and feeling, his way of speaking, his estimate of himself depended in no way upon social and intellectual traditions. If he had evolved from the Knights of the Round Table, Wister did not bother to mention that high fact.

Roosevelt, in short, lacked a sense of the vernacular. In spite of the value with which he theoretically invested the cowboy, in spite of earnest efforts at a personal range camaraderie with him, Roosevelt was never able to take the cowboy completely on the cowboy's own terms. He admired Wister's novel very much, but what he liked, as he wrote to the novelist, was "the broad humanity that comes when we deal with any men of strong and simple nature."[53] Lin McLean does perhaps represent broad humanity in a simple nature, but such abstractions say very little about him as a person and very little about him as a cowboy. When Roosevelt homogenizes all cowboys into such essentially romantic concepts, we gain a high principle of value, but we lose the cowboy as existing human being. And as historians we lose the concreteness which is the very stuff of history, the empirical evidence which suggests, at least confirms, any historical generalizations we may be inclined to make.

There remains nevertheless a rightness in Wister's claim about Roosevelt's way of seeing cowboys. The cowboy could not simply be looked at in all of his picturesqueness of dress and behavior. He needed to be understood, and that understanding required appreciating him not only on his own terms but also on society's terms, in the vision, as Wister put it, of "a civilized and enlightened observer."[54] If Roosevelt lacked the first appreciation, he did provide the second. We can be glad of that. But we cannot thus say that he made up for a deficiency in the first appreciation by the exuberance of the second. We can only say that understanding cowboys is a more difficult act than Roosevelt—and even Wister—realized, that it is a complicated act of mind and imagination, requiring as does any act of literary and historical understanding a sense of the human being both as self-aware subject and as social object.

V

Anyone who knows anything at all about Roosevelt's days as a rancher remembers his famous order to one of his men. Some cows gathered in the roundup had made a sudden bolt out of the herd. Roosevelt had tried to turn them back, but they had evaded him. It was then that he shouted to one of his men: "Hasten forward quickly there!"[55] The resulting laughter of the cowboys within hearing distance and generations of western readers since has helped confirm the cartoon of a tenderfoot (if strenuous) eastern rancher who might as well have been wearing a bowler and a frock coat as long as his cowboy talk so completely missed the mark.

It remains biographically true that Roosevelt probably never sounded like a cowboy, and it is critically true that he never wrote like one. His high-standard prose was never loosened enough to let the vernacular flavor and rhythms of the range come through. And yet no one in his time was more dedicated to the task of noticing and preserving the language of the range frontier.

Clearly the diction of cowboyland fascinated him. Lexicographers of western American will consequently owe him at least a long footnote of tribute for his pioneering efforts in their cause. Some of the evidence is again in the letters. To Charles Dana of the New York *Sun,* he wrote: "In your list of Indian words adopted into our language I did not notice that you included 'cayuse,' in use for small Indian horses in the far Northwest." In the same letter he added, "I was surprised to see your correspondent put down 'bronco' as a Spanish word. It is hardly ever used on the Mexican border, while it is in universal use on the northern cattle plains."[56] To Edwin Godkin, who had published a review of Emerson Hough's *Story of a Cowboy,* he wrote: "The reviewer's criticisms of Mr. Hough's Spanish give me a pang for the simple reason that I think I have committed every fault that Hough did, including the spelling of 'bronk' as if it were in some way connected with lung complaint. By the way, I wonder if the reviewer can tell me from what Spanish word we get the curious term 'Horsewrangler'? At least I suppose it is Spanish, for I should not think that such a term could have been invented."[57] A few weeks later he wrote to Charles Lummis: "Horsewrangler is such a well-known term in the West now. I wish you would sometime write out, and put in permanent form, an article on all these Spanish terms."[58] And the same day he wrote to Richard Watson Gilder suggesting that *horsewrangler* ought to be added to the *Century Dictionary.*[59]

This was what might be called the picturesque aspect of cowboy speech. The prose of the ranching sketches is sprinkled with its terms. There is thus a western flavoring, a linguistic dash of the cowboy's salt, if not his pepper. But the living tissue of cowboy talk, the little, more commonplace terms and the deviant grammatical structures, apparently escaped his notice or at least made little impact upon his own writing. But perhaps one desires too much; perhaps it is unrealistic to expect so brief a cowboy to have become so complete a cowboy.

VI

Whatever the critic's reservations, the sketches, one should finally add, won an official approval. In 1905, when Roosevelt was president of the United States, the National Live Stock Association honored him with a prominent biography in its *Prose and Poetry of the Live Stock Industry.* "His experience on the range and elsewhere," the writer observed, "added largely to his knowledge and to his admiration of his fellow-countrymen, and from it," the writer added, "he drew the inspiration and obtained the material for those of his books in which he so vividly portrays scenes, tragedies, characteristics, comedies, and incidents of the 'cowtown,' the ranch, the range, and the hunting trail."[60] In this context one might further suggest that the sketches had indeed the style of a president-to-be. Or put another way, perhaps there was always more president than cowboy in the rancher from the Bad Lands. But this, of course, was exactly as the leading stockmen of America preferred it to be.

Prose and Poetry of the Cattle Industry: Fact and Image as the Centuries Changed

For half a century the biggest and rarest book in the historiography of the cattle trade was *Prose and Poetry of the Live Stock Industry of the United States.* A full eight by eleven inches with the thickness of a three-inch beam, it tipped the scales at nearly seven pounds when it was published in 1905. The historian was lucky if he had a bookshelf on which it could stand. He was even luckier if he had the book itself. Ramon Adams, bibliographer of the cattle trade, wrote: "In my many years of collecting books on the cattle industry of our great West, I have never seen this rare book listed in any dealer's catalogue."[1]

Among historians of the cattle trade, however, the book's real importance is neither physical nor bibliographic. Adams believed *Prose and Poetry* "to be not only the most thorough, but the most important book on the range cattle industry yet written." Walter Prescott Webb called it "perhaps the most thorough and comprehensive work on the subject."[2] Still other historians undoubtedly put it high on their lists of basic works.

Given this historiographical reputation, one easily supposes that *Prose and Poetry* is a work of completeness, factualness, and objectivity and that as a work of this kind it differs clearly from much of the imaginative literature of the cattle trade, particularly fiction, being published in this same period. A critical reading of the work, however, shows it to be informed not only by the facts of the cattle trade but also by the images and ideologies of American culture as the centuries changed. It tells us as much about the minds and imaginations of livestock historians as it tells us about the world of cows and cowboys. Furthermore, a brief history of this history reveals not only how the cattleman saw himself in his present but also how he supposed he might find his proper place in Clio's company.

I

Few if any histories of the livestock industries have come out of plans as ambitious—one might even say grandiose—and official as those which led to the writing and publication of *Prose and Poetry of the Live Stock Industry*. By the end of the nineteenth century, some stockmen were beginning to look back on their frontier achievement; they were moved by a sense of the past.[3] Some of them had lived a good bit of it; they were indeed the pioneers.[4] One of them, John W. Springer, dreamed that some day "their history might be gathered from ocean to ocean, from the lakes to the gulf; that from Columbus, from the Spaniards, from Pilgrim Fathers, down through the centuries, we might trace the growth of . . . [the] chief source of man's food supply."[5] For the purpose of preparing this "complete, reliable and interesting history,"[6] the National Live Stock Historical Association was organized to become the sponsoring authority, and its secretary, Charles F. Martin, was directed to work with the historical association to ensure that the history would be correct and one which the Live Stock Association could stand by. Three volumes were planned, some two thousand or three thousand pages, "a colossal work" Springer called it.[7] In fancy one constructs a shelf to support the set; but then he despairs and leaves the volumes stacked like a great brown block on the heavy top of an oak-legged table.

However, the first volume was also the last. The great project remained unfinished. The reasons are not clear, but the difficulties in bringing the first volume to print may suggest a potential collapse of Springer's great dream. When the National Live Stock Association met in Portland in 1904, its officers were able to report considerable progress as well as some delays. "A corps of trained writers," President Springer noted, "are scouring the country and the libraries for all the historical data obtainable, while others are soliciting leaders of the present to permit their lives to be written and their likenesses handed down in the work. It has taken all of 1903," he added, "and it will take all of 1904, to bring out the first volume. The second should appear in 1905, or sooner, and the prices have been made reasonable considering the labor and expense involved."[8] The following year, at the convention in Denver, Springer talked of "the great historical work" being printed in Kansas City and ready for delivery a month hence. "It is," he remarked, "one of the handsomest works, typographically and every way, ever issued from the American press. While the set of books costs you [the stockmen] $27.50, it costs $25.00 wholesale to issue them, so it is no small undertaking, and with this Association getting a substantial percentage on every one sold, there ought to be a great many dollars in the treasury of the National Live Stock Association before January." In a final appeal for support, Springer indicated what was perhaps obvious to all closely concerned with the project, that great risk and expense had been involved.[9]

This was the last official report on the venture. The first volume was copyrighted in 1904 by the Hudson-Kimberly Publishing Company; but the expense of publication supposedly "broke" this firm, with the project consequently picked up by a new company, the Franklin Hudson Publishing Company. One volume only came from its presses,[10] and we are left guessing about what happened to the association's plans to make the history of livestock one of the biggest histories of all time. One suspects that however enthusiastic Springer, Martin, and others may have been, the ordinary stockman was moved, if moved at all, by a lesser and more practical interest. While he had no objection to someone making a book, between that acquiescence and putting down $27.50 lay a considerable distance. After all he could buy a pretty cow for that. One suspects, then, that the great project turned into a bookseller's disaster.[11]

The failure of the historical venture left other unknowns, not only further facts about the livestock industry but also additional notions about the nature of the three-volume work itself. Not the least of the unanswered questions concerns the curious title. Literary historians are hardened to titles like *Prose and Poetry of the Romantic Period,* but they may blink once or twice at *Prose and Poetry of the Live Stock Industry.* One supposes that old tough-minded cattlemen grunted a profane surprise or two, but accepted with final patience the prospect of a garland of verses celebrating the beauty of the sunrise over the old cowshed. The wives, they might have conceded, could enjoy at least that part of the book, and they could earn their enjoyment by having to put up with dusting around a volume that made the Sears Roebuck catalogue look almost as small as a pocket Bible. But, of course, the wives never got their garland, if garland there was to be. Ramon Adams suggests that the poetry was to come in the subsequent volumes,[12] but internal evidence hardly supports that suggestion. Toward the end of volume 1, the reader learns that fluctuations in market prices were to be treated in volume 2. Scarcely poetry as we usually know it. It seems clear, to this reader at least, that the title came from President Springer himself. The portion of his presidential address announcing the historical project was called "Prose and Poetry of Live Stock." Unfortunately that portion does not indicate what would be considered prose and what would count as poetry.

Since the available evidence does not make clear what was meant by "prose" and what was meant by "poetry," I should like to adapt these terms to my special critical purposes. In ordinary usage, "prose" may signify unembellished, unimaginative discourse; "poetry," on the other hand, is likely to mean writing or expression which is imaginative, writing marked less by a pattern or sequence of facts than by organized thought and feeling.[13] I shall therefore use *prose* to indicate the plain, seemingly factual aspects of *Prose and Poetry,* and I shall use *poetry* to indicate those aspects which in one way or another are primarily imaginative. Running the risk of simplification, I might call these different aspects the "historical" and the "literary."[14] It should be further understood that my intention is to treat these aspects as they are revealed in the text of the book, not as they may be found among the conscious purposes of the writers and the sponsoring stockmen. In spite of the title one supposes that the work was planned as history, not literature in the imaginative sense. However, as already suggested, the prose (the history) has a good bit of poetry mixed in it, and the poetry has important similarities to the poetry (the fiction) of the contemporary range literature that the history may have sought to correct.

II

Man is very much a creature of his surroundings.
Prose and Poetry of the Live Stock Industry

A history of the livestock industry might well begin with geography, and a critical study of that history might well begin with the images in that geography.[15] The cattle must have a place to graze; what they eventually become, whether they survive the hazards of weather, become meaty if not fat and marketable, depends upon the grasslands they occupy. Later, stored hay and grains and the comforts of shed and feed yard would break the grip of circumstance; but through the last decades of the nineteenth century a cow was pretty much a creature of her natural surroundings. Geographical determinism made sense.

But more important for history—even a history of the livestock industry—is the relationship of land to men. Were the stockmen in the late nineteenth century also creatures of their surroundings? They were, of course, cattle raisers and trail drivers rather than ministers and musicians, but did the environment have a deeper hold?

The human setting, insofar as it is rendered in *Prose and Poetry,* has little of the detailed or photographic hardness of objective geography.[16] It is instead a curious mix of images common to the literature of a century of transition. Compare, for example, the following passages: "The rolling prairies, covered at the same time with a luxuriant carpet of grass, appeared as verdant as on the morning of creation."[17] "The general aspect of the plains was, as it still is where the works of men have not disturbed it, one of sadness—even melancholy. The land seemed to be grieving over something that was lost forever. Then there was the silence of it . . . . The effects of the atmosphere of sadness, of the loneliness, and of the unbroken quiet of the vast stretches of the plains became oppressive, burdensome, maddening. . . . They bore down upon the mind as would a heavy weight upon the body; and a torturing heartache then kept company with a sense of exile."[18] In the mythic terms of the late nineteenth century, here was the West as Eden, and the West after the Fall, the West with a spiritual unity of man and Nature, and the West with man alienated from the world in which he exists.

The first of these images of man and nature had had a long and vital currency, although by 1905 it seemed to some more and more a literary vestige of an earlier time.[19] It was, of course, the ground (or should I say the garden) of primitivism. It indicated a central unity of romantic faith. Vestige or not, it revealed an abiding conviction about the West; its ideology spoke eloquently in *Prose and Poetry*. "This life upon the range," says the writer,[20] "brings one into contact with Nature, widens the horizons and instills a loftiness of soul that should be the inheritance of every human being, for in truth, there is greater real happiness in living close to nature than in breathing the smoke and dust of the greatest metropolis."[21] A splendid example of nature's cattleman was Charles Goodnight, who possessed "a breadth of view and fund of information upon a wide range of subjects that are surprising to persons whose lives have been spent among books, rather than in contact with Nature."[22] A further example was "the real mountaineer" of northwestern Colorado. "For him the majestic solitudes speak a language interpreted only by the heart, and the message is always one of pleasantness and peace."[23]

If the garden of the West was sometimes less verdant than vast, sometimes less conducive to peace than to bigness of conception, it was nevertheless the setting for a large moral fulfillment. Clearly bigness of land meant bigness of mind; implicit was bigness of soul. "It was a big country," says the writer in *Prose and Poetry*, "and its bigness broke down and suppressed small ideas and small things. Whatever it was, it must have size, largeness, to be worthwhile. The great range seemed endless—like the wide ocean; the trails were long—measured by hundreds of miles; and the herds were large—'hundred' being too small a unity for use in their counting. In this bigness of things there was no room for those that were little."[24]

That such images and ideas were generally prevalent around the turn of the century can be demonstrated by a sampling of western range rhetoric, historiography, and fiction. For example, primitivistic assumptions abound in the official oratory of the stockmen. Addressing the National Stock Growers' Convention in 1898, Governor Alva Adams of Colorado, himself a stockman, observed: "The world of the stockman upon the prairie had a broad horizon; it made him a broad man. There is a mental tonic in the atmosphere of the unfenced plain. . . . You may be short in society manners and society clothes, but the stockman is long in manhood."[25] John W. Springer, in his presidential address to the National Live Stock Association in 1901, warmed to the romantic vision: "Happy that man, and thrice blessed he who keeps in touch with nature, and can draw inspiration from the prairies, the valleys, the hills and mountains! . . . Little wonder is it that the western man loves his broad expanse of verdure-clad hills, prairies and mountains . . . . His nature broadens with his generous environment; while his soul attunes to the lowing of the herds."[26] Speaking to the same convention, C. C. Goodwin of Utah added a theistic touch: "While men in the cities are going wild over stocks, struggling to win against the sharp competition of their neighbors, Nature is calling on you to mark by day the marvels which have been spread out for your possession, and by night the processions of the stars sweeping on and on are the lanterns swung aloft that you may mark the order and the law and the splendor of the universe, and through them gain glimpses of the majesty of Him who sent them blazing on their shining courses."[27] In 1904, at the annual convention of the stockmen, Dr. J. E. Stubbs, president of the University of Nevada, spoke again the favorite thought: "There is something in the vast extent and varied physical aspects of the West that makes men broadminded. . . . They cannot look upon the mountains and valleys, upon the vast table-lands rising into magnificent peaks . . . without feeling that exaltation of mind which makes for greater freedom, more ardent love of home, deeper pride in our civic institutions, and loyalty and love for our common country."[28] "The broad horizon of the plain," said Governor Adams again in 1906, "gave them [the cattlemen] a keen and wide vision of life."[29]

In American historiography, the classic claim that bigness of land induces bigness of mind came from Frederick Jackson Turner. "The American," he had written, "had continually before him the vision of a continent to be subdued, challenging his courage and ambition, calling out his endeavor in the presence of unparalled opportunities, raising the competitive spirit to its highest point, stimulating nervous energy, inventiveness, optimism, practical capacity and largeness of design."[30] Amplitude of space meant amplitude of mind.

Other historians saw the West with a similar vision. "The great West," wrote Emerson Hough, "vast and rude, brought forth men also vast and rude. . . . Into their hearts came the elemental disturbance of the storm, the strength of the hills, the broadness of the prairies. . . . These babes of the West were giants, because that was a land of giants."[31] This broadness in the heart was of course good; it was related to what Hough called the "instinct for justice," the "faithfulness and manliness" of the cowboy.[32] As already noted, the big West as moral force was less explicitly argued by Theodore Roosevelt. Yet, to repeat, it seems clear that the western ranges were for Roosevelt a most suitable setting, if not the operating cause, of a heroic morality. "To appreciate properly his fine, manly qualities," wrote Roosevelt, "the wild rough-rider of the plains should be seen in his own home. . . . He lives in the lonely lands where mighty rivers twist in long reaches between the barren bluffs; where the prairies stretch out into billowy plains of waving grass, girt only by the blue horizon,—plains across whose endless breadth he can steer his course for days and weeks and see neither man to speak to nor hill to break the level . . . ."[33]

Later historians, following Turner, would seem to insist less upon nature as the cause of goodness than upon nature as the setting for freedom, where individualism, fostered by this freedom, might become good *or* bad. Turner, in his classic paper of 1893, had written of "that dominant individualism, working for good or for evil," but his style as historian argued nevertheless for a moral outcome to the westward movement. If, as he wrote in *Rise of the New West,* western democracy "came, stark and strong and full of life, from the American forest" or, as he clearly implied, from the American prairies, then the individualism engendered there must have worked for good rather than for evil. Frederick L. Paxson, in a Turnerian chapter on "The Westward Movement," emphasized frontier "qualities of positive force for good or bad." "The bad man," he wrote, "has been quite as typical of the frontier as the hero, but both have possessed its dominant virtues of self-confidence, vigor, and initiative."[34]

Need I suggest that most of this cannot be proved historically? If we believe it to be true, then the truth is in us, not in history. It is a poetic truth, not a prosaic truth. The historian can no
more measure the breadth of a stockman's soul than he can match
the riches of his rangelands against the pastures of Eden.[35]

The literary scholar will of course know the persistence of the
Edenic in the American vision of the West. From the discoverer
himself, Columbus, down into our own time, we have seemed to
need this mythic West. It shows in various ways in western historiography, and it is revealed abundantly in imaginative literature,[36] even in those works which purport to bring fiction closer to
history and therefore presumably away from myth.

For the literary rangelands of the West, two instances will
suffice as illustration. In *Reed Anthony, Cowman* by Andy Adams,
that writer so admired for his authenticity, even a part of Texas
near the Llano Estacado is made Edenic by the writer's imagery.

There was something primal in the scene,—something that brought back
the words, "In the beginning God created the heavens and the earth."
Men who know neither creed nor profession of faith felt themselves
drawn very near to some great creative power. The surrounding view
held us spellbound by its beauty and strength. It was like a rush of fern-
scents, the breath of pine forests, the music of the stars, the first lovelight
in a mother's eye; and now its pristine beauty was to be marred, as covet-
ous eyes and a lust of possession moved an earth-born man to lay hands
on all things created for his use.[37]

Another Edenic scene comes in Wister's *The Virginian*. The titular
cowboy has his island "deep in the unsurveyed and virgin wilderness," where he goes for many hours of reverie "in its haunting
sweetness." To Molly, whom he has taken to the island after their
marriage, he says, "Often when I have camped here, it has made
me want to become the ground, become the water, become the
trees, mix with the whole thing. Not know myself from it. Never
unmix again."[38]

III

It is, however, man's destiny as man to unmix, to feel his separation
and indeed his alienation from nature. And thus we come back to

that other image in *Prose and Poetry,* the West as a vast lonely stretch of plains upon which the stockman feels a sense of exile.

Insofar as rangeland anthropology was grounded in romantic primitivism, Nature was not only the place but also the sponsor of a joyful freedom. Hough stated the view explicitly: "Be sure, he [the cowboy] came from among those who had strong within them that savagery and love of freedom which springs so swiftly into life among strong natures when offered a brief exemption from the slavery of civilization."[39] Throughout his book on the cowboy, Hough sounded this note of freedom. On the Long Trail the vast processions of cattle were "guarded by men who never knew a master." "The natural fitness and natural longings of . . . [young men] led them readily into the free outdoor life" of cowpunching. The cowboy "followed . . . [this life] because he loved it for its freedom." The West was "the land *par excellence* of beef and freedom."[40] With even greater gusto, as we have already noted, Theodore Roosevelt also celebrated the freedom of the West. He had felt the charm of life on "the great free ranches," had "exulted in its abounding vigor and its bold, restless freedom."[41] "The hunter," thought Roosevelt, "is the arch-type of freedom," and the cowboy had followed the hunter, being moved too by a "bold, free spirit."[42]

This romantic conviction informs a good bit of the prose of *Prose and Poetry,* and being more personal faith than provable fact, more lyrical than literal in its presentation, it moves that prose in the direction of poetry. Roosevelt himself is one of its heroes. "Each return to his ranch," his biographer wrote in *Prose and Poetry,* "was with enthusiastic fondness for the free life in the open that it afforded him, and for the stout-hearted men of the range."[43] If there was monotony in the life of the cowboy, said the author of *Prose and Poetry,* there was also charm. In large measure it came from "the freedom, the occasional exciting episodes, but most of all from the vigorous good health that went hand in hand with it in the pure and exhilarating air of the plains."[44]

The rhetoric of the stockmen themselves added confirmation. Addressing the first annual convention of the American National Live Stock Association in 1906, Alva Adams declaimed the favorite scripture: the empire of the cattleman was "a vast territory of freedom." Cowboys, he said, have through the years grown gray hairs and become city millionaires, but "they have never discarded the brave and manly traits that were theirs in the wild, free life of the open range." Does the gray-haired, dignified cattleman, Adams wondered, perhaps "ever hunger for the license and the freedom of those lawless, wild days, when, as a cowboy, he was king upon the fenceless domain of the prairies?"[45]

But to repeat, if there was in *Prose and Poetry* an image of this kind of West, where the cowboy could be a free king upon the fenceless domain of the prairies, there was also another kind. Its presentation involved poetry too, but with a darker set of images, a less exultant song. Ironically, in this other kind of West, freedom was supported not by nature but by the debased civilization of the cowtowns.[46]

The ordinary cowboy is imaged in this West against a world vast, lonely, and fraught with dangers. He worked hard and long for little pay, moved by a sense of duty and a pride in his cowboy skills. If he felt a joyful freedom, he said little if anything about it. His situation in an alien natural world is suggested by the following passage from *Prose and Poetry:*

If the reader has ever been abroad upon the great, lonely, grieving plains, far away from any sign of the presence of his fellowmen, when a blizzard out of the north was sweeping in fury over the land, he will recall the sense of utter desolation by which he was seized, the feeling of helplessness that bore him down in the presence of such forces in such a situation. . . . In the opposite season, when the sun might burn and burn in a cloudless sky, week after week, even month after month, withering and shriveling the grass, glaring the land with its shimmering, blistering heat, and wasting the water of the streams and pools into nothingness, the cowboy patiently still went on with his work and did the best that was in him—for a few dollars for a month of his time, services, and for his knowing how.[47]

When he went up the trail north, he bound himself to a regimen of stampedes to be stopped, a ladder of rivers to be crossed, a thousand miles of monotonous work, bawling cows, and choking dust. But "when the herd is sold and delivered to the purchaser," wrote the author of *Prose and Poetry,* quoting Joseph G. McCoy, "a day of rejoicing to the cowboy has come."[48] In the cowtowns, the cowboys, "no longer the reserved, self-repressed men of the range," "threw off all restraint, and measured their 'enjoyment' of their few days of freedom and revelry by the degree of uproar with which they proclaimed their presence."[49] They could get roaring drunk, spend time with the whores, and maybe get shot in a brawl. But whatever they thought of themselves—and that we really do not know—it is unlikely that they saw themselves as kings proudly enthroned upon the fenceless domain of the wild prairies.

There are those who will say that this is the prose of the cattle industry. But I submit that historians can no more prove the philosophical and psychological meanings imaged here than they can authenticate the general spirit of buoyant freedom permeating the ranges of romantic primitivism. If Roosevelt said he felt a zestful freedom, I suppose we must believe him, but he could assert such freedom only as a personal truth. As historian he could not know it to be an objective condition of the cowboy's inner world. Certainly the author of *Prose and Poetry* offered little proof of the historical validity of his contrasting images of the rangeland West.

If the darker view can be said to be more realistic, if not more historical, then there is a further irony in the fact that imaginative literature did more to make it real than did historiography. The irony comes in the fact that historians—some of them at least—while seeking to dispel the romance of the range found in fiction, contributed more to that romance than did some of the writers of fiction.

Let us take as a central proposition in range anthropology the claim that the cowboy has a freedom guaranteed by nature. In literary romanticism dealing with the frontier, this freedom had always belonged to the heroic individual: Lord Byron's Boone had it as did Cooper's Natty Bumppo. Hough and Roosevelt found it in the cowboy. But in the West of the vast lonely plains, the cowboy seemed less heroic and he seemed less free. And even when he was heroic, his heroism involved acceptance of circumstances beyond his own making or control. The philosophical emphasis had shifted from freedom to destiny.

Although, as I have indicated, something of this darker image does show in the pages of *Prose and Poetry,* it remains true that in the stockman's official view of himself he was still at home on his great free ranches; he still thought he was moved by a bold, free spirit. He knew that times were changing; he could speak sentimental elegies about the good old days; he had, as the efforts to get out a three-volume compilation show, a sense of a monumental past. But there was no doom in this changing past; it had no tragic prospects.

At the century's turn, however, the fiction of the cattle industry was revealing a different mood. It was still romantic in many ways, not the least in its heroes whom it had not yet broken to the closely delineated probabilities of everyday life. It had not yet always found with confidence its appropriate style, that literary vernacular suitable to both the raw vitality of new range experience and the need to articulate the meanings of that experience artfully. It still wavered uncertainly between the tragic and the comic. But it showed nevertheless the darker shadows of destiny.

A few examples will serve to illustrate. Alfred Henry Lewis's "The Man from Red Dog," *Wolfville* (1897), may seem to be simply another local color story in the manner of Bret Harte. Yet beneath the sentimentality and in spite of the comic grotesqueness of the Old Cattleman's telling, there remains a starkness, an unromantic acceptance of the fact that men die in predicaments in which they find themselves. In "Destiny at Drybone," one of the stories Owen Wister used to make up *Lin McLean* (1897), we are a long way down the trail toward a full literary realism. If Miss Molly Wood, in the novel that would follow, sometimes seems cut from the pattern of the genteel heroine, Mrs. Lusk of "Drybone" does not. But more to the point here is the conviction that the cowboys who bury her face down in a used coffin are a long, long way from celebrating the rites of freedom. Finally, there is Stewart Edward White's "The Rawhide," a short novel that concludes his *Arizona Nights* (1907). When Buck Johnson dispels the "shapes of illusion," he sees his own West in a sharply different way. "Mile after mile it swept away before him, hot, dry, suffocating, lifeless. . . . Here and there rock ridges showed with the obscenity of so many skeletons, exposing to the hard, cruel sky the earth's nakedness. Thirst, delirium, death, hovered palpable in the wind; dreadful, unconquerable, ghastly."[50] More important, he sees his wife as she really is. Indeed, it is the discovery of her infidelity that opens his perspective on a different world. If one here needs a symbol of that world, it might well be the stuff of the title itself. Estrella has learned in fascination the terrible power of drying rawhide. Imprisoned with her lover in a fresh cow skin, she will die as the day's sun slowly dries the rawhide. Again, scarcely a paean to man's freedom. And Buck's possibly sentimental decision to release the pair does not in any way soften the harshness of the world in which in so many ways we are bound.

IV

Thus *Prose and Poetry* shows us two quite different images of western man: man bold, self-reliant, naturally free; and man profoundly conditioned by the circumstances which surround him. If these images, at least as they emerge in a single work, seem incompatible, if they seem to suggest philosophical uncertainty and confusion, one can further argue that taken together they image the curious mix of ideas old and new that flowed in the intellectual currents of the century's changing.

There was first of all the ambiguity of nature. If the natural heart of the cowboy knew instinctive justice, then clearly to be natural was to be good. Had Emerson known about cowboys, he might well have included them, along with farmers and Indians, among his men *naturel*. But if the cowboy was in a different way a creature of his environment and that environment was conceived as the push and pull of amoral biological forces, then nature was quite another matter. Indeed, this Darwinistic nature *was* matter, and not transcendental spirit.

There was the further ambiguity of history itself. If the livestock industry, its animals, its practices, the men whom it involved, had developed out of the past under the grip of old and continuing historical forces, if in short the industry had evolved as other social institutions had evolved, then the cowboy was indeed a product, a human resultant determined wholly by antecedent forces. The design and some of the detail of *Prose and Poetry* suggest this kind of Darwinian history.[51] Defined in the context of this sort of history, the cowboy could hardly be a great man riding his unfenced ranges. But transcending this sense of an evolutionary past in *Prose and Poetry* is a view of another kind. In his

"Introductory," James W. Freeman struck the different note: "The world is moved by thought."[52] The biographer of Charles Goodnight added: "The chief worth of any human being is in the illumined soul."[53] And near the close of the book, the writer of *Prose and Poetry* focused the whole way of thinking in the proposition "history itself really is biography."[54] Taken together, these statements provide a succinct summary of Emersonian, rather than Darwinian, ideology.

Defined to embody such high principles, the cowboy could become a romantic hero. Philosophically he could become a representative man. However, in *Prose and Poetry* the cowboy did not become a representative man. In this text he merely lives and works and dances in nameless indistinction. No ordinary cowboy seems to deserve individualized, hero-making attention. It is the important cattlemen like Charles Goodnight, Richard King, and Theodore Roosevelt who are imaged in some biographical fullness. Indeed, it is as if social (or class) position dictated the kind of history to be used. Clio's cowboys are the unnamed products of range evolution; Clio's cattlemen are great men with bold ideas and free, illumined souls.

It should be added finally that neither version of history is presented with compelling evidence and persuasive rigor of concept. Both remain deductive rather than inductive, sketchy notions drawn from the curious mix of American ideologies. There is, one might say, more metahistory than history. And thus, to return in conclusion to my earlier distinction, if hard history is the prose and all else is the poetry, then the title fits. The literary scholar need not have waited for volume 2.

Classics of the Cattle Trade: A New Look at Some Old Standards

There is in economic history so little of the dramatic and heroic interest that we cannot wisely compete with political and military history in those appeals.

Abbott Payson Usher, Conference on Economic History,
29 December 1920

There is no Herodotus or Thucydides for the cattleman's frontier.

Louis Pelzer, *The Cattlemen's Frontier*

In the works of one decade, between 1929 and 1939, the historiography of the cattle trade can be said to have reached a professional maturity. While, as we have seen, many basic works had been published earlier, few of them were the products of historians thoroughly and rigorously trained in the methods of historical scholarship.[1] Frederic L. Paxson's "The Cow Country," the first full-length article on the subject to receive space in the *American Historical Review,* had appeared in 1916; under a different title, "The Evolution of the Live Stock Industry," it had come out again in 1925 in *Readings in the Economic History of American Agriculture.*[2] However, the larger evidence of a professional science of range historiography was issued impressively in 1929 in Ernest S. Osgood's *The Day of the Cattleman* and the following year in Edward Everett Dale's *The Range Cattle Industry.* Both histories, it should be noted, had come out of the dissertation-making process; Dale had completed his doctoral work at Harvard in 1922 with "A History of the Range Cattle Industry in Oklahoma," Osgood at Wisconsin in 1927 with "The Northern Cattle Country, 1865–1890." Additional major studies of the cattle trade came from academic historians in 1931 in Walter Prescott Webb's "The Cattle Kingdom," a central part of *The Great Plains,* and in 1936 in

Louis Pelzer's *The Cattlemen's Frontier*. Still other histories would
be written, other facts and conclusions added; but among professional followers of cows, cowboys, and cattlemen, these four
works would remain standard classics of a thorough, objective,
unromantic historiography of the range frontiers.[3]

   In addition to their rigorous scholarly method, these works
shared certain important assumptions about the nature of the
frontier history with which they dealt. "The range cattleman,"
wrote Osgood, "has more solid achievements to his credit than the
creation of a legend. . . . He built up a great and lucrative enterprise . . . and laid the economic foundations of more than one
western commonwealth."[4] This building of enterprise and laying
of economic foundations was the "story" of *The Day of the Cattleman*.[5] "The emphasis," wrote one reviewer, "is economic."[6] Dale's
work was even more explicitly economic. Begun under the aegis
of the Bureau of Agricultural Economics, it was intended to add
to the larger account of American economic development. "The
spread of the range cattle business," wrote Dale, "over this enormous region [the western cow country] was one of the most
significant events in the economic history of the United States
during the latter half of the nineteenth century."[7] J. Frank
Dobie's terse description of Dale's book read "Economic aspects."[8] Webb sought to provide a necessary geographical context
but found, like the others, the historical consequences in social
and economic forms. The cattle kingdom, he concluded, was "the
most natural economic and social order that the white man has yet
developed in his experience with the Great Plains."[9] "Motives in
occupying and stocking the range country," wrote Pelzer, "were
fundamentally economic." Economic influences, not the "more
colorful aspects," thus constituted the "principal theme" of *The
Cattlemen's Frontier*.[10] Reviewers read Pelzer at his word. The
book, said Walcott Watson, "deals primarily with the most important economic aspects of the cattle kingdom." Pelzer "has recorded," he went on, "the fundamental economic processes
through which this Western industry developed . . . and a sound
analysis of the economic causes of its termination."[11] Dale found
the work a "real contribution to the literature of the West, and to
the history of an industry that has such a far reaching effect upon
the economic history of this country and upon American life."[12]

"Economic treatment," observed Dobie in a bibliographical note, "faithful but static."[13]

But in spite of such authorial pronouncements and such critical acceptance of these proclaimed conceptions, it should have seemed evident to perceptive readers that these works were not just scientific studies of impersonal economic developments on the range lands. To begin with, their titles were misleading: they provided almost no hint of the economic intentions. Reviewing *The Day of the Cattleman,* Douglas Branch noted that the book has "no such inclusive scope."[14] He might have remarked further that the book is ostensibly not about a *day,* in the historian's usual sense, and that it is not about *the cattleman,* in the historian's usual sense.[15] *The Range Cattle Industry* is perhaps a more accurate title since it does point toward an economic concept, yet the concept of industry does not really organize Dale's book.[16] Although Webb's title, "The Cattle Kingdom," has acceptance in popular tradition, it does not clearly denote the social and economic features he sought to analyze.[17] Pelzer's history was also by intention not about cattlemen and for the most part referred to the frontier as a place rather than as a historical economic process. One can say, then, that the titles do not fit the books they name. Or one can argue that perhaps they do fit: that these works of history are not simply what some reviewers took them to be.

Read carefully, with as much concern for style and shaping image as for avowed professional intentions, these histories provide some interesting, and even ironic, critical results. The histories, through the detached, disciplined factualness of the historians, sought to be objective, impersonal, and unromantic. Yet in a number of ways they are subjective, personal, and even romantic. As economic histories, they sought to deal in statistical patterns, not in personalities. Yet in neglecting some elements of personality, they weakened their grasp of the very reality they hoped to represent. Four historians with strong personal identification with the range West attempted, in the discipline of the new history, to remain disinterested observers rather than participants. The tension which resulted from this effort shows on almost every page. In a further irony, while heroically committed to facts and figures, as professional personalities they bridled themselves with the new blinders of a historiographical fashion—and failed to see some of the personal dimensions of their chosen economic events. Thus these four classic histories tell us finally not so much about the history of cows and cattlemen (although they tell us a good bit) as about the history of a certain period of western history.

The first sentence of *The Day of the Cattleman* struck a dominant note: the concern was to be with "solid achievement" rather than with "legend." This achievement, since it was economic, needed a "straightforward and unromantic" presentation.[18] Pelzer characterized Osgood's style as "one of distant detachment rather than one of sympathetic appreciation."[19] Branch called Osgood's research "thorough and painstaking."[20] J. Evetts Haley called Osgood's book "a scientific product," illuminating and interesting to "every 'puncher' of statistical and historical cows."[21] Yet there were signs in the reviewers' responses that an emerging scientific history of the ranges had not yet put a firm lid on romantic pressures. Pelzer found Osgood's book "evidence of continuing interest in one of America's *picturesque* frontiers."[22] And Haley's metaphor of the historian as puncher scarcely suggested the scholar with his cold file of factual information.

It can be demonstrated, I believe, that whatever the scientific intentions of these historians, the historical landscape of these histories retained some of its traditional picturesqueness or, if not picturesqueness in the traditional sense of that term, a romantic aura clearly at odds with a concept of economic setting.[23] And it can be further demonstrated that these historians were in spirit punchers, to borrow Haley's metaphor, men who, whatever their academic training, retained a deep personal identity with things western, particularly with the cowboys and cattlemen who worked the ranges. Whatever their mortar boards and doctoral gowns, they were, at an important layer of their sensibilities, cowboys. The point can be imaged in a scene as Dale crossed the final summit on his way to a Ph.D. When he returned to the examination room to hear his committee's decision, he found that Turner, his chairman, had been showing other members of the committee a photograph of Dale in cowboy costume.[24]

To begin with, there was the special sense of the cow country itself as it was described in the pages of history. Paxson, quoting Roosevelt, had struck a lyrical note in speaking of "the great unfenced ranches, in the days of 'free grass,' "[25] but Osgood evoked a more somber mood, drawing upon a landscape imagery made popular by Washington Irving nearly a century earlier and reworked by Roosevelt and others in the intervening years.[26] In a glance at the historical background, Osgood noted the movement of Lewis and Clark up the "lonely reaches" of the Missouri, the activity of the "lonely trappers" far up in the mountains. Beyond the wagon track to Oregon "a vast waste stretched away on every side to the far horizon." Herds of buffalo moved over the "face of these great solitudes." The impression of such a "solitary vastness" had indeed helped to create the myth of the American desert. Now into "this great solitude," "these unfamiliar wastes, where nature appeared so strange and formidable to his unaccustomed eyes," rode the cattleman.[27]

Describing "this interesting and romantic region," as he called the cow country in a review of Pelzer's book,[28] Dale was seemingly more restrained, willing to use only a few general notes. Yet even these rather abstract notes were themselves sometimes charged with a special intensity of literary meaning. "For a century and more it [the frontier grazing land] was there, a kind of twilight zone with the light of civilization behind it, and the darkness of savagery before."[29] It was the chiaroscuro effect of romantic painting.[30] Pelzer too seemed restrained, yet he like the others added some touches of color. The longhorns grazed not just on grass, not just on the specific buffalo grass, but on "buffalo grass ranges dotted with skeletons and staring skulls of buffalo."[31] The ranges became a "winter purgatory" in 1886 and 1887.[32] And in an elegiac note reminiscent of Roosevelt, he asked, who are there to recall "the days of unfenced ranges"?[33] Finally, in this summary sketch of the historical landscape, there was the special plains world of Walter Prescott Webb. In keeping with his special thesis Webb needed to establish the plains not just as a stage on which events could happen, but as an environment that would shape these events. He might have called his work *The Plains Determine*. "The Plains worked their will, and man conformed."[34] Western life was "in accord ultimately with the laws laid down by the inscrutable Plains."[35] But however well such inferences might perhaps accord with scientific geography, Webb's definition of his historical landscape was sometimes as romantic, as moody, as any work in western historiography. The environment of great distances and sparse population "engendered self-reliance," fostered "a rather distinct type of Western man," "a distinct Western psychology."[36] Yet the same plains, in another mood or perhaps in another mood of the historian, could have a quite different effect. "Mysterious, desolate, barren, grief-stricken," the plains oppressed the women who settled there, sometimes driving them to insanity.[37]

In this historical settling of the cow country, the cattle trade or the cattle industry had its beginning and grew to importance during the last decades of the nineteenth century. Insofar as this development consisted of wrangling cows, stopping stampedes, shooting up cow towns, and events of a similar nature, its story could perhaps be told, as it had been told, in a straightforward narrative of men and cows in action. But if this development was indeed economic, then perhaps there were other more appropriate structural concepts by which this development needed to be ordered for the purposes of historiography. There is little evidence, however, that these historians seemed to consider that economic history might require its own design,[38] that an unromantic historical method would require an unromantic style and structure. To be sure, they slowed the narrative pace and thickened the exposition. To be sure, they substituted statistics for heroes in chaps and spurs. But the histories which supposedly organize the new kind of "story" show that however important economic elements had become, their importance had not yet seriously altered the older ways, indeed the heroic ways, of western historiography.

Consider some of the terms used to name and characterize parts or the whole of their "story," for example, *American saga, eloquent story,* and *history picturesque and tragic.* These must, I believe, be regarded as literary terms, terms more easily associated with Parkman, Motley, and Prescott than with writers of twentieth-century economic history. The textual presence of these terms, or more particularly the historians' feelings that seemed to charge them, gave these histories of the cow country some curious effects. "In after years," wrote Osgood, "the drive of the Texas men became little short of an American saga." This could have meant that the drive would be taken up by other writers, perhaps the fictionists, and elevated into a saga. However, what followed in Osgood's brief elaboration was indeed *his* sense of saga. "To all those who saw the long line of Texas cattle coming up over a rise in the prairie, nostrils wide for the smell of water, dust-caked and gaunt, so ready to break from the nervous control of the riders strung out along the flanks of the herd, there came the feeling that in this spectacle there was something elemental, something resistless, something perfectly in keeping with the unconquered land about them."[39] The peculiar incongruity between substance and form, the special tension between objective matter and subjective interest, was even more strikingly revealed in Dale's *Range Cattle Industry*. In some respects it seems the most scientific of the histories under consideration. For that very reason the literary features, slight though they may seem to be, must push stiffly against the economic grain of the book. Two brief passages will illustrate my point. "The tables of figures showing market receipts and shipments, the price of farm lands and of corn, the number of homesteads taken, the number of sheep in certain states, and the volume of exports of cattle and beef, tell an eloquent story."[40] But in what way do tables tell a story, particularly an eloquent story? One may possibly invest statistical patterns with dramatic meaning; we do speak of dramatic rises and drops in stock market values. But is this the sort of story Dale was alluding to? Or did Dale mean rather the sequence of human events, the personal enterprise back of the data which make up the tables? Such enterprise could, of course, be economically conceived, the motives of the cattlemen reduced to the quest for economic power and profits;[41] but Dale seemed unwilling or perhaps unable to see his cattlemen in these terms. Identifying closely with the cattlemen, he was perhaps reluctant to strip them to their economic skin and bones. But even if, in the unromantic discipline of the new economic history, he had wanted to do this, his documents would not have convincingly supported such economic inferences. "The early history of the grazing industry," he wrote at the close of his book, "in any part of the Great Plains region is a story of men who met hardship and danger and financial reverses in a fashion that must prove an inspiration to those who have succeeded them."[42] Thus the story became eloquent and heroic not in the matter-of-factness of statistical numbers but in the personal memory and tribute of the historian.

Implicit in Pelzer's history was a similar story. Insofar as he stuck to profits, wages, interest, dividends, and increase of herds, this story was perhaps, as he intended, subordinated. However, as any student of western rhetoric knows, to subordinate is not necessarily to put out of mind and feeling. A story of economic factors would be neither picturesque nor tragic in its ending, for these terms suggest a human drama, not the closing of an economic cycle or the reaching of bottom in a business downturn. Yet Pelzer saw his history finally in this dramatic mode. "The era of free grass was gone," he wrote. "The exuberant spirit of the cattle boom of the early eighties had neither forerunner nor guide. Born of freedom, it had flourished for a few years on the frontier where nature and the march of events did not permit it to grow to seasoned maturity. But a history picturesque and tragic in its ending is one of its legacies to the west."[43] The abstraction *spirit of the cattle boom,* whatever the statistics used to measure it, meant in human terms a heroic enterprise of cattlemen. To try to deal with that enterprise as abstract spirit, as if it were as impersonal as a prairie wind, was to empty it of the real historical motives that made it move. Ironically, in this new economic historiography,[44] if we know little of what the historical cattlemen felt, we do learn the feelings of their surrogate, the historian himself.

If the trail drive from Texas to Montana could be called a saga, it could be called an epic too. A daring venture of men across the entire breadth of a nation showed a truly heroic dimension of setting and action and theme. Andy Adams's *Log of a Cowboy* has seemed to some readers more than a log, more than a novel; the scope, if not the literary manner, has suggested the epic. Webb, so far as I know, did not apply the term to Adams's book, yet central to his own sense of the cattle kingdom was what I think may be called the epic spirit. In Webb's re-creation of the western past, cattlemen spread the institution of ranching over "the empire of grass" in the space of fifteen years; it was, he said, "perhaps one of the outstanding phenomena in American history."[45] Yet *phenomena,* at least in most of its common meanings, was scarcely a term to carry the heroic feel of the cattle West. In Webb's version,

Abilene, Kansas, became more than a functioning trade center; it became a symbol, standing "for all that happened when two civilizations met for conflict, for disorder, for the clashing of great currents which carry on their crest the turbulent and disorderly elements of both civilizations—in this case the rough characters of the plain and of the forest."[46] And if a cowtown needed a grand symbolism, life on a ranch required more than the matter-of-fact rhetoric of a geographer's prose. "Hot days in the branding pen with bawling calves and the smell of burned hair and flesh on the wind! Men in boots and big hats, with the accompaniment of jingling spurs and frisky horses. Camp cook and horse wrangler! Profanity and huge appetites!"[47] If this is prose, it is prose in the spirit of Whitman, not in the style of a practiced social science.[48]

Besides the explicit concepts of saga, story, and picturesque tragedy, and the implicit sense of epic, there was in these histories a distinct habit of metaphor which must be called literary rather than scientific. And because it appealed to a sense of grandeur if not sublimity, it must be called a mode of romanticism rather than a mode of realism. Derived, it seems, from earlier historiographical practices and warmly supported by unchanging frontier values, it continued to flourish unconditioned by the new kinds of data. It was, in short, a way of imagination rising from tradition and subjective conviction, not from the shaping pressures of a supposedly rigorous and scientific social study.

From one point of view, the problem may have seemed simple. The history of the cow country meant the movement, sometimes slow, sometimes fast, of men and cattle. What would be the appropriate metaphors of such a movement, noting now that such special western movements were parts of a larger American historical destiny, the tide of advancement westward, and beyond that, the tide of social progress upward? Turner had classically defined the movement. Was it any wonder that others picked up his paradigm of western historical process?

"Any history of the ranch cattle industry of the Great Plains," wrote Dale, "is merely a part of the history of a much larger movement, that of the settlement and development of the American wilderness. This is a movement that has been characterized by the appearance of successive stages of society—that of the hunter and trapper, the herder, and the pioneer farmer following one

another within the same region in more or less rapid succession
according to conditions of topography and climate."[49] The agricultural occupation was a "steadfast march across the continent."[50] The metaphors of *stages* and *march* thus suggested a
philosophy of frontier history happily combining the higher
drive of destiny and the optimistic advancement of societal states.
Jefferson had expressed the same view a century earlier:

Let a philosophic observer commence a journey from the savages of the
Rocky Mountains, eastwardly towards our seacoast. These he would
observe in the earliest stage of association living under no law but that of
nature, subsisting and covering themselves with the flesh and skins of
wild beasts. He would next find those on our frontiers in the pastoral
state, raising domestic animals to supply the defects of hunting. Then
succeed our own semi-barbarous citizens, the pioneers of the advance of
civilization, and so in his progress he would meet the gradual shades of
improving man until he would reach his, as yet, most improved state in
our seaport towns.

"I have observed," added Jefferson, "this march of civilization
advancing from the seacoast, passing over us like a cloud of
light . . . ."[51]

By 1929, however, the assumptions underlying the idea of
history imaged in these metaphors were being questioned. It
should have seemed more and more intellectually anachronistic
to suppose that the westward expansion of the cattle industry
conformed to Enlightenment notions of historical progress. It
should have seemed more and more doubtful that economic
development in the West marched in stages. It should have
seemed less and less satisfactory to use the data gathered by the
Bureau of Agricultural Economics merely to give a quantitative
precision, a scientific veneer, to old historical structures. Stage
theories, of the sort used by Dale, were under particular attack
from economic historians. Werner Sombart noted that such
theories related to the condition of production were used by the
philosophers of the ancient world and were popular in the
sociological literature of the eighteenth century. "But this so-
called 'condition of production,' " he argued, "is not an idea
which serves to give mental unity to the chaos of scattered particulars with which the economic historian is concerned."[52] One

supposes that the newly important particulars scattered on the ranges of the West would have required a new concept, a new historical structure to give mental unity. Yet there is, I believe, no evidence that Dale attempted to validate his historical pattern by letting his special gathering of economic evidence break through traditions and perhaps ask for a new, more appropriate pattern. There is, I believe, no evidence that he thought his scattered particulars, to repeat Sombart's language, needed a new kind of unity, with possibly a new kind of historical structure. The result in Dale's work was a curious dissociation between substance and form. If the economic substance was scientific, in the sense that it was gathered by rigorous research in the documents, the form was not. The latter could be no more documented than could the metahistorical design of Whitman's "Passage to India."[53]

When Paxson had written of the "Cow Country" in 1916, he had written of the "forces" generated there and of the "new forces" started by the beef industry "that continue to touch American life on many sides."[54] The language of forces was, of course, not new in American historiography; it had been used by Turner in the essay of 1893,[55] and it had been rhetorically basic in the scientism of Henry Adams. It had not, however, become an intellectual fashion in the historiography of the ranges. Yet if events in the cow country were to be seen as impersonal results, if economic pressures were to be analyzed in the manner of a true social science, then *forces* must have seemed an appropriate term. The "greatest moving force" of the "flowing stream of history," wrote Harry E. Maule in his introduction to *Cattle*, "has always been economic pressure."[56] At one level of their theory, the professional historians of the cattle trade seemed to agree.

Yet while perhaps denoting overwhelming forces, the imagery used by Dale and others tended to remain literary, dramatic and colorful, rather than scientifically precise and neutral. And further, even as literary imagery, it held problems in meaning, for it suggested a heroic natural determinism which seemed incongruous with, indeed antithetical to, a sense of heroic personal freedom. The point can be illustrated with two passages from a work in what I would call the popular tradition of range historiography. "The old-timer . . . was a chip tossed on a great stream of life that flowed up from the South . . . . Each of them [the pioneers] was singularly forceful, tough as hickory, enduring as steel, a man of character expressing himself in original energy."[57] Here we have force exterior, impersonal, acting upon man, and force interior, personal, acting from within man. The difference from the philosophical and literary point of view, as well as from the economic point of view, is critically important.

Viewed from the air or even from a prairie butte, a herd of cattle strung out along the trail would perhaps have looked like a great stream. The image thus had visual accuracy. However, the metaphor as used historically suggested more than the sinuous movement of a line of several thousand head of beef. It dramatized the vast push of economic pressures. "In the years following the Civil War," wrote Dale, "this flood of Texas cattle pent up within the state through the four years of conflict burst its bonds and flowed northward in a great stream."[58] Some pages later the metaphor was repeated: "Finally, there was by this time a great stream of Texas cattle flowing northward over the trail."[59] Where were the men who gathered and drove the cattle, who gave them a daily momentum and direction? It was as if the whole great action had become impersonal, as if the cattle as flowing force had assumed their own economic destiny.

Other developments had a similar imagery. The Indian Territory having been excluded from grazing and settlement, it was, wrote Dale, "as though a dike, or wall, had been built about this region, a wall impervious to the waves of civilization that beat against it." However, the cattle industry, "more fluid in its character than is agriculture, soon began to penetrate it and to spread itself over the rich pasture lands within."[60] As already noted, Webb saw in Abilene "the clashing of great currents which carry on their crest the turbulent and disorderly elements of . . . [two] civilizations."[61] And finally, as Pelzer told the frontier story, the free-range industry was coming to an end with "the approach of nesters and small ranchmen who, like a glacier, were to spread over the estates of the cattlemen."[62] The simile of a glacier may seem to slow the historical momentum, but it nevertheless reinforces the sense of the impersonal and the inexorable.

The deterministic implications of these images were supported by a more literary kind of statement. Circumstances, not individual free choices, sometimes dictated what might happen. Thus, as Osgood saw the historical process, when the ranges became crowded and a system of organization began to emerge, "frontier individualism surrendered to economic necessity."[63] In the evolution of ranching, according to Webb, "the Plains worked their will, and man conformed. The ways of life in this region appear [geographically] logical, reasonable, almost inevitable." In a return to metaphor, Webb added: "Society was highly rarefied, the human particles were far apart, and they oscillated over wide spaces."[64]

The image of human particles oscillating over wide spaces was perhaps philosophically defensible. If man was, as some late nineteenth-century writers put it, an atom adrift in the flux of things, then there could be no good reason for believing a cattleman was a more heroic particle than any other. Such anthropology might not be easily adapted to economic history—it seemed grounded in a physics (or metaphysics) of society that seemed to have little if anything to do with economics—but it was at least compatible with concepts of large impersonal forces which might be vaguely labled economic. However, it is the thesis of this study that whatever the theoretical gestures in seeming adherence to a historiography of impersonal forces, the historians themselves were temperamentally incapable of accepting such unreliance of self. As a result, quite aside from certain problems in economic history, they were caught in philosophical and literary difficulties. While making gestures toward a sort of naturalism, they seemed convinced that their story had the character of high tragedy. "Literature," wrote Webb in an essay explaining the adventure of writing *The Great Plains,* is "the flower growing out of the compost of human effort and physical forces." M. Zola could not have said it better, with such a curious mixing of sentimentality and pretentious science. However, the great French naturalist would not at the same time have justified ploughing through "geology, climatology, botany, [and] anthropology" in order to write "heroic tragic history."[65]

Put in another way, the histories of Osgood, Dale, Webb, and Pelzer are haunted by the presence of the old range cattleman. One says *haunted* rather than *dominated* because the old pioneer cattleman does not ride in full concrete gusto upon their pages.

There is not even a small explicit image of Haley's Goodnight or
Emmett's Pierce; in fact some of the great cattlemen are barely
mentioned. The statistics, the institutions, the economic ups and
downs have seemingly taken over. And yet there lurks in the
minds of the historians, there rises in their western sensibilities,
the personal importance of the frontier great ones.

When Osgood wrote of the range cattleman as a "frontier
figure, operating with little or no capital outside of what he had
invested in his herd," or when he noted that "the old cattlemen
who had kept the calf tally on a shingle, whose only book had been
a checkbook, . . . found themselves sitting in at directors' meetings where eastern capitalists deferred to their business experience and judgment,"[66] he was as much paying tribute as he was
marking economic change. When Dale told the "remarkable"
history of the cattle industry, he believed it to be inspiring not
because it revealed how to become a shrewd investor in cows, but
because, as noted earlier, the men involved in it "met hardship
and danger and financial reverses" in a stalwart manner.[67] Although Webb mentions Goodnight as a source only, surely that
great cowman helped give meaning to the historian's assertion of
frontier values. "The Western man of the old days had little
choice but to be courageous. . . . The great distances and the
sparse population of the West compelled and engendered self-
reliance."[68] Finally, more than the others, Pelzer dealt, at least in
brief mention, in personalities. The rise of the cattle industry, he
said, exhibited a "freedom and an individuality." Yet certain men
constituted the "solid element"; however strong their indi-
vidualities, they furnished the "backbone" of association. Such
men were Shanghai Pierce, "who in dramatic and powerful voice
recounted stories of the Texas trail," and Alex Swan, who held "a
considerable faction of cattlemen" "under his spell and magnetic
personality."[69] My point again is that while association was indeed
a change of economic structure, it was not the economic motives
of these men so much as their heroic independence and self-
reliance that stirred the almost eulogistic interest of the historian.

History, as every historian must realize from the inside of his
task, has never been written from a complete file of objective data,
using a disciplined method of machinelike analysis.[70] It has, in
various ways, been autobiographical, in some instances blatantly

so. However, by the 1930s the historiography of the cattle industry had seemed to become a science, and the historian knew very
well that, as he might have put it, he had damn well better keep
himself out of his pages—except as he might observe, report, and
document. Yet a reading of Osgood, Dale, Webb, and Pelzer
shows nevertheless that in attempting to write impersonal history,
they were sometimes distinctly personal. If they tended to leave
out the historical persons of the cowboys and cattlemen, they
nevertheless as historians, to repeat my figure, continued to wear
their spurs and chaps. For many readers, this no doubt added a
pleasing western flavor.[71] After all, these readers might have
argued, you can't keep a self-reliant man, even a historian, out of
history. Still, one must insist, the historian's self-reliance was
against what should have seemed the proper professional grain.
No doubt, as we have come to realize, economic history needs
beneath its markets, prices, gains and losses a sense of self, the
person as he lived the concrete events of obtaining a living.[72] But
ironically, whatever the shaping presence of the personalities of
the historians themselves, the historical cattlemen, who were the
concrete economic persons who motivated events, were not revealed as central figures in this new version of the range-land
story.[73]

Freedom and Individualism on the Range: Ideological Images of the Cowboy and Cattleman

A<small>LMOST</small> coeval with his first actual venture on horseback behind a herd of cattle came the fictional cowboy. It was not perhaps so much an instance of a writer consciously "making up" a fiction as letting an interested, even excited imagination respond to a colorful figure found riding across the world.[1] Some time later, a more matter-of-fact observer thought he caught a serious discrepancy between actuality and literary image. He decided to correct the fiction, to substitute the truth for an untruth. Perhaps this observer was a journalist. In any case the effort of correction, of truthtelling, of re-creating the cowboy as he actually was became one of the primary missions of the western historian.[2]

A typical statement is that of Edward Everett Dale in *The Range Cattle Industry*. Fiction, poetry, and painting, said Dale, have in many cases given "an entirely false conception of the industry and the region in which it was carried on."[3] One supposes that Dale here also implies, within the false conception of the industry, a false conception of the cowboy and the cattleman. What is the true conception? Although *The Range Cattle Industry* is by intention an economic history of the industry and thus concerned primarily with acres grazed, cattle counted, profits or losses ensuing, it does nevertheless suggest some features of the men involved. Indeed, the final paragraph of the history, with its perorative emphasis upon the men "who met hardship and danger and financial reverses" in an inspirational manner, clearly implies a certain conception of the cattlemen.[4] And one supposes that this conception should be regarded as a *true* conception.

Although Dale at no point defines the cattlemen's philosophy explicitly as *individualism,* one nevertheless supposes that he shares with other historians a conviction about the central rightness of this term. "It was quite natural," he wrote at one point in *The Range Cattle Industry,* "that the ranchman should cling closely to the old idea that 'a government governs best which governs least,' and should even at the present time be somewhat chary of government efforts to help the range cattle interests."[5] Along with this political view, sometimes labeled *rugged individualism,* has come the identification by other historians of yet other kinds and degrees of individualism.

One historical conception of the cattleman, then, is that he was an individualist, that he was a believer in individualism. Is this indeed a *true* conception?

While academic historians of the cattle trade have said little about the cowboy's freedom, the traditional view has tended to see him as "fascinated with the free untrammeled life of the west."[6] Economic or geographical historians like Osgood, Dale, Webb, and Pelzer might well have trouble fitting a personal freedom into their sometimes deterministic worlds. Furthermore, since this freedom was often guaranteed by nature, the modern scientific historian might well deemphasize it as he shied away from the mythic ground of romantic primitivism.[7] Yet other historians, or at least other writers purporting to deal with historical reality rather than with myth or fiction, have persisted in defining the cowboy as a lover of freedom.

A handful of statements, over three-quarters of a century, will illustrate this conception of the cowboy. "The charm of ranch life," wrote Theodore Roosevelt in 1885, "comes in its freedom and the vigorous open-air existence it forces a man to lead."[8] According to William MacLeod Raine and Will C. Barnes, the cowboys with a trail herd from western Texas had "a wild, free life, far from most of the restrictions that residents of towns and cities accept without question."[9] Finally, in 1965 Ramon F. Adams observed of Bob Kennon: "A typical cowboy, he did not marry until late in life because of his love of the freedom of his profession: that right to wander as he pleased, see new country, and make new friends."[10] Freedom from town restrictions may not, of course, be exactly that freedom that Roosevelt valued; freedom to wander may not be the same as freedom from a city's legal restraints. However, all of these observations seem to recognize in the cowboy a personal sense of impulse unconditioned by close social pressures. Maybe he wanted to ride upon one grass-covered hill instead of another; maybe he wanted to see if the boss and biscuits at the next ranch were better; or maybe he merely wanted to fire his six-shooter at the moon.[11] Being a cowboy supposedly opened and increased his options. And supposedly this mattered to him to the point that whatever the low pay and the many hardships, cowboying was the best of all possible lives.

Another historical conception, then, is that the cowboy was free, that he valued freedom in the cowboy way of life. Is this a *true* conception?

I

Although the cattleman has been portrayed as an individualist by many historians, a critical consideration of the historical validity of this image can be focused in the writings of two major scholars of the cattle trade, Ernest Osgood and Lewis Atherton. *The Day of the Cattleman* and *The Cattle Kings* provide a sufficient textual base. Other writings may enlarge and thicken the historians' consensus; some may perhaps modify the emphasis or shorten the reach of the proposition; but the conception in these two works is nevertheless sufficiently typical to represent the central historiographical issues.

In Osgood's work, the claim of individualism for the cattleman, one notes, is an assumption rather than an argued proposition. The historian's study of organization indicated a slow formation of social groups, a fundamental change of circumstances necessitating a fundamental change in frontier character. In his first isolated location, the cattleman was "perforce unsocial," but with changed conditions "the characteristic frontier individualism" succumbed "to the equally characteristic need for group effort."[12]

That the frontier individualism was characteristic of the cattleman apparently needed no proof here. At least Osgood offered none, as if proof was unnecessary. But while the claim that the cattleman was perforce unsocial may perhaps be accepted easily, at least in the sense that isolation made organized society difficult if not impossible,[13] the individualism is another matter. It cannot be assumed that frontier isolation led to an individualization which fostered individualism. On the contrary, as sociologists, psychiatrists, and novelists will testify, it may indeed diminish the sense of self and intensify the human need for a group identity.[14]

Apparently Osgood could start with the assumption of the pioneering cattleman's individualism because he (Osgood) accepted as historically given the thesis of America's most influential ideologue of frontier character. Although Osgood does not cite Turner at this specific point in *The Day of the Cattleman,* it is safe, I believe, to call him a practicing, if not devout, Turnerian.[15]

Frederick Jackson Turner's classic formulation came of course in the essay of 1893, "The Significance of the Frontier in American History." "To the frontier," said Turner, "the American intellect owes its striking characteristics." Among these is "that dominant individualism, working for good and for evil, and withal that buoyancy which comes with freedom."[16] That it works for more good than evil is perhaps suggested in an earlier passage: "The frontier individualism has from the beginning promoted democracy."[17] What was the historical evidence to justify this conclusion about the frontier genesis of individualism? Turner's documentation is at this point unfortunately thin.

One turns, then, to a history of the historical idea itself, to Ray Allen Billington's *Genesis of the Frontier Thesis.* Where did Turner get the idea that the frontier generates individualism? Did he go to the frontier where he could discover the attitudes of frontiersmen? Did he read frontier journals, letters, and newspapers? Did he hear the gospel of individualism in the rhetoric of official spokesmen, behind the pulpit and on the stump? Billington's sources are curiously of a quite different sort. Turner may have read an essay by Edwin L. Godkin, editor of *The Nation,* noting that frontier life fostered individualism. He may have read William Graham Sumner's articles crediting vacant lands and underpeopled territories with stimulating individualism. He may have absorbed the ideal of individualism from the agrarian myth of the nineteenth century. He took note of some conclusions in Herbert L. Osgood's "England and the Colonies": "No conditions are so favorable to the growth of individualism as frontier life. . . . Society is atomized." He was pleased, says Billington, with Robert Baird's *View of the Valley of the Mississippi; or, The Emigrant's and Traveller's Guide to the West* with its gallery of traits, including "independence of thought and action." And he probably found support in Achille Loria's claims that free land "infused a conscience [*sic*] of liberty," that it fostered an antisocial tendency.[18]

All of this source material is of course secondary. In Billington's account of the genesis, there is not one piece of firsthand historical evidence, not one scrap of proof that Turner knew frontier individualism in any immediate form, not one instance of grounding his generalization in the individualism of concrete historical persons. Thus one cannot say, following Billington's analysis, that Turner demonstrated historiographically that the frontier engendered individualism. One can say only that he thought it did. There is indeed a compelling logic in the views of Godkin, Sumner, and others, and there is a compelling logic in the thesis of Turner. The argument, however, is ideological, not historical. The conception of the frontiersman as a believer in individualism is perhaps a true conception in the sense that it is coherent within the structure of the American democratic ideology,[19] but this proposition is quite different from saying that it is true to the concrete nature of historical frontier persons.

This is not, of course, to deny that individualism was a frontier characteristic. The evidence so far considered does not justify that sort of negative proposition any more than it justifies its affirmative opposite. We are left suspended in a world of ideas and counterideas. But presuming to ride point in the venture of finding our way out, one can reaffirm that in writing history we need to know individualism inductively from concrete evidence, not deductively from ideological principles. In the instance of the cattlemen, we need to know from the cattlemen themselves. Where better to make a start?

As historian, Lewis Atherton seems at first reading a good bit closer to these cattlemen. "Ranchers and cowboys alike," he writes, ". . . expressed allegiance to individualism from the earliest days of the cattle kingdom. In describing ranchers and drovers, Joseph G. McCoy used word after word that correlated nicely with that concept. Such men were hardy, self-reliant, free, independent, and acknowledged no superior or master in the whole wide universe. Possessed as they were with a strong innate sense of right and wrong, they quickly resented any infringement on their freedoms."[20]

If Atherton seems closer to the cattlemen, that closeness is mediated wholly by *Historic Sketches of the Cattle Trade.* If that work is a faithful mirror of concrete attitudes, a field guide to the thoughts of existing cattlemen, then we are on sure ground. But as we have seen, while *Historic Sketches* does, as its author intended, give much "practical and correct information," it is scarcely a compendium of objective fact and interpretation.

Undoubtedly McCoy knew a good many cattlemen. Yet again let us ask if his conception of them in *Historic Sketches* was unbiased and objective. Consider three observations in the text partially cited by Atherton. "They [the cattlemen] are disposed to measure every man's action and prompting motives by the rule of selfishness." One may suppose that McCoy as a businessman had learned in experience this characteristic of many cattlemen although it seems likely he meant self-interest rather than selfishness. The *Sketches* as autobiography would show that he encountered some truly selfish men in his Abilene years, particularly railroad executives, but the evidence of his book does not reveal the "selfishness" of the cattlemen. Atherton, it should be noted, does not take from McCoy this negative aspect of the cattleman's individualism. "With a strong inate [*sic*] sense of right and wrong . . . ," McCoy wrote in a passage used by Atherton, "they [Southwestern cattlemen] are, as would naturally be supposed, when the manner of their life is considered, a hardy, self-reliant, free and independent class, acknowledging no superior or masters in the wide universe."[21] As already noted, this is a tribute, not a factual observation. But whether or not it says anything verifiable about the existential nature of historical cattlemen, it does epitomize a basic notion in the frontier ideology of the nineteenth century. An innate sense of right and wrong sanctioned a natural independence and self-reliance. Emerson and Thoreau could believe this sincerely. McCoy could utter the same faith in a rhetorical echo of an earlier persuasion. But as historian he could not prove the innate sense to be a fact of human nature. We can say that it is a historical fact that McCoy believed in a form of individualism, but we cannot extrapolate from that fact a reliable generalization. McCoy's faith is historical in the sense that it was uttered in the context of a work of history; more important, it is also historical in the sense that it is a faith possessing historicity. It is an intellectual artifact to be gathered into our museum of range ideas.

The most striking, indeed the most radical, proposition in McCoy's formulation of the cattleman's individualism is the following: "Each man seems to feel himself an independent sovereign, and as such capable of conducting his affairs in his own way, subject to nobody or nothing save the wishes, tastes and necessities of himself."[22] To match the radical individualism of this sentence, one must go to the writings of the philosophical anarchists, Josiah Warren, Stephen P. Andrews, and Benjamin Tucker. But did McCoy really mean what these anarchists meant, that the individual self is sovereign and thus not only entitled to its own unique identity and integrity but also respectful of the sovereignty of other individual selves? It is, I submit, difficult, if not impossible, to search out the evidence of this kind of philosophical individualism in the sources close to the historical cattlemen themselves.

As historians we do not know that the frontier life of the cattleman "atomized" his society. While society was "highly rarefied," to use the metaphor of Webb in *The Great Plains,* we do not illuminate the resulting human and social condition by adding that "the human particles were far apart, and they oscillated over wide spaces."[23] Even if the image could be validated historically, it would be a strange conceit with which to represent the heroic individualism valued by Turner, Webb, Dale, and almost every other frontier historian. If it had an aptness in the historical writings of Henry Adams, it seems incongruous when related to the persons of John Chisum or Shanghai Pierce or Charles Goodnight. To thin society is not to atomize it. To force men to become self-reliant does not force them to regard their selves as sovereign. There is no evidence, so far as I know, that Goodnight, for example, however independent and self-reliant he may have seemed to be, regarded himself as sovereign. And certainly there is no evidence that he regarded all other men as having a unique value in their individual persons.

Historiographically there are two sorts of difficulties in the conception of the cattleman as a believer in individualism. There is first of all the problem of knowing what the term signifies, and then there is the problem of knowing that the signification truly rises from the concrete thoughts and actions of historical persons, that the abstraction issues from the attitudes of existing cattlemen.

It seems reasonable to suppose that R. H. Williams was making a verifiable observation when he wrote, "The range problem of management is more individualistic than any other system of agriculture."[24] In the sense that management decisions and the tasks of implementing these decisions fall upon a man alone on his own ranges, the management function is clearly individualistic. And this would have been more generally true a hundred years ago than today. It would have been particularly true of trail driving, for even several years' experience, the emergence of routine practices, and the structuring of the long event into a plan could not eliminate the chanciness and the consequent need for urgent decisions and impromptu actions. Trail driving must have developed self-reliance.[25] Isolated responsibility must have developed self-sufficiency.[26] The cattleman may indeed have grown accustomed to having his own way.[27] And when organized society crowded in and began trying to solve his problems for him, he may well have resented this social and governmental interference. When he spoke politically, he spoke in tones of self-reliance. Even his organizations ironically advocated a rugged individualism.[28]

But this is about as far as one can go. When William Graham Sumner wrote about individualism, he probably meant a laissez-faire doctrine seemingly sanctioned by the new social Darwinism. Individuals in this natural competitive environment must indeed be rugged. With its emphasis upon natural right and power, this individualism was of course a new kind of primitivism. But whatever the pride in ruggedness, it had little to do with a philosophy that gives metaphysical and moral sanctity to the individual person. If the frontier fostered only a rugged individualism, it did little to engender democracy.[29]

Yet the frontier ideology was democratic. It put value upon individualism, upon the unselfish as well as the selfish kind. And after the frontier was gone, as we continued to value a democratic individualism, perhaps in the threatening pressure of what we have called the Great Society to value it even more, there developed an ideological need to make history prove what morally we knew to be true.

Perhaps this ideological pressure can help explain the curious gap which sometimes seems to exist between the reluctant evidence and the historical interpretation of it. A case in point: in his introduction to James C. Shaw's *North from Texas,* Herbert O. Brayer notes that "the cattleman and his family were wedded to the concept of unlimited time and space, freedom of movement, and individualistic action characteristic of the West." To this observation he adds that "though militantly independent and individualistic throughout his entire life, he was a firm believer in the efficacy of cooperative action within the cattle industry."[30] These claims about Shaw may prove to be true, but at the close of his book we can only hope that they are true, that Shaw was indeed the typical individualistic cattleman we want him to have been. His text does nothing whatsoever to support his editor's image of him.[31]

Is, then, the conception of the cattleman as a believer in individualism a true conception? True, we must answer, only in a limited sense of that term and only in particular instances of the cattleman. The grand generalizations we have been accustomed to reading must be regarded with continuing historiographical skepticism. The ideological image of the individualistic cattleman may prove to have little correspondence to existing historical cattlemen.

II

The passing of the unfenced range brought many changes in the cattle trade, and many of these have been dealt with in fullness and authority by the economic historians. But for reasons which I have already suggested, one aspect of the fenced world has been left to other writers. I mean the absence of freedom and the sense of loss that supposedly went with that absence. A maker of cowboy doggerel spoke the lament: "We've been too used to Freedom on the Ranges Nature growed."[32]

Whatever the objective reality the historian might seek to know, a prevailing view of the ranges has valued their frontier freedom, not merely because they were there to be used without ownership but also because they were presumably the invigorating setting of personal liberty. Certainly this was what might be called the official view at the close of the nineteenth century and in the decades immediately following. A free frontier was basic, one might say, in the ideology of the western ranges. It can be called the official view because it was spoken so frequently on ritualistic occasions when the cattleman idealized himself and his world. For example, speaking to the American National Live Stock Association in 1906, Governor Alva Adams of Colorado, himself a stockman, described the ranges before fences and ditches as "a vast territory of freedom." Cattlemen, he added, "have never discarded the brave and manly traits that were theirs in the wild, free life of the open range."[33] From somewhat different perspectives, others would sound a similar note. Walter Farwell, of the wealthy family that owned the gigantic XIT Ranch in Texas, reminisced: "It is a compensation to have known the Panhandle at the turn of the century, when the frontier was free and unregenerate, with civilization and decorum still in the future."[34] And the historian of the XIT wrote in one of his books: "There was the freedom of the frontier, and a breaking of many of the bonds of propriety that cramped some men in a settled land."[35]

These three claims about the frontier, however, leave us with no clear idea about its freedom. We are left with possibilities of meaning, with ambiguities hovering like distant heat waves on the mind. If freedom is a kind of wildness, the absence of decorum and the bonds of propriety, we may seem to have the unrestrained behavior of a cowboy shooting up a cowtown. This letting loose, as we shall see, was indeed one way in which the cowboy acted out his freedom. However, the good governor probably

meant wildness in a gentler sense. The freedom of the primitivistic wilderness is, of course, a wild freedom calling up no natural
image of violent and erratic behavior. The wilderness freedom
mentioned by Turner in his famous essay enticed Americans
westward not so they could raise hell but because it supposedly
opened their spiritual possibilities. This freedom may be the mere
absence of restraints, a state as amoral as the condition of water in
a turned-on tap. Providing he escapes the trap and rifle of the
wolfer, the wolf in his wildness may be said to be free. Or freedom
may be a sort of unconditioned condition in nature, a state as
moral as a fellowship in Christian service. Although these different, indeed contrasting, meanings are possible, although the
cowboy insofar as he thought about freedom may have seen it as
the chance to cut loose, it seems clear that when freedom became a
scriptural term of value it implied a natural morality. It affirmed a
central idea in the frontier ideology of the West.

It is useful to establish this ideological base before considering the cowboy and his freedom. More than any other man of the
frontier, he became the embodiment of its freedom. "The basic
reason for the differences between the cowboy and other men,"
wrote Stewart Edward White, "rests finally on an individual liberty, a freedom from restraint either of society or convention, a
lawlessness, an accepting of his own standard alone."[36]

This account of the cowboy, it should be clear, is implicitly
primitivistic. It rejects for the cowboy the order of society and
conventions; it supposes in their place a natural standard. If the
cowboy is lawless, if he lives outside of statutory rules and regula-
tions, he does not thus fall into moral anarchy. If he is like a bird
of the wilderness, he is not like a wolf on the prowl. He possesses a
natural sense of goodness. Guided by his instinct of rightness, he
is free to disregard all of society's artificial mandates. This, to
repeat, is the cowboy according to frontier ideology.

But if the cowboy is to be defined in terms of his work—many
historians and literary critics insist on this—then cowboying was
primarily a matter of riding horses, driving cows, roping and
branding calves. And if the cowboy was truly free, the freedom
should have been in his cowboying. If his work was an integral
function of his existence on a free range, his freedom should have
been a function of his range life.

However, at the existential level, insofar as our sources permit us to reach this level, the sense of freedom is hard to find. On the contrary, the cowboy's world seems closed, marked by monotonous routines and binding group loyalties. "If I could go up the trail," thought young Billie Timmons, "I'd have a freer life."[37] The young cowboy worked for Charles Goodnight on his Cross J Ranch, and Goodnight could have told him that the trip up the trail was "a rough, hard, adventurous life" but that "when everything moved smoothly the trip was an agreeable diversion from the monotony of the range." This was, Goodnight said, "its sunny side."[38] As one cowboy remembered in his autobiography, when the drive had reached Miles City and the cowboys were to be paid off, "We were *wild to have our freedom,* and now, at least, we were one happy bunch of cowpunchers."[39] So the cowboy escaped the monotony of the range by going up the trail and then escaped the monotony of the trail by getting wildly drunk in a cowtown. But what kind of freedom was this?

It is a curious fact, or at least an informed impression, that *freedom,* like *individualism,* has been a much more active word in the vocabulary of historians than in the vocabularies of the cattlemen and cowboys themselves. Almost anyone writing an introduction to a cowboy book cannot seem to get along without it. One suspects again the ideological need to affirm a frontier value. A case in point: in 1957 Will Tom Carpenter's *Lucky 7: A Cowman's Autobiography* was published with an introduction by Elton Miles. On a single page of the introduction the following bits of frontier rhetoric are gathered: "a man's love of the freedom of the cattle trail," "half a continent of unfenced prairies that seduced a man and held him jealously," "the unfettered life of the cattle-driver," "the free and flat grasslands," "his joyful independence," "limitless freedom of movement," "his freedom-loving spirit."[40] The text of the autobiography, while it does speak of "the wide, wide world," shows nothing and says nothing about freedom. On the contrary, it says a lot about the hard, hard work. A similar absence of the experience and idea of freedom can be noted in other diaries and so-called autobiographies. For example: in 1876 seventeen-year-old William Emsley Jackson helped drive a herd of cattle from Oregon to Wyoming. His diary gives no sense whatsoever of a cowboy living a life of freedom. In fact the word *free* is used only once, and that use is unconsciously ironical. When he has been paid off and his chores have been turned over to someone else, he says, "I am like that little darky now, 'I'se [a] free nigger.' "[41] E. C. Abbott, in the classic autobiography *We Pointed Them North*, tells of the cowboy's independence, wildness, and love of fun,[42] but he says almost nothing about freedom. The two instances, as I shall point out, are revealing. He does, I should add, say a good bit about the long hours and the hard work.

That many of the supposedly historical claims made about the cowboy are ideological can, I believe, be further indicated by a critical consideration of two of the western conceits associated with Will Tom Carpenter: *limitless freedom of movement* and *freedom-loving spirit.* The historical experience of Americans "proved" to them that in movement lay freedom, that distance and extended space were essential to the geography of freedom. Go west across the Atlantic. Go west across the Appalachian Mountains. Go west across the rolling prairies. Westward, said Thoreau, is the direction of freedom. If you can move, you are free.

Americans moved, however, not because they were sucked into the great vacuum of the West but because, as Turner said, they loved freedom. Love of freedom was natural, inherent in the make-up of human nature. If cattlemen, as McCoy said, had an innate sense of right and wrong, the cowboy, others could insist, had an innate love of freedom.

Applied to Will Tom Carpenter, then, these notions have been deduced from a democratic frontier ideology, not induced from the concrete existential feelings, thoughts, and actions of a historical cowboy.

In historical retrospect, we should have seen, as Jefferson did see, that physical liberty is not moral liberty. And had we as historians looked closely at the supposed geography of freedom, had we mapped it in its concrete details, we would have seen that movement was never limitless, that a cowboy did not even have the full measure of physical liberty attributed to him.

Was the cowboy, then, free? Was he a lover of freedom? I assume when we ask these questions that we mean something more, or other than, the freedom to leave the ranch or the herd in order to have a wild time in Dodge City. Our answers here will depend upon our data and the metahistorical assumptions we use to interpret and organize these data. From the Marxist point of view the cowboy was not free. The socioeconomic data may be thin, to say the least, but this thinness did not prevent Marx's daughter and her husband from asserting that the cowboy's "supposed 'freedom' is no more of a reality" than is the factory worker's freedom.[43] But this conception of the cowboy may, of course, be simply another ideological version. In the context of the social Darwinism of the late nineteenth century, the man of the range should have been seen as a product of environmental forces acting to make the new social species cowboy.[44] And if the ranges were included in the block universe, the pervasive determinism should have left the cowboy a mere pawn of an impersonal biological destiny. This too would have been an ideological conception. The historian could not possibly demonstrate empirically the causes and effects of a Darwinistic development. He could only speak, as some did, the key words *natural selection* and trust that this uttering of apocalyptic phrases would somehow illuminate the course of history.

But if one started not from a covering principle of some kind but from what the concrete evidence might tell, what answers to questions about the cowboy were possible? E. C. Abbott, as previously noted, mentioned *free* or *freedom* twice in his recollections. What did he mean? Was he naming a central quality of cowboy existence?

Speaking of the Cheyennes and their desperate return to their homelands, Abbott says, "You couldn't blame them for that because they were only savages and were fighting for their freedom like savages."[45] However, this is little more than a primitivistic cliché, doing almost nothing to illuminate the concrete motivations of the Indians and throwing even less light on the cowboys' sense of themselves. The other reference, though seemingly slight and casual, is nevertheless revealing. "When I was eighteen or nineteen," the cowboy remembers, "I was so full of that shooting business I couldn't be free to enjoy myself, anyway not like I did later."[46] In one popular version of the cowboy, what is sometimes called the mythic version, he is free to arm himself with a six-shooter, free to engage in random shootouts, dying if he dies in total self-responsibility. However, the version is humanistically false, not because it leads to more gunfire than history perhaps warrants but because it is psychologically superficial. It says nothing about the anxiety that goes with a lonely and potentially violent responsibility. The cowboy in such circumstances may not have felt free at all, and if he did believe he acted freely, his freedom may have been at best an anxious freedom.

Is, then, the conception of the cowboy as a fervent believer in freedom a true conception? We must answer again that it is true, if true at all, only in a limited sense and only in particular instances. We really know so little about the cowboy, about historical persons who were cowboys, about the concrete sense in which they knew themselves or by which others could perceptively know them, that we should only with caution and a certain historiographical reluctance make generalizations about them. As much as we may value the image of the free, fun-loving cowboy, as much as we may need him to embody the lighthearted openness of our western dream world, we should not suppose that we can easily find him in history.

III

Beyond this inconclusive conclusion, the critic of history can, I believe, make some useful observations. Obviously a major problem in the historiography of the cattle trade at the point of better understanding the men involved is the scarcity of reliable concrete information. We have an abundance of statistical materials, cows driven, sold, slaughtered, acres fenced, miles of wire strung; we have an abundance of details about the kinds of saddles, numbers of cinches, diameters of spur rowels, designs of chaps. But we do not have adequate personal information, the inside concrete particulars by which the nature of the person can be known. Yet even if our study tables are heaped with notes bearing a richness of such detail, that richness will be a pedantic chaos unless we also have reliable ways of sorting and organizing the facts into valid historiographical conceptions. I suggest three revisions or additions toward a better historical philosophy and methodology.

At the point of some historical concerns, particularly at the point of such conceptions as range individualism and range freedom, we need a better anthropology, a doctrine of man that will enable us to hold the human facts in a convincing human coherence. This means that the pieces of cattleman fact or cowboy fact must come together in human wholes not because they point out of the documents to the same figure, but because as historians we are willing to assume an inner structure that draws the pieces into a unity we call man. Such a structure, from which we flesh out our model of historical persons, may itself be historical in yet another way. Unless we are prepared to accept the notion that anthropological concepts, like mathematical equations, escape the hold of history, we must concede that any idea of man, no matter how steady and enduring it may seem to be, is at best tentative and temporal. Nevertheless, as historians we are allowed a brief stay against the forces of change. Our model holds long enough for us in our time to understand the man beneath the chaps, the woolen shirt, and the work-stained Stetson hat.[47]

As historians we need new historical sociologies. To say that isolated ranchers were unsocial, that lonely line-riding cowboys existed wholly outside of any kind of social tissue is a reductive evasion of our need to develop a sociology of the range. We have so long celebrated the independence of range people, seeing them as reluctantly, begrudgingly brought together in association, that we have tended to believe that vacant space is necessarily as empty of society as it is empty of churches and call girls.[48]

Finally we need new ideologies, or better still no ideologies, if freedom from ideology is indeed possible.[49] Ideologies do provide a sustaining tradition of concepts, a context of values important to the sense of purpose of a people or a nation. But if writing history means getting back to the way things were, not the way we prefer them to have been,[50] if ideological principles substitute their meanings for the meanings we ought to pursue with some sort of empirical rigor, with a willingness to let the past speak to us in its own terms, then we are getting tradition or the treasured past instead of history.[51] Thus history must be radical in the sense that it insists on going back to a maximum concreteness, being willing, if necessary, to throw aside some of the conceptual baggage it has gathered so far. For what historians seek after all is truth, not time-honored conceptions, truth about concrete persons existing in historical times and places. The cowboys and cattlemen were such persons. Surely they, as much as presidents and kings, deserve our best efforts to understand them.

The Fence Line between Cowboy History and Cowboy Fiction: Frontier in Dispute or Meeting Ground of Human Understanding?

To speak of a frontier between cowboy history and cowboy fiction is merely to recognize an aspect of their relationship which has obtained for more than a century. Novelists have of course often borrowed from history. Sometimes they have seen their own work as primarily historical, even though designed as fiction. Usually it has been the facts of history, not the fictions, which they have chosen to use. Few if any western novelists, so far as I know, have shouted from the ranchhouse step that the novel has its own kind of meaning, that it owes little to history, that historians therefore have no special mission and monopoly of western truth. Historians have, of course, sometimes praised fiction. They have found it entertaining or they have found it historical. Rarely have they delighted in its truthful fictions. So if peace has seemed to prevail on this frontier, it has prevailed because historians wrote the articles of agreement.

Frontiers may of course be friendly places where two worlds face each other and touch in mutual respect, but they may also be settings of contention. If we assume, as we can easily assume, an adversary relationship between history and fiction, we may even suppose the frontier to be a buffer zone protecting history from fiction, fiction from history. Scholars need not be diplomats; indeed like Vance Palmer they may find comfort in boundaries. It is the unknown, not the fighting, that arouses them to their tasks. So if the frontier between history and fiction is an incompletely explored territory or if the map of it is perhaps out of date, it is time to have another look; it is time to venture onto that frontier with new questions and reexamined assumptions. We can then hope, if historians and novelists are finally found rightly separated, that the line of separation is a rigorously considered philosophical and methodological boundary and not merely an archaic mete of intellectual tradition.

After a great bibliographical roundup, the literature of the cattle trade, that sprawling collection of history and fiction dealing with cows, cowboys, and cattlemen, proves to be a mixed herd indeed. To suppose a frontier may at first glance seem to suppose a facing relationship between worlds so far apart, so differently constituted that only the sturdy enterprise of the wandering scholar can join them in intellectual experience. Between Wayne Gard's *The Chisholm Trail,* a history, and Emerson Hough's *North of 36,* a novel, may lie a considerable distance. But between Ross Santee's *Cowboy,* a novel, and Edward Dorn's "Vaquero," a poem, may stretch the distance between earth and Venus. What is assumed in this study, then, is not that all history and all fiction should be considered vis-à-vis, but that some history and some fiction approach each other in material and method and that here, in this apparent converging, lies the supposed frontier. One identifies this frontier specifically by noting, for example, the similarities and yet the great differences between Osgood's *The Day of the Cattleman* and Wister's *The Virginian.*

I

A venture onto this frontier may rightly begin with a brief survey of present historical positions. This is good scholarly protocol, and it is to put most important matters first. (Remember it was the historians who compiled the rules of procedure.) A lingering glance at popular cow history will show that some writers continue to be perhaps more literary than historical. Whatever the historiographical evidence, they continue to impose grand traditional forms upon their material, untroubled by their apparent subjectivity, happy to celebrate the past rather than to understand it. Thus, as one of these popular historians sees "the rawhide years," the cattle drives up the long trail become a "great pageant of western romance."[1] Another glance may seem to find professional history and fiction happily sharing their truths in the ecumenical spirit of the new academic universalism. While some historians continue to suspect the writers of fiction, insisting, for example, that the literary image of the cowtown marshals "violates reality"[2] and that if there is romance associated with cattle trailing, it was created by "naïve novelists,"[3] others are even recommending novels as historical sources. Years ago, when the new history was still relatively new, James Harvey Robinson set a national example by suggesting that "future historical writers when they come to describe our own days will be forced to assign the modern novel a high place in the hierarchy of sources."[4] From time to time a similar view has appeared, if not prevailed, in the historiography of regions. Western historians dealing with the cattle trade have occasionally offered lists of western novels as useful sources. However, the limitation, indeed the one-sidedness of this apparent humanistic merger, is often revealed in the choice of novels. High, if not first on the lists, will likely be Andy Adams's *The Log of a Cowboy;* low, if not last on the lists, will likely be Wister's *Virginian.* The historians are, of course, not saying by means of this sort of ranking that *The Log* is a better novel than *The Virginian;* they simply mean that it is better history. Thus they are not recommending novels *as novels* at all. What interests them is the factual content of the novels, not their imaginative structure and style.

A further and closer look will show that recent professional historiography of the cattle trade, instead of closing the distance between history and fiction, has moved away from those features variously and pejoratively called romantic, novelistic, and literary. Described generally, the result has been to turn from the personal to the impersonal, from the concrete to the abstract. Need one say that fiction without concreteness and without person is indeed empty. Two instances will illustrate this sort of history. Jimmy Skaggs's *Cattle-Trailing Industry,* while it gives a sketchy biographical attention to the leading trail-driving entrepreneurs, seeks to reduce economic history to a relationship, as the subtitle indicates, "Between Supply and Demand." Thus the railhead markets do not teem with cowboy riotousness; the marshal does not confront the gunfighter. They teem with "economic activity as buyer and seller" meet "at the end of the trail. It was there," notes the historian, "that supply first confronted demand."[5]

The ultimate—and one of the most recent—in historiographical abstractions is David Gallenson's equation for profitability of the long drive. In this venture in western Cliometrics, the central concern is obviously with finding empirically valid quantitative values. Thus the data accumulate to the point where, for example, the historian can assert that Q_2 (cattle reaching market) equals $0.984 Q_1$ (original trail herd). Back of this equation remain, of course, the traditional factors, the hazards of Indians, rustlers, stampedes, and river crossings, but these are now weighted quantitatively. The first two, the historian notes, declined in importance, but stampedes and river crossings remained "quantitatively" constant and thus historiographically important. In spite of high risks, in spite of the fact that a herd of five thousand lost an average of eighty head to these assorted hazards, the rates of return were high. Needless to say, as the historian does say in his conclusion, these rates "were not realized by the drovers who were shot by irate homesteaders, scalped by Indians, trampled by stampeding cattle, or drowned while crossing flooded rivers."[6]

II

One particular phrase here provides the necessarily limited focus for an exploration of the frontier between cowboy history and cowboy fiction. If it indicates nothing of Cliometric importance, perhaps it nevertheless holds something of historical value. And certainly, as we shall see, it marks a human moment over which the literary imagination has often pondered.

The phrase is *trampled by stampeding cattle,* and I choose it among the others not because it pushes into our attention fraught with significance—shooting and scalping may seem more traditionally exciting—but because it challenges us with appropriate questions. Reduced to its simplest terms, the historical event indicated by the phrase offers us little more than a dead cowboy, probably nameless, and a small group of living cowboys, also probably nameless, obligated by circumstances to bury their dead.

What if anything should the historian do with this event? What if anything can he do with it? The documented instances of cowboy death by trampling are statistically unimpressive. Thus if we insist on number and number, we had better turn to other matters, say to counting cows or acres or miles of barbed wire. An enterprising Cliometrician could probably work out an equation for death on the trail, but of what use would his equation be? Say thirty thousand cowboys and fifty dead by trampling. Cowboys reaching Abilene equals 0.998 times cowboys leaving Texas. Furthermore, it seems doubtful that any death or any sum of deaths contributed to changes, even minor, in trail routes or herding techniques or overall operating costs for the driving contractor. So how did it concern history that a cowboy was trampled? The death of Jedediah Smith at the hands of the Comanches in 1831 may not have further altered history, but at least we can say that here was a man who had mattered, his end being, as the philosopher of history might say, a significant terminating motif in the story of western exploration.

Thus some will say, let us leave all trampled cowboys to folk song and sentimental fiction. Whatever the historical authenticity of the dead cowboys who inspired the ballads whose sad strains we occasionally hear, some will say that history has nothing to do with dead cowboys. As historians, let's not get sentimental.

No one believing in the high importance of the craft will suggest that history should become sentimental. Sentimental history is bad history just as sentimental fiction is bad fiction. Both are motivationally superficial; both fail to do what history and fiction in their own ways ought to do, that is, bring understanding to human existence. However, I am suggesting that fear of sentiment, as a part of a larger fear of subjectivity, has sometimes turned the historian away from what I am prepared to call his humanistic responsibility.

Put in its most radical form, in the context of this study, that responsibility is to understand, insofar as possible, the individual cowboy in that moment of ultimate historicity, death. Such a proposition will no doubt provoke from some detractors of the cowboy the response that the argument has now become philosophically sentimental. In some critical circles, to attach such

importance to the cowboy is to arouse more than a ripple of intellectual sniggering. For the cowboy, these amused dissenters
will answer, cannot possibly carry all of this historical significance,
however well he totes his six guns. Yet we do not really know as a
matter of historical fact that he cannot carry it. The simplicity we
have habitually taken as the historical cowboy perhaps cannot
carry it, but we are after all not dealing in simplicities. Simplistic
history, like sentimental history, works no better for cowboys than
it works for poets and kings. Thus I am suggesting what perhaps
should be assumed as professional horse sense, that we take for
granted no established boundaries around the historical cowboy,
that we assume instead an open frontier of humanistic knowledge
into which we can yet venture, with some risks, to be sure, as may
be appropriate on any frontier, but also with the possibility of
fresh discoveries.

The further special assumptions that give warrant to this
venture can be briefly put. At the risk of repeating what has been
earlier stated and elsewhere implied, one needs to say again that
the individual is historically important. Whatever the historian's
focus upon the group, the class, the cultural type, he cannot disregard the individual, the individual discovered as person; for
groups in their historical concreteness are after all aggregates of
persons. Obviously the historian has neither the time nor the
methodological means to deal with all particular persons, but
knowing and valuing even one out of a hundred or one out of a
thousand adds an important dimension to historical understanding. The individual cowboy, the unique cowboy, is thus important to history first of all not because he was a cowboy but because he was a person. We can say the same thing about congressmen and kings. And if this importance should seem a negative importance, in the sense that uniqueness may seem to stand
against the very way of historiography, that cannot matter. History, one hopes, must ever recognize and push against its limits.

The collective *cowboys* is at best a loose term of nominalistic
convenience. The discreteness of the persons it collects into a
group ought therefore to retard the homogenizing habits of historians. Thus we ought to discard all of the slick, easy generalizations which bring the mind to comfort and to rest. Cowboys
were freedom-loving. Cowboys were intensely loyal. Cowboys

were lonely and illiterate. Most of such generalizations as they appear in history are, in my judgment, ideological or literary notions, inadequately supported by concrete historical evidence.

Furthermore, the historical existence of the cowboy held the possibility of significant experience. Without philosophical ostentation we can project over him a proposition which an influential contemporary thinker posits of all men: the "history of the human person comes into being in the encounters which man experiences, whether with other people or with events, and in the decisions he takes in them."[7] For the cowboy I do not of course mean experiences in roping and branding cows; I do not mean experiences in shooting up cow towns. I mean, within the special focus I have established, experiences in encountering fortuitous death, that hardest of all human facts, in a world which was, whatever its thin and transient covering of trail camp amenities and pieties, starkly alien to human concerns.

Finally, the most important aspect of the cowboy was what he thought and felt, not what he wore on his head and feet, except perhaps as the hat and the boots can be taken as objectifications of his inner life.[8] If, as Marc Bloch observed, the subject matter of history is human consciousness,[9] then we are not writing the history of the cowboy unless we are dealing with his consciousness. Some doubters will persist: Did he have a consciousness? At least did he have a consciousness worth taking account of? Inferred from most works of cattle trade historiography, our answers may well be that he did not. Yet surely this inner void comes from the empty-headedness of historical method, not from the nature of the cowboy himself.

These propositions, it should be clear, add up to no argument for the special importance of the cowboy. They apply with equal rightness to the historical mountain man, prospector, homesteader, schoolteacher, cattle queen, and whore. Whatever the western area, the critical historiographical need is to understand the historical persons who lived and worked and died there.

We cannot, of course, deal with the trampled cowboy; he has indeed become object. But those who must find and bury him, who doing so confront in him their own finitude, are another matter. What meaning, if any, could they find in this seemingly senseless and violent event? What meaning, if any, can the historian find for them? We are now, I believe, beyond the usual borders. We are, I believe, moving in the yet unexplored country where western history has so far been reluctant to go. I submit, however, that if we can respond to these questions we can perhaps illuminate not just the existence of the cowboy but also that of all western men who pitted their possibilities against the dangers and the indifference of a wilderness world.

Let us, however, back up for a moment to familiar ground, to this historical event as we find it in two well-known books, the first a standard work on the Chisholm Trail, the second an "unconventional" history of the cowboy. "There was no one," writes Wayne Gard, "to conduct funeral rites for the cowpuncher who was drowned or crushed to death. Usually the trail hands wrapped the body in a blanket and, without ceremony, laid it in a shallow grave. Heavy boulders, if any were within reach, were placed on top to keep out coyotes. Some of the graves beside the trail had crude wooden headpieces, but most of them had no marker to tell what ill-fated cowboy had reached the end of his trail on the lone prairie."[10] After a more detailed account of discovery and burial, Philip Ashton Rollins added an individualized note: "At the foot of one of the noblest peaks in the Rocky Mountains lies a grave. Its occupant died in a stampede. All that was said at the interment came out hesitantly and as follows: 'It's too bad, too bad. Tom, dig a little deeper there. Hell, boys, he was a man,' and presently, when the burial had been completed, 'Bill, we boys leave you to God and the mountain.' "[11]

As historians like to ask, was this the way it actually happened? Are we thus left with a sentimental image of death at the end of the trail on the lone prairie and with a halting passage of mountain piety? Indeed, can we really believe that Rollins heard what he here tells us as history? Or had the boys perhaps been watching a bad western movie? And yet, if this seems inadequate as history, how can we make history tell us more? How can we move deeper into our supposed frontier?

III

To anyone who has worked in the field of cattle trade history, the many problems in dealing with events of this kind are obvious.

The business history of ranches is possible because in many instances ranch managers kept thorough, if not meticulous, business records. The social history of cattle towns is possible because with the development of towns came municipal governments and courts with their records, newspapers with their often detailed reporting, and even citizens with the time and interest to keep up the local annals. But the human history of the trail drive is another matter. Few if any drovers had the time or the interest to keep daily journals. Insofar as such sources are available, they are likely to be a gathering of the tersest of notes, with little or no putting down of reflection or feeling. "Swimming Cattle is the order," one of the few participant-observers wrote on May 31, 1866. "We worked all day in the River & at dusk got the last Beefe over—& am now out of Texas—This day will long be remembered by me—There was one of our party Drowned to day (Mr Carr) & Several narrow escapes & I among the no." The entry for the following day opens with mention of a stampede "last night" and closes, "Many Men in trouble. Horses *all* give out & Men refused to do anything."[12] It is perhaps as close as the sources will take us directly. Yet it is only one source, and we must be careful about making it typical.

The richest storehouse of historical information has been *The Trail Drivers of Texas,* a hefty compilation of more than three hundred pieces of biography and autobiography. Assuming the accuracy of some of these memories, we can perhaps reconstruct the outer movements of certain inner events, for example, the finding of a dead cowboy, his burial in his own blanket in a grave scratched out of the plains earth with axe and shovel. But beyond such simple historical configurations we cannot easily move with confidence. The soft aura of old dreams floats easily in what purports to be a factual text.[13] This sort of trail history rarely if ever buries its cowboys on the open plains; it buries them on the prairie, more exactly on the lone prairie. Furthermore, it buries them where the wild roses bloom. As one trail driver remembered, "Some few [cowboys] never came back, but were buried along the lonely trail among the wild roses, wrapped in their bed blankets; no human being living near, just the coyote roaming there."[14]

Thus what purports to be a history of the trail and ranch life is often a selective, nostalgic memory. "We have forgotten the hardships and remember only the pleasant things," said one trail driver.[15] "It seems now as though it was in some other world and under fairer skies," said another.[16] Granted that history cannot be written free of present perceptions and meanings, it remains true nevertheless that even the most idealistic of histories must seek rigorously to probe back through the obscuring fogs of regionalistic sentiments and pieties, back through the drifting shadows of lore and legend. When we ask as historians, what was the meaning of death beneath the hoofs of stampeding cattle, when we try as historians to understand that cowboy moment of shock or grief or anger, can we find answers in the comfortable pieties of nostalgic old men? "Looking back," wrote one of them, "it seems that Providential guidance has been instrumental in my living through the many harrowing experiences of the early days."[17] Did the cowboy thus feel the voice of God even in the thunder of running cattle? Perhaps he did, but we must in effect ask him again if we are truly to know. Teddy Blue, who also pointed them north, remembered a quite different sort of conviction: "You could pray all you damn pleased, but it wouldn't get you water where there wasn't water. Talk about trusting in Providence, hell, if I'd trusted in Providence I'd have starved to death."[18] May it perhaps be true that the impieties of youth sometimes become the pieties of old age?

If, then, the historian has relatively few sources, if these sources are often sketchy at best, having almost no concrete immediacy, and most important if they give him only the outer shell of the event and the men involved, can history go on, can it push still deeper into the yet unknown? My answer is that it can, that it has not yet reached whatever absolute boundaries the divine map of history may have marked out for curious man.

We must begin our venture not with the hope of discovering rich deposits of new source material, but with the conviction that the old sources can perhaps tell us more than we have so far allowed them to tell us. New documents will undoubtedly be turned up along with the old spurs, rotting saddles, and other artifacts of the cowboy past, but these sources are likely to seem as apparently unyielding as those we already know. Thus our conviction must be based on the possibility of new ways of historical understanding. And these ways must involve what for some historians may seem radical changes in the traditional relationship between the historian and his evidence. Indeed these ways may seem to involve radical redefinitions of both *historian* and *historical evidence*. I say *may seem to,* believing that modern historiography has long sanctioned these ways, that what is new, and perhaps radical, is only their application to historical problems in the West.

The new relationship means that the historian cannot wait like a blank roll of tape for his supposed facts to speak. To learn what they mean, to give them the coherence, the meaningful structure they may at first seem to lack, he must do more than record human events; he must in a sense participate in them. He must come to his task with a capacity for empathy, re-creating, and indeed reliving. If the old empiricists, who still ride firm in the saddle, object, let us say at once that we are not thus abandoning history to the vagaries of subjectivity and idealism. To say that the historian is not subject is of course to utter nonsense; to suppose that being subject he must corrupt and distort all that he knows is to reveal a naïve kind of cynicism. To argue that history must be wholly free of idealism is to favor the impossible; and to suppose that such idealism necessarily means the uncritical imposition of innate ideas upon the pure objectivity of history is to reduce history and the historian to caricature. Surely we have reached the point in the epistemology of western history where we can recognize that the historian understands by means of structures he bears within himself but that these structures may themselves be historical in the sense that they too have been established by historical experience.[19]

Thus, to understand that historical moment out of the past, we start with whatever facts and artifacts scholarly enterprise and good fortune may have provided us. We fasten ourselves, one might say, to whatever seems given.[20] But then we let our perceptions make their own inquiry. We let our imaginations hover over that moment, exploring relationships, critically trying out possible patterns of meaning, not with the intention of making something up but with the hope of understanding what in an essential way is already there. That these imagined patterns or configurations are nevertheless similar to fictions should be obvious,[21] and thus we may seem to have reached our boundary line, if indeed we have not already crossed it.

Such historical ventures into new territory or such new historical ventures into old territory are clearly fraught with risks. Any well-trained graduate student can perhaps write the sort of history that consists in heaping up and arranging notes gathered from a multitude of sources, but only a sensitive, disciplined, and responsible humanist can presume to give himself to the further difficult task of understanding what these sources mean, to trusting his perceptions as well as his acquired habits of historical method.[22] To abandon what Robert Lifton calls "exaggerated concerns with detached objectivity"[23] may not be easy, for there is comfort and safety in impersonal objectivity, even when there may not be understanding. To venture without the usual trappings may seem risky and very lonely. The bibliography may shrink; the footnotes may grow fewer and fewer. Imagine the terror in looking down a page of historical assertions and not being able to find security in the thick supporting layers of documentation.

While yet on the historical side of our supposed frontier, let us then have one further look at the cowboy in the particular trail situation upon which I have placed our focus. Our bibliography has diminished to a single title, and a lonely footnote will account for all citations. A cowboy named Davis has been killed, "killed," as our informant puts it, "deader than hell." "Our outfit," he goes on, "laid off that afternoon to rest the herd and help bury him, and I remember after we got the grave dug one of the fellows said: 'Somebody ought to say something. Don't nobody know the Lord's Prayer?' I said: 'I do.' So they asked me to say it over him, but I only got as far as 'Thy will be done,' and got to thinking about my brother and had to quit. You know why. I was kind of rattled anyhow."[24]

We cannot corroborate this account from other sources, but we can nevertheless give it historical credence. And even more important we can find meaning in it in the sense that all of its parts can be seen to cohere into an understandable human whole. First of all it has the advantage of coming within the context of an extended autobiography. Although we may perhaps not believe every autobiographical assertion, we are nevertheless persuaded by this self-history as a whole. It suits our perception of an authentic person. Thus when that authentic person participates in the trail event, the actions, the hints of inner response seem authentic, and not just the unmotivated gestures granted to stock figures in fragments of official memory. It is not perhaps much that we understand here. Certainly we must wish for a richer sense of this moment. And yet what we do learn is important. For the historical "I" is no longer merely a dumb object, a mute "him" who might as well be an "it" for all we know of his nature as man. It is not a full burst of consciousness, yet slight as it seems the association of this new death with the death of a brother is a kind of inner meaning, truer, one believes, than the conventional pieties with which the cowboy past is so often garnished. Truer, we should add, not just to the way the cowboy was, but truer too to the way man is. Indeed, we understand this cowboy in the past precisely because we identify with him as we claim his identity in us. To deny the use of such anthropological transferences in history would be to reduce history to the story of unknowable strangers, to leave historical cowboys as little more than quaint objects preserved in the museums of time.

If we seem now even closer to the ways of fiction, that closeness is fitting. For it is time to see the lay of the frontier from the other side.

IV

Anyone even casually acquainted with the literature of the West will remember many novels dealing with the epic drive of cattle from Mexico and Texas to the northern markets and ranges. From *The Log of a Cowboy* to the latest variation on an old theme and structure, the march of trail drive fiction goes on, apparently without end. If the last cow has been driven, the last novel has yet to be written. No one, so far as I know, has attempted an accurate tally of these books. In a variety of modes, at differing levels of sophistication, these works delineate the experience of moving great herds of longhorns up the ladder of rivers, through dust, Indians, storms, stampedes, and the civilized violence of cow towns.

It is not, however, in one of these novels that I propose advancing into the unsurveyed range between history and fiction. Some of them perhaps might serve us well in this study, but if we are again dealing with a single brief trail event, we can, I believe, rightly find our appropriate texts in the shorter forms, in the short story and in the one-act play.

When J. Frank Dobie included "Longrope's Last Guard" in his book *The Longhorns,* he called Charles M. Russell's story "perhaps the finest . . . that has ever been written about cows or cowboys."[25] Fifty miles south of Dodge City, in the worst stampede the narrator has ever seen, Longrope, a trail-driving cowboy, is trampled to death. Alerted by the shots of discovery, the trail men gather and are moved to silence by what they see. The narrator observes, "Let death visit camp an' it puts 'em thinkin' . . . . He's never welcome, but you've got to respect him." Some of the men are for taking Longrope to Dodge and getting a box made for him, but a cowboy called Old Spanish says: "Boys, Longrope is a prairie man, an' if she was a little rough at times, she's been a good foster mother. She cared for him while he's awake; let her nurse him in his sleep." So wrapped in his blankets, Longrope is put to bed. And what remains to be said in the story is a sort of epilogue: after twenty years the end-gate marker has disappeared; the burial spot has returned to grass. "It sounds lonesome," the story concludes, "but he ain't alone, 'cause these old prairies has cradled many of his kind in their long sleep."[26]

It is not difficult to understand why Dobie valued this story so highly. "Longrope's Last Guard" shows a writer with an ear tuned to authentic western speech, an eye sharp for the authentic details of men and cattle, and a heart warm to Dobie's own brand of western mysticism. In my judgment, however, it does not as fiction take us where we need to go. At the point of deepest imaginative concern, it falls into a reverential literary hush; it withdraws from concreteness and turns to the abstractness of standard, if not sentimental, personifications. If death does indeed put men thinking, what do they think? As one interested reader, I refuse to believe that they think simply that death is to be respected, that the prairie has been a good mother, that there is a kind of earthly brotherhood in her caring soil. Fiction, I believe, can do better than this—if the writer will but use it with more seriousness and sophistication.

To do better, fiction must advance into our supposed frontier. And here there are no established obstacles and limits, no academic guidebooks, no walls of high tradition. If in the judgment of some critics there seems to be presumption in the historian's effort to answer our questions, there can be no risk of presumption if the effort comes within the art of fiction. For pushing on toward the limits of imaginative perception, even at the risk of wandering in a mapless inner world, is to show fiction's own proper boldness. Technical problems may slow the venture, timid imaginations may choose to turn back, but final boundaries, if indeed there are any, are themselves yet to be discovered.

A second work in another literary form may give us better, at least different answers. Late in 1923 the Pioneer Players of Melbourne produced Louis Esson's one-act play "The Drovers." Written in a Bloomsbury flat, half a world away from the author's remembered Queensland, the play sought to evoke a sense of vast arid plains and dramatically to define the tragic predicament of a man trapped there.[27] On the long drive across the Barklay Tableland, the thirsty cattle have rushed in stampede. Briglow Bill, one of the drovers, has been badly trampled. He knows himself he's done.[28] There is nothing to do but leave Bill with a strong shot of pain-killer and get the mob going. As the boss says, "How in Hell can we travel with an injured man?" Thus Briglow Bill dies, his passing sung in the sympathetic pidgin chatter of a watching black boy.

What is the meaning of this western death? Briglow has made no tragic mistake. The jackaroo, the greenhorn, who has shot at a dingo, tries to claim responsibility, but as the boss says, "It's all a damned accident." To Briglow it doesn't matter. He says, "It had to come sooner or later. I've lived my life, careless and free, looking after my work when I was at it, and splashing my cheque up like a good one when I struck civilization. I've lived hard, droving and horse-breaking, station work, and overlanding, the hard life of the bush, but there's nothing better, and death's come quick, before I'm played out—it's the way I wanted."[29]

As an eloquent bit of bush stoicism, it will perhaps do. A man lives a good hard life; death comes before he is weak and whimpering. Maybe, as Briglow muses, the bush'll miss him a bit, the tracks he's traveled, a star or two, and the old mulga.[30] But it is a hope, not a conviction. He knows as well as those who leave him that the dry plains do not care, that, as an American cowboy might well have put it, they do not give a good goddamn whether he lives or dies.

It is simple, stark and simple, as understated as anything in the theater of its time. Compared to the American cowboy melodrama of the same period, it is strangely underwritten. Little happens on stage; gunsmoke does not fill the air; human voices quietly sound against the vast silence of the empty plain. Perhaps the short play could say no more.

It is not, however, as deeply into the matter as I believe the imagination can go. However eloquent the drover's stoicism, it does not speak ultimate and universal answers to the question of death. The great anxiety is not so easily reckoned with. A heroic fatalism requires that man accept the fates, but is it not yet more manly to tell the fates to go to hell, to define oneself in one last gesture of rebellion against the indifferent world? There are, to be sure, no possibilities that will change the final fact of death; indeed it is the most certain of all human possibilities. However, that certainty need not mean that man merely lives to die; on the contrary, it can mean that even in dying man lives.

If we seem to have moved away from the cowboy and drover, it is only the traditional versions of these fictive persons that we have left behind. I grant that the standard cowboy of most westerns cannot hold the sorts of meanings I am suggesting. However, I believe this incapacity reveals not so much the inherent weaknesses of the fictive cowboy as the imaginative weaknesses of the western writer. I have mentioned technical problems. There is, for instance, the matter of point of view. As long as we seem stuck with a choice between innocent eastern greenhorns and quaint old-timers whose brains and nerves are made of saddle leather, we haven't, I'm afraid, much hope of moving on. The innocent has been a sensitive instrument with which freshly to see the ranges, deserts, and mountains, and of course from Mark Twain to the present we have used him for initiation in the western rites of manhood. The old-timer has had his uses too. We could always look at him and see the enduring habits of work and survival. But neither innocence nor habit is worldly and open enough to serve as the mode of consciousness. If the fictive cowboy is to represent not just the dumb kid or the brush buster who follows cows up the trail but men as they deal with their condition as man, then a structure much more complex, with a wider capacity of thought and feeling, must be imagined.

We left the historical frontier at the point of its concern with the way man is. I have now moved fiction to a similar position. Has the frontier thus entirely disappeared? I think not, if this disappearance means that history and fiction have merged. To be sure, they have met at a juncture of shared humanistic interest, but their materials, their approaches, their perspectives remain nevertheless different. They meet at this common point, yet they stand apart. Using what I trust is an appropriate metaphor, I say that they remain separated by at least a single strand of fence wire. But that wire, I should add, need not be barbed.

There is a final way of mapping the meeting ground between history and fiction. "History alone," wrote an influential philosopher of history, "shows what man is."[31] Some will prefer to say that history alone shows what man was, not what he is. And some will insist that it is fiction and the other imaginative forms that show what man is. In the classic distinction, history tells what happened, poetry tells what happens. History deals in the unique, poetry in the universal. Thus to say that history shows what man is, is somehow to speak unhistorically just as to say that fiction (substituting that term for poetry) shows what man was, is somehow to speak unpoetically.

We can, however, resolve the difficulty by philosophizing a bit further. At least we can reach an anthropological position which history and fiction can share. History shows what man is, and what man is is historical. That is to say, man in his very nature possesses historicity. He is historical not because he stands in history, surrounded and swept willy-nilly by the passage of time, but because he is temporal in the very basis of his being. If this seems to be an ontological statement, so be it. Whatever its high ethereal ring of rhetoric, it does not free man from historical existence. The study of man's past shows this anthropological truth; the imaginative study of his present and his future shows it too. Historical researches lead to this insight; imaginative studies of existence confirm it.

So what shall we make of our trampled cowboys? Shall we say that they represent the human risk, the chance of failure, even death? Shall we say that they prove that destiny, not freedom, often prevailed? But even quantified, with all trampled historical cowboys stacked in one pile, boots out for easy counting, they may seem to prove nothing but the relative smallness of their own statistic. I have suggested a further effort toward understanding this human datum, a joint inquiry by both history and fiction. A dead cowboy is not just a number, not just a body, not just a name abstracted from the trail roll to be sent home for the family tears and rites of memory. He was a person; he was a self who asserted his "I" in and even against the world. Indeed, that was and is his meaning. We know this because even now, in an act of projected identification, we can understand him then.

We say that the history of the West was violent; we say that the literature of the West is violent. There are those who would change the image by a change of proportion: give more attention to the goings on in the little house on the prairie, less emphasis upon the brawlings, shootings, and lynchings. And perhaps this gentler reading of the western experience is indeed the corrective historiography and fiction need. But however well-intentioned these efforts may be, it is possible that they obscure a deeper problem. Sentimental peace in the West is just as bad as raw violence. Western violence, one might say, is sometimes violent only in its rawness. Understood violence, violence perceived in its delicacy and fullness, may be humanistically redeemed, gentled if you will. Such perception should be the way of both history and fiction.

Thus, while there may be petty quarrels and active skirmishes, there need be no field of bloody contention between history and fiction. If the historian observes that a fictional cowboy violates history because he (the cowboy) wears an unauthentic pair of pants, he (the historian) may be right, right that is about the pants. However, such observation has really nothing whatsoever to do with the cowboy's existence in history. And if the novelist claims that he is being properly historical by documenting his setting as the original Abilene or Tombstone or Los

Angeles, he may be right too, right that is about the accuracy of his setting. However, such documentation has really nothing whatsoever to do with a character's historical existence. The claims and counter-claims, the storing up of extraneous facts like ammunition, the manning of forts of disciplines in academe are thus so much thrashing about beside the important point, so much show obscuring what truly matters. Facing each other across that barbless wire, the historian and the novelist, one comes to believe, have finally nothing to shout or shoot about.

Theory of the Cowboy Novel: Some Ranch-house Meditations on Its History and Prospects

> Cows and men don't have a hell of a lot in common. I studied that old vet's handbook for three days running, and I didn't ever get clear whether he should kiss the girl or just leave her standing at the gate to the pasture.
>
> The author of *The Romance of Allis Chalmers*

IF the cowboy is worth writing about, observes William Savage, Jr., then he deserves "the best and most sophisticated of literary treatments."[1] For the serious writer interested in the cowboy as literary subject, this surely is a statement of the obvious. American writers from Owen Wister to Larry McMurtry, Argentine writers from José Hernandez to Ricardo Güiraldes and Jorge Luis Borges, Australian writers from Louis Esson to Douglas Stewart have supposed that any subject—including the cowboy—that deeply engages the imagination is entitled to the best of a writer's artistic skills. What makes a subject worthwhile is after all not its historical, economic, or sociological importance, but its capacity to be invested by the imagination with significance.[2]

Why then this new call for a higher, more serious literary treatment of the cowboy? The answer relates to the persistence of a sad statistical fact about cowboy novels: out of every hundred novels written perhaps only one has literary sophistication. Using a small sample of seven trail-drive novels, Savage points out that only Robert Flynn's *North to Yesterday* uses "the fictive possibilities afforded by the long-drive motif." The others tend to "reproduce history" rather than to "produce literature."

Savage's point is well taken, but his suggested solution to the problem may not be adequate. Indeed it may even aggravate the weakness we are hoping to overcome. Savage believes in fictive possibilities. He believes in the significance of myth. However, he argues that the myth of the cowboy has arisen from "mediocrity" and will not long survive. To find the basis for a sophisticated literature, supposedly to develop a more enduring myth, and thus to elevate the acceptance of the cowboy to "some rational plane," we must, Savage concludes, return to "the sources of the historical cowboy." "We must turn the cowboy inside out and learn more about him."[3]

We are here, I am afraid, exactly where we have been for three-quarters of a century, in a critical dead end, or, to shift metaphors, in a chute without a gate. It is true that the cowboy deserves the best and most sophisticated of literary treatments. This means all of the seriousness and craft the fiction writer can bring to his task. But it is equally true that the cowboy deserves the best and most sophisticated of literary criticisms. And this for the most part he has not received.

A brief review of some of the major statements in this century should reveal the basic assumptions that have prevailed. Perhaps, when these controlling notions have been recognized for what they are, we shall be better able to see around or beyond them to the more fruitful prospects the writer needs opened to his view. For if there is in these assumptions a fierce honesty, a regionalistic pride, a defensive commitment to one kind of truth, there is also a blinding naïveté, a failure to understand some of the most elementary principles of imaginative art.[4]

The beginnings of a literary criticism dealing with the cowboy are understandably obscure. Who first took up pen or pencil to say to the world, "That's the wrong way to write about cowboys" or "That is the right way"? One supposes that before such an act of criticism could happen the critical subject itself must have acquired a certain importance, perhaps in the form of a work or a body of works serious enough to invite analysis and judgment.[5] A sustained criticism, what might be called a body of theory, must obviously have awaited the emergence of something which could be abstractly called the cowboy story or the cowboy novel. With due awareness of earlier writings, we can I think mark this full emergence with the publication in 1902 of Wister's *The Virginian.*[6]

It is perhaps true, as Russel Nye observes, that Wister "invented" the cowboy—if one means that he gave him literary seriousness and complexity.[7]

If 1902 was the year of the cowboy's rise to literary distinction, there is irony in the fact that some critics were already beginning to predict his disappearance from literature.[8] His historical heyday had passed, they argued. What right then did he have to exist in fiction? "Some keen-eyed genius," wrote Arthur Chapman just before the publication of *The Virginian*, "who recognizes the theatrical untruth of the accepted school, will catch the interesting phases of actuality. Then we shall get some capital stories of . . . the ranch, minus the cowboy and the round-up . . . . The actual people of the West," he went on, "will be introduced in fiction, and the change from artificiality to reality will be welcome . . . ."[9] The "actual people" of course did not include the cowboy.

Chapman was not perhaps an important critic, but his assumption has nevertheless persisted, perhaps indeed because it appeals to no faith in the imagination, because it requires little elaboration of critical argument. It takes the common-sense view that the only reality is the reality out there in the world. It equates the real with the actual. If there is a real cowboy, he is out there, tanned by the world's sun and surrounded by actual cows. Thus, to put reality in fiction, the writer does not need to create a cowboy; he simply reports on the one already riding the ranges.[10]

Two decades later Philip Ashton Rollins published *The Cowboy*, the first of several books committed by Rollins to an "accurate" portrayal of the "bygone puncher."[11] Like other works of their kind, these books sought to distinguish the "real" cowboy from the "synthetic."[12] While many features of cowboy character and life were detailed by the author, two in particular will serve to illustrate Rollins's thesis about the cowboy in fiction. "The keynote of his [the real cowboy's] existence," Rollins wrote in the preface to *Jinglebob*, "was hard work."[13] Thus, to present the reality of the cowboy, the writer must present him fully in his cowboy work. A different sort of feature was the cowboy's use of guns. The gun was, Rollins acknowledged, "an integral part" of the cowboy's "full dress," but it was the synthetic cowboy of the fictionist, not the real cowboy, who was "heavily freighted with weapons" and who carried them in "melodramatic fashion" and discharged them in a "theatric manner."[14] In sum, the real cowboy, though he carried a gun, mainly worked hard; the synthetic cowboy does little work, being occupied mainly with theatrical shooting.

For Rollins, as for Chapman, reality was thus found in what could be observed on the ranges. The synthetic cowboy of fiction, whatever pleasure he might give, was a different order of creature.[15] The term *synthetic* clearly denotes a quality not to be taken seriously.

Here again is the common-sense view, with all of its suspicion of that which is made-up, imagined rather than copied. The literary naïveté is as striking as the subject in his big hat and boots. Apparently it did not occur to critics of this kind that Oedipus, Hamlet, Quentin Compson, and Willy Loman, among others, in the many-peopled world of literature, are all synthetic too, that what finally matters is not that they are made-up but how completely they are made-up, how totally they persuade us of their imagined being.

The thesis about the cowboy work and the guns would prove an enduring if naïve notion. In 1923 Eugene Manlove Rhodes, whom some critics would come to regard as one of the best writers of the range lands, contributed his own bit of argument in the essay "The Cowboy in Fiction." Like Rollins, he emphasized the cowboy's work, noting that it is seldom touched upon in fiction. "If work is mentioned at all, it is usually the obvious and external phases of it, such as calf branding or steer shipping." "There *was*," he added, "gunplay amongst the cowboys; but what the cowboys did best and most was to work the cattle. It was not unnatural to write up the fighting days of the cowhands; but the skill, the daring, the fine faithfulness, and the splendid fun of the workdays has been neglected."[16] Andy Adams "wrote of those working days, truthfully and lovingly," Rhodes added further in a brief tribute. One supposes that Rhodes also approved of Adams's seeming unwillingness to use gunfire as a dramatic solution.[17]

That the work of the historical cowboy was important one cannot deny. We perhaps exaggerate if we claim for it collectively that it was "dominant in the shaping of civilization in Texas and in America's West," but without being Marxists we can agree that how a person makes his living, particularly since he spends so much time at it, is important in defining his nature. To some extent personal identity may lie in the individual ways a man responds to economic needs, in his habits of work, in the work values he lives by. From historical sources the western scholar knows that the cowboy did indeed work and work hard, that his days were filled with long hours of tedium, dust, sweat, and sometimes loneliness. One suspects that the average cowboy experienced little of Rhodes's splendid fun. A contemporary acquaintance with ranch hands will confirm that ranch work is still hard work, with little fun or excitement and a whole lot less glory.[18] Thus that there was more sweat than shooting may well be historically true. As Teddy Blue remembers: "I saw a lot of hard work on the range but very little shooting."[19]

That the fictional cowboy has often engaged melodramatically in gunplay one also cannot deny. This should be evident to any reader of even a fraction of the hundreds of novels exuding smoke and thunder across the range lands and through the cow towns. The reader of popular westerns may well need an adding machine to tote up the unmotivated uses of the cowboy's six-guns.

Neither of these truths, however, has final importance in a literary criticism of the cowboy novel. Consider how little we learn of "princing" in *Hamlet,* how little we learn of selling in *Death of a Salesman,* how far removed we are, in spite of a documentary sort of detailing, from the work of selling real estate in *Babbitt.* In Patrick White's novel *The Vivisector,* we learn relatively little about the work of being a painter but a great fullness about the humanity of the painter. The critical truth is that novelists, playwrights, and poets have never been particularly interested in the work of their characters.[20] It is of course good for society that men work, that they work with pride and skill, but the way a plumber fits a joint tells us less about his humanity than the way he accepts the death of his child or the way he adjusts to going blind. How a cowboy braids a hackamore is obviously less fraught with dramatic importance than how he carelessly—but perhaps tragically—uses the gun which he carries on his hip.

The fact that cowboy fiction has often been melodramatic in its use of gunfire means not that the guns are an inappropriate, perhaps unhistorical addition to authentic cowboy character, but that guns have been used without enough attention to motive, without concern for the human meanings to be realized through violence. Violence for the sake of violence has of course no more justification in the cowboy novel than in *My Antonia* or *The Song of the Lark*. One can in fact easily rewrite *Hamlet,* leaving out important lines, and make the killing of Polonius and Hamlet as senseless as the fatal falling of a thousand cardboard cowboys.

The first book-length study of the literary cowboy came in 1926 with the publication of Douglas Branch's *The Cowboy and His Interpreters*. While the author dealt with a sizable number of more or less serious writers, the assumptions related to his theory of the cowboy novel are clearly implied in his judgments of three novelists: Owen Wister, Emerson Hough, and Andy Adams. The negative judgment on Wister's *The Virginian* seems based on the following propositions: There are no cows in the story. The Virginian is not a type; indeed he is not really a cowboy. The heroine is not natural to the cattle country; on the contrary, she is "a commonplace little prude from Vermont." The novel is not true to its historical intentions.[21] And underlying this whole prejudiced reading of Wister was, one suspects, the further and perhaps absolutely limiting biographical principle that Wister was an easterner.

Emerson Hough, however, was a different sort of writer, a writer, Branch seems to assume, equipped with the proper set of western notions. Hough knew the West from his own experience; "he knew and understood the cowboy"; he had the wisdom to know that "the cowboy and the range were inseparable." *North of 36,* Branch concluded, was "the most faithful story of the cattle-industry ever written by one not a cowboy himself." Unlike *The Virginian,* it had cows, a whole herd of them. Unlike Wister's titular hero, Dan McMasters "could have lived only on the Western range." Unlike Molly Wood, Wister's heroine, Tasie Lockhart was herself "a part of the cattle-country." Furthermore, the novel was a "faithful" "mirror of its chosen day"; that is, it was historically authentic.[22]

The supreme achievement came, however, from Andy Adams. *The Log of a Cowboy,* said Branch, is "the finest piece of literature that the cattle-country has produced." It lacked, one supposes, the faults of *The Virginian,* and it improved upon the achievements of *North of 36*. Adams was a cowboy, not "a literary connoisseur out of the East." If he was not a sure grammarian, if he lacked a knowledge of academic technique, this did not matter. He was faithful to his materials; his incidents were a "rich metal that needs no polishing"; he let the narrative move of its own free will; he disregarded plot "as though implying that a yarn needs no structure to be interesting, if only it is a Western yarn."[23]

One is struck here by what should perhaps be called a kind of western primitivism or a sort of western puritanism. The best writer about cowboys is the natural writer who lets the materials speak for themselves, who has an instinctive faith in their worth. It is, in a sense, a call for a western plain style. At the very beginning of American literature, John Cotton wrote in the Preface to *The Bay Psalm Book* that God's altar needs not our polishing. He was, of course, rejecting the sophisticated manner of Anglican writers. Now Branch speaks of a western literary metal that needs no polishing. He is, of course, rejecting the sophisticated manner of eastern establishment writers. It is thus surprising, after all of this, that Branch quotes, with no sense of incongruity, a curious declaration by Adams: "the human imagination is the source of all that is imperishable in literature." However much there is of faithful remembering and honest reporting in *The Log of a Cowboy,* there is very little imagination.

The critical principles thus presented in *The Cowboy and His Interpreters* have kept their adherents for nearly half a century, perhaps because these ideas have had the serious force of a book-length format and because Branch has been regarded— even honored—as a scholarly and eloquent advocate of a western ideology. Yet whatever their sincerity, these ideas are finally artistically limiting, more appropriate, one might say, to the historian than to the literary critic.[24]

One of Branch's original discoveries may have been his realization that there are no cows in *The Virginian*.[25] He was at least the first critic to make the bovine absence important. In retrospect and with a little hyperbole, one might identify a whole school of western critics who have made cows the *sine qua non* of a good cowboy novel.[26] But whatever the obvious importance of cows to the cattle trade, the insistence on the cow-man relationship as essential and definitive is to put the writer in a curious and

self-defeating position. As any stockman knows, cows are interesting if sometimes stubborn animals. They perhaps have their
own point of view about life, as witness Frank Davison's novel
Man-Shy. They can even become heroes of a sort, as witness J.
Frank Dobie's story of Sancho in *The Longhorns.*[27] The work
involved with cattle can be interesting too, as witness the many
accounts of branding, herding, and driving.[28] A good roper
might well take pride in his useful skill.[29] Nevertheless, the
working relationship of a man to a cow, however skilled it may be,
has limited significance. If the cowboy is to embody more universal features of the human condition, he must be dramatized and
defined in a larger human context. He cannot be held to the
branding corral or the trail drive or the feed yard. His generic
name, which tends to bind him like a semantic strip of rawhide,
needs to be loosened and opened to a larger range of human
experience.[30]

Critics of the cow school are ironically limited in still another
way. Although they insist on cows, they do not seem to insist on
what I would call "cowness," that is, the concretely rendered
reality constituted by the presence of cows. Of the writers praised
by Branch, Adams is perhaps best at presenting cowness, yet
there is nevertheless a whole cowyard full of sights and sounds
and smells missing from *The Log of a Cowboy,* and a novel like *The
Outlet* has even less of this sensory detailing.

For Branch, however, it was enough to have cows in the
background, for they made that background range land. Because
the cowboy and the range were inseparable, the range was, as we
say philosophically, his ground of being. Yet there is a continuing
naïveté in this. The novelist, if not the critic, should know that a
character does not become real because he is placed in a certain
setting, because the stage is filled with grass and sagebrush, because he stands or rides surrounded on all sides by cows. No
matter how authentic the cows and sagebrush, the cowboy will
remain a mere figure unless he is characterized, imagined into a
person in whom we can believe and who dramatizes in his way not
just a cowboy problem but a human problem.[31] The inadequacy,
if not the western wrong-headedness, of Branch's assumptions is
clearly revealed in his condemnation of *The Virginian* and his
praise of *North of 36.* It may be true that McMasters could have

lived only on the western range; it is also true that he has little if any life beyond that range. Tasie Lockhart is supposed to be real because she is "a part of the cattle-country." Involve a woman in a trail drive and *ipso facto* she becomes an accepted component of a cowboy novel, even though she does none of the real work of the drive, even though she is, as Andy Adams said, a fifth wheel on the wagon, even though she is, in the Howellsian sense, pure cardboard.[32] But put a woman in a schoolhouse in Wyoming and *ipso facto* she has no more rightful place in a cowboy novel than a camel driver or an English barmaid, even though the novelist may use considerable skill to define her there.[33]

Explicit in Branch's praise of Adams are two assumptions which deserve special discussion for the reason that they have continued to be central in theories of the cowboy novel, shaping the judgments of even such influential critics as J. Frank Dobie and Bernard DeVoto. The first of these assumptions is that the cowboy novel must be faithful to history, and the best-known consequence of this assumption is a critical preference for *The Log of a Cowboy* over *The Virginian*. The same assumption, in the instance of DeVoto, resulted in the highest acclaim being given to the writings of Eugene Manlove Rhodes. Branch wrote: "The tendency of the writings of Andy Adams and the others I have named with him [including Rhodes] is to preserve the cowboy and the range in the clarity of history."[34] As already noted, in Branch's judgment, Wister did not do this; Hough did, providing, Branch thought, a faithful mirror of the range world of the 1860s, and Adams, because he was there as a cowboy himself, wrote even better about what happened. Above all, then, Branch seemed to argue, the cowboy novel should *preserve* in *the clarity of history*. Dobie and DeVoto seemed to agree. Dobie thought *The Log* the best piece of literature the cattle country had produced. DeVoto thought Rhodes was the only artist that country had produced. But it is clear that the versions of literature and art used in these high claims are heavy with historical meanings and that they have little to do with the imagination in its creative sense. In what purported to be literary criticism, neither Branch nor Dobie nor DeVoto dealt with what might be called literary and artistic features. They remained historians making historical judgments.

Even within the context of history, the ideas which lead to

these judgments seem stiffened with curious antiquarian loyalties. Traditionally it has perhaps seemed one of the historian's functions to preserve.[35] He has sometimes sought to do with words what museums do with artifacts. A work of history may seem to hold a bit of the past stopped in time, insulated from change as if caught in a universe of transparent plastic. So if the historian can find the cowboy of the past and fix him in this permanency, good. Our antiquarian curiosity about what he looked like will thus be satisfied. But the novelist should never suppose that his function is to preserve. Anything preserved is lifeless, and if there is any one thing the novelist deals in it is life. If the literary cowboy cannot be made to come alive in the pages of his natural home, the novel, not the historical ranges of the past, then he had better be left to the professional preserver. If the only life he has in fiction is the life the author asserts was robustly lived back there in the 1860s and 1870s, if he cannot be made to live again in 1980, then literarily he is dead and should be buried along with the worn-out saddles, steer bones, and the ashes of old branding fires. Branch wanted to preserve the cowboy in the clarity of history, but even if one supposes that he meant something other than the shiny distinctness of a well-made wax statue of Wyatt Earp, the clarity of history has little to do with the richness of a novel. It may be that history seeks to be clear, although great works like *Montcalm and Wolfe* and *The Conquest of Mexico* do not easily reduce to the rightness of this adjective.[36] But what great novel do we admire because it has clarity? *The Log of a Cowboy* is perhaps clear. But it is not a great novel.[37]

There remains the further assumption that only the westerner can speak with ultimate rightness about the West. Literary philosophies and techniques brought from Europe and the East cannot substitute for regional experience. Only that experience can provide the intimate felt-in-the-blood certainties from which a cowboy novel is authenticated. The best novelist dealing in cowboys must therefore be born a cowboy and remain a cowboy.[38]

Such a view cannot perhaps be called a literary theory. It is rather a regional *mystique*. And were it to be found only in the mind of Douglas Branch, we could dismiss it as the cranky position of a somewhat eccentric critic. However, this conviction has been almost as pervasive as sagebrush, and any move toward sophistication in our criticism must question its validity as a guiding principle or feeling. For it is neither as right nor as ineradicable as sagebrush.

Philosophically it closes rather than opens to possibilities. It suggests a cultural determinism, for it implies regional ideologies in which there is no conscious control and no genuine choice. One is reminded of leftist debates during the 1930s when writers seemed locked permanently into bourgeois or proletarian ways of seeing. The question what is the proletarian novel sometimes became the question who can write that best kind of novel, with some partisans answering, only the novelist who is of the proletariat. For the student of regional cultures the westernist view is additionally confining because it denies the possibility for the comparison of cultures, the advantages of seeing from the outside as well as from the inside. It is as if to say that Veblen could not understand the leisure class because he had not been born into it. From the point of view of the literary theorist, the westernist view is particularly narrow. It reduces, if not impoverishes, the writer's resources; it denies him a usable relationship to national and world literary traditions, to nonregional forms, to a technical richness that ought to be available to any writer, whether he deals with the West, the East, or the farthest reaches of the Arctic wastes. It leads to all sorts of dubious suppositions: that *The Virginian* would necessarily be a better novel if Wister had been a western cowboy; that Adams and Rhodes did not need to learn anything from Hawthorne and James.

Nearly thirty years after *The Cowboy and His Interpreters,* another book-length study of the cowboy was published, in this instance the combined effort of a historian and a professor of English. In two chapters of *The American Cowboy: the Myth and the Reality,* J. B. Frantz and J. E. Choate survey cowboy fiction from 1890 to 1915, justifying their special historical focus by noting that in these years this fiction changed from the subliterary to the artistic. Compared to Branch's treatment, theirs is more comprehensive and in some judgments perhaps more sophisticated; the literary record is filled out with additional works and some of Branch's exaggerated enthusiasms are considerably modified. Nevertheless, as literary criticism, *The American Cowboy* is inadequate. It proves to be a loose gathering of unelaborated critical gestures, in which it is impossible to find the principles of which the artistry of the cowboy novel is constituted. Insofar as theoretical assumptions do show through the discussion, they are for the most part the old ones.

Once again *fidelity* is a key critical term. *The Log of a Cowboy* is dominated by "accuracy and a fidelity to the true West." *Reed Anthony, Cowman,* another of Adams's novels, is told with a "sincere devotion to frontier facts." Hamlin Garland had tasted enough blowing dirt "to write of the West with considerable fidelity and disenchantment." Only *The Log of a Cowboy,* say Frantz and Choate, was written with the same "feeling of artistic responsibility" shown by Garland in *They of the High Trail.* Artistic responsibility here seems to mean a serious fidelity to the true West.[39]

But if in these judgments the historian's values seem to prevail, other bits of discussion hint at another dimension to their critical theory. In some introductory generalizations, Frantz and Choate point out that while there have been good stories which have captured the cowboy with fidelity, there have been other good stories which have captured him with imagination and some stories which have combined fidelity and imagination.[40] But what they mean by imagination and how it effectively combines with fidelity remains unclear. Unfortunately the chapters that follow provide no critical illumination. In an interesting and perhaps ingenuous scheme of distinction, the authors separate Wister from the dime novelist by putting him in "a somewhat higher caste," but at no point do they clarify his literary success and failure. *The Jimmyjohn Boss* is "not convincing," but we are given no critical reason why it is not. "Faults abound" in *The Virginian,* but insofar as they are specifically indicated they seem to be faults of historical inaccuracy. *"The Virginian,"* the writers announce, "whatever its faults, whatever its banalities, is no common book." But what justifies this reluctant praise? Other writers and other works get the same superficial treatment. Arthur Paterson's *A Son of the Plains* "works out a story of rather high literary quality." But we are not given the faintest notion of the principles on which this judgment is based. Reading the novel should perhaps enable the fellow critic to make some guesses, but reading this novel, whatever its interesting antique touches of an earlier time, leaves one still beating the textual bushes for the signs of a quality story. Hough's *The Girl at the Halfway House* is "unquestionably the best" of his western novels; in that novel a description of a booming frontier town is "particularly well handled." However, we are given no guidance to the literary principles which support such praise. Hough's description of the cowboy is "colorful" and "exaggerated." In other words, it deviates from historical accounts; it is not faithful. Here the principle of judgment is implicit, but the principle is historiographical, not literary.[41] Frantz and Choate further agree that Rhodes was a "rare craftsman," but nowhere are we given any critical proof of his craftmanship.[42]

One further critical point in *The American Cowboy* needs special consideration. Although it seems relatively minor and although one has difficulty fitting it into the larger intellectual context of the book, it is nevertheless important, for it points away from earlier prevailing assumptions. "The realism of *Moby Dick*," the authors observe, "may contribute to that novel's value, but its mysticism and symbolism have made it great. And it is here that Rhodes fell down, that, in fact, the whole realm of cowboy fiction falls down, for the fiction of frontier days won't be truly accepted as classic unless and until the archetypal myths are woven into the story, for they are a part of the American folk mind." Stewart Edward White, they further note, showed the ability, as did Wister, "to work with myths and legends which are accepted if not understood by the American folk."[43]

We are here in heady critical country, and one wishes that the critics had marked a clearer trail. The reader finds himself in this country in a mild state of surprise, for he might well have supposed that the book would keep a steady course over the more familiar ground called reality. The dust jacket says that the cowboy "deserves to be understood in terms of reality, as distinguished from myth." The introductory chapter notes that "a discrepancy exists between the range cowboy as he has been presented fictionally and he actually was." To be sure, this hard historical line is softened enough to allow truth to be not "strictly factual if it will just capture the essence."[44] But one supposes nevertheless that this essence is real too, and not something mystical and mythic. Furthermore, the very structure of the book, from its subtitle to its final chapter called "The Truthtellers," seems to organize the historian's traditional contrast between myth and reality (truth).

What, then, is to be made of this venture into myth? The allusion to *Moby Dick* helps very little; indeed the implied critical comparison seems curious to say the least. What are the archetypal myths supposedly basic to the American folk mind? How does the writer know them? How does he know them as literary truth? Certainly he does not weave them into his story.[45] How then do they function as integral form and substance in the mind of the novelist and in the structure and substance of the cowboy novel he writes? These and other questions *The American Cowboy* does not answer.[46]

For some students of the cowboy novel, the ultimate word was spoken late in 1954 and again late in 1955 when, comfortable in his Easy Chair, Bernard DeVoto issued to the world a pair of essays having the style of authority and the format of high sophistication. W. H. Hutchinson thought them the beginning of a book which "would have discussed the 'western' probably beyond further need."[47] Taken with some earlier writings, particularly an essay on Rhodes, "The Novelist of the Cattle Kingdom," they comprise a formidable body of critical dogma.[48]

Had DeVoto lived to complete his book, one wonders what he could have said further about the horse opera, as he insisted on calling the cowboy novel. It is not that he had already said everything that needs to be said but that he had shut himself into a critical shack where there was nothing left worth discovering, or to change the figure, he had ridden down a narrow trail, with blinders on himself as well as his horse, and had blocked with boulders all the passes behind him.

In "Phaethon on Gunsmoke Trail," after surveying a considerable body of cowboy fiction, DeVoto concluded that the writer of the horse opera is in a closed predicament: he must choose between the mythic West and the historical West; he cannot have them both at the same time. But if he chooses the mythic West, he cannot expect to deal with it in acceptable human terms; and if he chooses the historical West, he cannot continue to feature the sun gods.[49]

Here again is the abiding assumption that the West gives the artist his possibilities and imposes his limitations: the writer has only the history, the folk myths, the traditional forms which the region has given him. When DeVoto says that the writer *cannot* do this or do that, he is not pointing to an imaginative incapacity or failure; he is talking about what he perceives to be an intrinsic weakness in the cowboy materials themselves.

It is, I submit, a curious position, particularly for a critic of almost pugnacious independence and what might be called frontier self-reliance. One might describe DeVoto's own predicament—not that of the western writer—as that of a critic who has trapped himself, to change the figure again, in his own reductive conceptions. He defines the horse opera—the term itself cheapens whatever it will come to signify—in such a way that all complexity, all subtlety, all richness are excluded. His examples for the most part justify his simplistic model. But to suppose that this critical model establishes for all time the possibilities of the cowboy novel is to suppose that the western writer is swept along willy-nilly in popular literary history, that he has no genuine choices in substance and form, that imaginative innovation is powerless against the regional grain. Yet suppose a critic in the mid-1920s in another region, after looking over a cotton wagon full of southern novels, including *The White Rose of Memphis,* finally pronouncing: nothing here, turning at the same time to a young man named W. Faulkner, says, you better get back that job at the post office.

DeVoto further defines the myth of the West as the myth of the sun gods. Given this celestial context, it takes little imagination to see serious novelists scurrying for surer ground. Tell a novelist that he's going to be working with sun gods, and he'll sensibly reply, no thanks. I'll try to make an honest living selling buggy whips. DeVoto knew this as well as any novelist. He knew that novelists don't begin with a belief in sun gods; they begin with a belief in people. Nevertheless, he seemed to think that the dream of sun gods held a fatal fascination. It was as if the West had set a trap for weak and wandering imaginations. But surely here DeVoto was making too much of myth, too little of novelists. If the novelist starts with an ordinary cowboy and that cowboy becomes too heroic and loses his humanity in a literary deification, let us blame the novelist, his lack of understanding, the deficiencies of his craft. Let us not blame a popular myth.

For DeVoto the one chance for the novelist of the cattle kingdom seemed to lie in the historical West. Cowboy fiction of a serious sort had no place for myths; its riders could not be sun gods. On the contrary, its only ground of reality was the historic rangeland West as it had been known by those who experienced it. There, and only there, lay the prospect for literary truth. And there, in the judgment of DeVoto, Eugene Rhodes firmly took his stand and became the kingdom's only artist.[50]

The nature of Rhodes's artistry, the nature of his practice as a novelist, is thus the crux of the critical matter in a discussion of DeVoto's assumptions about the cowboy novel. DeVoto in effect called Rhodes a historian of the cattle kingdom; he called him its archeologist.[51] But he also called him its artist and its novelist. In the use of these terms, what did he mean? How was the historian a novelist? How was the archeologist an artist? The answers, it seems to me, are far from clear. Indeed, although DeVoto was himself a novelist and wrote a good bit about the novel, his theory of the novel remains vague to say the least.

One can, however, discover a few general principles. It is safe to say that for DeVoto a good novel was a realistic novel. For him as for Howells, the novel and realism were closely related, if not inseparable. When he wrote that a writer cannot deal with the mythic West in "acceptable human terms," he meant, one may suppose, that the cowboys of that West cannot be defined as believable, realistic human beings. Yet DeVoto's idea of realism as he presented it in his essay on Rhodes, while it does support a favorable judgment on Rhodes, nevertheless leaves the critic a long way from a fully reasoned literary theory.

Consider two claims about Rhodes's realism. "The man was," said DeVoto, "a rigorous realist." "Drouth is drouth in his pages, thirst is thirst, heat is heat, and dust, dust. When a remuda comes in, that is the way remudas come in. Water in barrels at a cook wagon stinks as water does stink when carried fifty miles and left under the desert sun."[52] Furthermore, many of the characters in Rhodes's fiction, like the dust and the stinking water, seem taken directly from the actual world. However, all of this, while it does provide an authenticity of detail and person, has little to do with novelistic realism. It has almost nothing to do with making cowboys acceptable in human terms, almost nothing to do with the basic work of the imagination in making fictive persons real.

For many readers two of the least acceptable character types in Rhodes's gallery of range people are the heroines and the villains. In DeVoto's own judgment, both types are romantically drawn. The women are "incredible"; the villains are "astonishing." Yet, according to DeVoto, both the women and the villains are nevertheless "immensely true," true "not to life, but to the sentiment of the society he [Rhodes] writes about." This involved a more important realism, the recording of "the deposit which experience in the range country left on the minds of those who underwent it." "I am willing," DeVoto said, "to let that define realism in fiction."[53]

But did not DeVoto thus open the pasture gate to all sorts of unwanted strays? Can we say with confidence that the sentiments in Rhodes are any more true than the sentiments in Zane Grey? How does the historian—and here obviously the novelist has become the historian of sentiments—prove the rightness of claims about sentiments? And there is a further problem. Whatever the historian can or cannot prove about the sentiments of a society, sentiments are novelistically true *only* when they function believably within the imagined situations defined by the novelist. They are validated within the novel itself, not by vague assertions about the social feelings of a time past. Howells and James knew this. Anyone writing about the cowboy ought to know it too.

I return finally to William Savage's concern for a sophisticated treatment of the cowboy. To restate his thesis, we must go to the historical sources, turn the cowboy inside out, develop a myth freed from mediocrity, and thus lift the cowboy to acceptance on a rational level. In my judgment, however well-intentioned this thesis may be, it does not provide an adequate critical strategy by which we can develop a sophisticated theory of the cowboy novel. Even with its forthright acceptance of myth, it leaves us essentially where we have been before.

There are, it seems to me, two major misconceptions in Savage's position. As historians we do need to know more about the cowboy; if the historical remains are available, it is not only useful but essential to turn him inside out. For only then can we approach that maximum of concreteness to which all history aspires. It remains true nevertheless that what we find, however important it may be to the art of history, may not be useful to the art of the novel. Suppose we find that the typical cowboy was sweaty, dusty, and unbathed for weeks at a time;[54] suppose we find that he was hard-working, skillful with the rope, the branding iron, and the cutting knife; suppose we find that on the trail he was raunchy as a barned bull, brutally reckless in the cow towns, guilty and mean-mouthed afterwards.

For these facts, if facts they prove to be, the historian will be grateful. It is his professional obligation and pleasure to know and accept whatever concrete humanity he finds in his chosen part of the past. Whatever he writes starts with this concreteness and always points back to it. The novelist, however, is in a different situation. He too hopes to make all humanity his subject, but his abstractions are of a different order. In them he seeks to represent not the maximum concreteness of a particular past time and place, but the universal concreteness of all men in all times and places. One doubts that Faulkner found the significance of Flem Snopes by turning the southern redneck inside out or that James found the significance of Christopher Newman by turning the typical American tourist inside out. Novelists after all are not so much finders as they are makers.[55] Thus much of what goes into the cowboy of a sophisticated fiction will be put there by the novelist's imagination, not grubbed out of the historical sources.

The second misconception concerns the nature of myth. The mythic dimension of any literary character, including the cowboy, is an enlargement, not a distortion, of his reality.[56] A sophisticated theory for a sophisticated fiction will recognize this critical truth. But the claim that we can find ground for a better myth by going to historical sources betrays a misunderstanding of the myth-making process, and the further claim that a better myth will lead to a rational acceptance of the cowboy betrays a misunderstanding of what might be called the esthetics of myth, that is, the way readers respond to mythic features in a piece of fiction.

The notion prevails that the myth of the cowboy is given. If you are a writer willing to use it, you accept it. It then in a sense writes the novels since it dictates the conception of characters, the necessary settings and actions. A further notion prevails that this myth is, by virtue of its grounding in mediocrity, second-rate, if not downright cheap. Thus if you take the myth, you cannot possibly write anything of high literary value. But here again De-Voto has let the writer become passive victim; he has conceived him as taker, not maker. I suggest again that we stop blaming our mediocrities on a myth and start blaming the novelists for a weakness of creative vision.[57]

If, however, the writer seeks another sort of myth or if he seeks elements to add a deeper complexity to the myth at hand, he will not likely find what he looks for in the historical documents. Since mythic structures are abiding forms in the nature of man himself, they may of course be revealed in history as they are revealed in painting, poetry, and religion. Yet it is naïve to suppose that a writer can take up his notebooks, venture to a library, dust off the old accounts, and find the components of that profoundly vital sense of mythic man he seeks. The mythic vision, the mythopoeic power, is in him, if he will but be aware of it. It is an understanding not learned in a scholarly seminar.

If, further, he sees the cowboy with this vision, he will not necessarily have made him rationally acceptable. Indeed, if the writer is a good novelist, he may have made him acceptable in a highly irrational way. We do not accept cowboys because they have been rationally presented. Rationality in fact has little bearing on the art of the novel.[58] Cowboys are acceptable in fiction because the imaginative logic of the novelist has convinced us that along with their sweat and dust and smell of cows they have a measure of human significance. But that significance may finally be no more reducible to rational analysis than is the madness of Ahab.

The Left Side of the American Ranges: A Marxist View of the Cowboy

"Out in the fabled West," wrote a visitor to America in the late 1880s, "the life of the 'free' cowboy is as much that of a slave as is the life of his Eastern brother, the Massachusetts mill-hand. And the slave-owner is in both cases the same—the capitalist."[1] What makes this observation noteworthy is not its sociological acuteness, although that might be argued, but its authorship. The leftward-seeing traveler in this instance was Edward Aveling, the son-in-law of Karl Marx. Aveling and Marx's daughter Eleanor had come to the United States in 1887 for a fifteen-week tour, traveling westward to Cincinnati and Chicago, interested in, among other things, cowboys and anarchists. Their conclusions they shortly put into a book, *The Working-Class Movement in America,* published in London in 1891. They were, they said, "driven" to the impression "that the condition of the working class is no better in America than in England."[2] And prominent in this working class, judging from the spatial emphasis of a substantial chapter, were the cowboys.

That the Avelings were driven to the conclusion that the cowboys were little-known proletarians[3] is perhaps evidence of how easily they found what they had set out to discover. Their case for the cowboys rested not on a field study of ranch and trail conditions, but on a conversation in Cincinnati with a singularly handsome, blue-eyed cowboy named Broncho John and on the contents of a little pamphlet which he gave them.[4] "No class is harder worked," their informant told them, "none so poorly paid for their services." The cowboys "have no organization back of them," while their employers have "one of the strongest and most

131

systematic and, at the same time, despotic unions that was ever
formed to awe and dictate to labour." Yet, said Broncho John,
there is hope for change: so many cowboys have "awakened to the
necessity of having a league of their own" that a Cowboy Assembly
of the Knights of Labour or a Cowboy Union is sure to be started
in the near future.[5]

If the Avelings ever learned of the cowboy strike of 1883,
their writings do not betray this good news from history. There is
probably much more that escaped their notice, and there is much
more that got into their book by way of dubious, left-pulling inference. No doubt the historiography of the cattle trade is not
seriously weakened by the omission of their evidence. Needless to
say, Ramon Adams did not include their book in his bibliography.
Nevertheless, the wrench of their radical point of view stirs interesting questions. Given the evidence from reliable sources that
the cowboy was underpaid and overworked—such testimony
comes even from that scriptural document on trail driving, Andy
Adams's *Log of a Cowboy*—why has he not been seen as the
exploited victim of cow-country capitalism? Whatever the cowboy's sense of himself, whatever the traditional image of him in
lore, legend, and literature, why has he nevertheless not been creatively imagined in a more radical perspective? Indeed, this second question is clearly implicit in the Avelings' book. Following
the topical question "Where are the American writers of fiction?"
they note that "of the American novelists none of repute has pictured for us the New York or Boston proletariate [*sic*]."[6] Having
discovered the cowboys to be proletarians, they might well have
further asked, why has no novelist pictured the proletariat of the
range lands?

In response to these and other questions, the following discussion must for now be sketchy rather than exhaustive, suggestive rather than definitive. Indeed, what may purport to be a small
hold of modest answers may prove instead to be a stirring about of
further questions.

I

If we are inquiring into the literary way of the leftist observer, we
might well start with Edward Aveling himself. Whatever his social

theory about cowboys, his design and style for dealing with them are curious to say the least. In his book-length account of his American journey, the note on the cowboys comes at best as a sort of afternote, three brief paragraphs at the end of a twelve-page chapter dominated by the heroic presence of Buffalo Bill. Obviously Marx's son-in-law was fascinated by Cody's wild West show, the most interesting show, Aveling said, in a most interesting country. "The Wild West," he wrote, "is an attempt to bring home to the mind of the town dweller, life and death in the Rocky Mountains, where the wave of savage life is beating itself out against the rock of an implacably advancing civilization. Over a large open space, partly surrounded by raised seats, Indians, Mexicans, cowboys, mustangs, elks, and buffaloes process, race, shoot, dance, jump, throw lariats, carry imaginary mails by pony express, rope and ride Texan steers, attack stage coaches and settlers' cabins, kill one another, and generally carry on after the wild, free, and not very easy fashion of the West." The intense fascination the show exercises upon the imagination "is in part due," Aveling added, "to the coming face to face with conditions that in some sense represent our ancestral ones."[7] The Republican Roosevelt could not have said it better. Nor could Leslie Fiedler have presented the mythic vision with more eloquence and fervor. Only two men, Aveling admitted, had produced on him the effect produced by Buffalo Bill. They were Charles Darwin and Henry Irving.[8]

Whatever the abstract social theory Aveling brought with him on his American journey, the concrete "merry men" (as he called them) of Cody's camp were scarcely proletarians of the ideal sort. Although some of them, to be sure, were not perhaps cowboys, they were nevertheless of the cowboy type. As a group they were perhaps as close to a cowboy class as Aveling ever came directly. Having spent "happy hours" with them, he was moved not to protest but to tribute: "to the ease and grace and simple refinement of these most manly men."[9] It is so charming, so personal, so primitivistic a tribute that we have to remind ourselves that we are reading not Francis Parkman, not Frederic Remington, not Owen Wister, but the son-in-law of Karl Marx.

Two other left-seeing visions of the cowboy reveal a similar gap between abstract social theory and concrete representation.

In 1932 V. F. Calverton published his *The Liberation of American Literature,* a work trying, as he put it, "to get at the root-factors in American culture which have determined the nature of our literature." "It is," he declared, "only by an appreciation of the class psychologies dominant at the time, as Marx has shown, that we can understand the nature of a culture or the direction and trend of a literature."[10] Turning briefly to the cowboy in his final major chapter, he noted that through the propaganda of the cinema "many Europeans came to think of America as an extended wild-west show," but that in 1908 "the serious study of the cowboy commenced, and cowboy lore began to take on literary dimensions." The date here marks the beginning of John Lomax's long search for cowboy ballads. Calverton, obviously more interested in cowboy songs than in cowboy novels, mentions further collections, gives the text of "O Bury Me Not on the Lone Prairie," and names four additional songs which, as he puts it, "best succeed in preserving something of the spirit of cowboy life." A final comment on cowboys follows in a footnote: writers like Charlie Siringo, Andy Adams, Emerson Hough, and Will James "have helped dispel the myth about the cowboy which has been created by the cheap wild-west magazines and the cinema." Citing J. Frank Dobie as his authority, he further notes that *The Log of a Cowboy* is "perhaps the best book in this whole field."[11]

It is, I submit, a strange bunch of critters to be gathered by a Marxist rope. A song like "The Texas Cowboy" may succeed in preserving something of the spirit of cowboy life. But how do we know that it does, for how do we know that the spirit of the song was the spirit of history? Certainly Calverton suggests no clear way of knowing. Even more critically demanding is our supposition here that *best succeeds* ought to mean best succeeds in preserving the class psychologies dominant on the western ranges. However, at this point the textual material remains fiercely unyielding. It is like trying to get milk from a longhorn steer. One might suppose, further, that if writers dispel myths created by cheap magazines and movies, they then leave exposed a social and historical reality marked by appropriate class structures. It is doubtful, however, that the writers Calverton names dispelled myths, and it is almost certain that they did not reveal the social complexity of cowboy life. I am of course trying here to hold the literary historian to his prefatory assumptions, yet the truth is that he long ago escaped the matters within my scholarly loop. At the point of the cowboy, Calverton is no more Marxian than he is Manichean. If Adams's *Log of a Cowboy* is the best book about the cowboy from a Marxian point of view, then J. Frank Dobie sure as hell did not know that it is.

A third radical portrait of the cowboy is in a still different artistic form although it shares the same problem of joining social ideology and concrete representation. In 1930 Charles Boni added Frank Harris's *My Reminiscences as a Cowboy* to its paperback list. The book is perhaps of little consequence—Dobie held it in contempt—and Harris himself was scarcely a penetrating social critic. It is nevertheless at least worth noting that like Aveling he too had three heroes: "Wild Bill, Shakespeare and Cervantes—all dead."[12] The Bill in this instance was Hickok, not Cody. But what makes the book relevant here is not Harris's story, but William Gropper's illustrations. Gropper was at this time perhaps America's leading radical cartoonist, contributing regularly, as he would throughout the Angry Decade, to *The New Masses* and other left-wing journals. Yet if Harris's cowboys could even in slight ways give in to the pressure of the artist's radical impulses, be shaped into images of protest, the drawings do not show it. On the contrary, the horses buck and the men pose in mythic vitality. Obviously, one quickly suggests, the radical artist was merely doing a job for his capitalistic employer, merely illustrating a text. Yet the drawings have even less social realism than does the story, and whatever their assigned or unassigned relationship to the text, they have indeed been drawn in a characteristically Gropper manner.[13] I do not know for certain that Gropper ever saw a mounted cowboy, but I will guess that seeing one, his artistic eye responded to the cowboy's energy and motion, not his proletarian look, whatever that might be.

In sum, the proletarian cowboy has been difficult to see, even when the observer has looked through a framework of radical theory which ought, one supposes, to make him seeable. Is it that the mythic is even more immediately visible than is the socially real? Or is it that mythic structures are even more primordial and universal than class structures? In my judgment, the literary history of the cowboy began with Walt Whitman. Observing cow-

boys on the plains of Kansas a century ago, Whitman wrote an
archetypal description: "The cow-boys ('cow-punchers') to me a
strangely interesting class, bright-eyed as hawks, with their swar-
thy complexions and their broad-brimm'd hats—apparently always on horseback, with loose arms slightly raised and swinging as
they ride."[14] The literary account from the left, insofar as there
has been one, has not deviated from that beginning.

II

For more than three-quarters of a century the economic complex
of cattle raising in western America has been called an industry.
From James Cox, *Historical and Biographical Record of the Cattle
Industry,* 1895, through Edward Everett Dale, *The Range Cattle
Industry,* 1930, to Jimmy Skaggs, *The Cattle-Trailing Industry,* 1973,
historians of the cattle business have followed this industrial
usage. And for an even longer period historians have called
cowboys *laborers* or emphasized their role as workers. In 1874
Joseph G. McCoy defined the cowboys as "the common laborers";
in 1886 Joseph Nimmo described the cowboy's "duty as worker in
the cattle business" as riding the range, driving herds, and
rounding up dispersed cattle;[15] for nearly a century a whole
string of writers, including Andy Adams and Eugene Manlove
Rhodes, has insisted that what the cowboys mainly did was work,
not engage in gunfights or rescue pretty maidens from runaway
stagecoaches. Yet so far as I know, no one, in this long period of
discussion, has called the cowboys *industrial workers.*

There are, I believe, a number of interesting reasons for this
fact. It is first of all almost unthinkable to call the cowboy an
industrial worker. To do so is clearly against the traditional grain.
If the term *industrial worker* connotes a close containment within a
binding system of orders, tasks, and wages, the term *cowboy* can-
notes openness, freedom, and self-reliance. The social reality of
the cowboy might involve low wages, long hours, and little freedom, but we are of course thinking here—if we are indeed
thinking—outside the context of social reality.

There are, however, other explanations or at least other
dimensions to this first fast-gun rejection of what might seem an

accurate and appropriate term. Almost from its inception the historiography of the western cattle industry has been shaped by a variety of kinds of cow sense. On the one hand have come the works celebrating the heroism of cows, cowboys, and cattlemen. Even McCoy's pioneering effort, which was, as we have seen, devoted "to a plain exposition of the manner of growing and marketing common live stock," was alive with wild cowboys and stalwart cowmen. And from 1874 to the present this sort of history has flourished, giving a sizeable cut of books with such titles as *The Trampling Herd, The Longhorns,* and *The Rawhide Years.* Even the major bibliography of the cattle industry bears a heroic title, *The Rampaging Herd.* On the other hand, since around 1880, when census and other data seemed to make economic history possible, a series of historical studies has sought to deal impersonally and scientifically with the economic forces permeating the range lands as well as the urban markets. Here one might add to the titles named earlier *Range and Ranch Cattle Traffic* (the so-called Nimmo Report of 1885) and *The Colorado Range Cattle Industry.*

In relationship to an industrial conception of the cowboy, many of these economic histories show interesting conceptual and rhetorical features. In some, the cowboy and, to a lesser extent, the cattleman have very nearly disappeared. This is true, for example, of Dale's *The Range Cattle Industry* and Osgood's *The Day of the Cattleman.* Thus while one may still assume that cowboys were working in the cattle industry, he learns almost nothing about their nature as workers within that industrial system, for the historian has simply failed to deal with this aspect of their industrial history. However, if the cowboy and the cattleman are not explicitly present in these works, something akin to their spirit lurks nevertheless on many of the pages.[16] Furthermore, even to the extent that these histories are economic histories, they do not, in my judgment, deal adequately with the cattle industry as industry. The concept *industry* has only the vaguest of meanings, being easily and freely exchanged for business, trade, operation, and other terms which loosely gather up a herd of activities associated with the raising and marketing of cattle.

It can be argued further that the resistance to industrial conceptions runs even deeper, not merely against the western grain but against the American grain itself. "The values and beliefs of this country," wrote Peter F. Drucker in 1942, "are values and beliefs of a society in which there were no large corporations, no mass production, no permanent working class, no management power. At heart, the average American is a Populist; and the essence of Populism today consists of a refusal to admit as valid the reality of the industrial system."[17]

III

These observations, I trust, indicate something of the historical problem of trying to understand the cowboy from the left side. But are there not perhaps other possibilities? Putting aside what the historical and literary record so far shows, is it not possible to make a fresh start with new assumptions? If a yet unidentified observer armed only with the preconception that a cowboy is a man were to ride over the pass into cowboy land, what might he speculate philosophically and, given a new concrete social definition of the cowboy, what might he project as appropriate in fiction?

Elsewhere I have argued that if the cowboy is to be taken seriously in history and fiction, he must be understood in terms of man's existence, with a sense, to use another term fashionable in our time, of his human condition.[18] This critical argument rests of course on the assumption that all men, in all times and places, whether congressmen, cowboys, or kings, are subject to the same primordial conditions of existence. They suffer anxiety, they endure meaninglessness, and they die. As the philosopher says, they have been thrown into the world and must consequently make-do with that original human fact.

There is, however, a possible objection to this analysis. Put in the simplest terms, it is that this analysis of existence is not historical. Although insisting on man's historicity as a feature of his existence, it makes this historicity specious by considering existence as if it were the same in all times and places, as if, in short, it were not subject to history. It avoids, writes Marvin Farber, "the pressing problems of human existence as they have appeared historically—the concrete conflicts between slaves and slave-holders, serfs and feudal lords, workers and capitalist, and the numerous concrete problems and tensions of our existing socio-economic system . . . . 'Human existence,' " Farber goes on to say, "is not an undifferentiated thing, or essence; it must be considered as human existence in a slave economy, or in a capitalist economy; and, again, as human existence in the form of a worker, or of an employer of labor."[19] In the words of a distinguished Marxist critic, all men, even solitary men, are involved in a "specific social fate, not a universal *condition humaine.*"[20] In what to some may seem a radical shift of focus and tone, we can say that even the lone cowboy was not alone.

Whether or not one agrees with this Marxist anthropology, he must recognize that putting these assumptions against our traditional version of cowboy life further exposes a weakness in our understanding of that life. What might be called cowboy sociology remains for the most part an unexplored and un-mapped field. Indeed, even to speak of a cowboy sociology may strike the intellectual ear with some surprise, not because the cowboy was unimportant, but because, seeming to exist outside of society, he has seemed to need no sociology.

The reasons for this apparent sociological neglect are, I believe, easily suggested. More than perhaps any other frontier type, the cowboy has been defined as a child of nature. Primitivis-tically conceived, he has been a son of the plains or a son of the sagebrush.[21] "Like a bird of the wilderness," wrote John Clay, he was "accustomed to freedom, not trained to be interfered with."[22] Thus to be a cowboy was to identify with nature, not civilization, to choose freedom, not the chains of society. And even when the natural parentage became less metaphorically explicit, the defining emphasis was still upon freedom outside or at best jux-taposed against a social context. "The basic reason for the differences between a cowboy and other men," observed Stewart Edward White in 1904, "rests finally on an individual liberty, a freedom from restraint either of society or convention, a lawless-ness, and accepting of his standard alone."[23]

Surely, however, this primitivistic version of the cowboy ig-nores historical and social realities. It is no doubt difficult, perhaps impossible, to work out a thorough historical sociology of the cowboy—the sources of appropriate evidence are simply rare or nonexistent—but insofar as we can make informed guesses we can confidently question many of the traditional claims made by history and literature. Elsewhere I have sought to demonstrate, for example, that the image of cowboy freedom comes less from the cowboy's sense of himself and the world in which he lived than from the historian's ideological need to project that value-charged image into the frontier past.[24] But quite aside from the scattering of evidence in historical sources, we are clearly entitled to an a priori doubt about the human validity of the primitivistic cowboy. One supposes that the cowboy, whatever his willingness to engage in solitary work, was nevertheless frequently and acutely lonesome. His intense pleasure in group activities such as storytelling, poker playing, and collective hell-raising suggests that he was not by nature a loner. The thesis that the frontier with its vast spaces atomized society is very likely a distortion. To say that it stretched society thin would be a better way of speaking.

Thus one does not have to be a Marxist to believe in the fundamental importance of a cowboy sociology. To see the cowboy as a *naturel* riding in Emersonian communion across the pastures of Eden or as a particle oscillating across the great empty spaces of Texas is not to see him as a person existing in a truly human world.[25] The Marxist view would, however, assume not just a set of relationships called society but a close social matrix of historically determined class structures. In this radical perspective, the cowboy, whatever his sense of himself, would be seen as a worker involved inextricably in a capitalistic range enterprise of national and international dimensions. But, to repeat, such a view would proceed from general philosophical assumptions, not from compelling empirical evidence. The absence of leftist range historiography stems perhaps as much from the difficulty of such historiography as from the rugged individualism of those who have traditionally been historiographically interested in cows, cowboys, and cattlemen.[26]

The lack of such historiography, however, in no way cancels the possibility of insights to be gained through a radical perspective. Even if we look closely and steadily at only a few of the cowboy situations where his economic predicament, if not his social fate, is at least faintly visible, we can modify the simplistic figure we have grown accustomed to believing was the real cowboy. But the greater prospect lies perhaps in what can be imagined in fiction, for here what is missing in the sources, all of the evidence to which footnotes ought hopefully to point, can be provided creatively. And further, the novelist's presumption of intimacy can, if he does his work well, expose the inner social condition, if not class psychology, of the individual cowboys involved.

IV

We can best sketch the nature of this radically different novel by projecting it against a particular piece of range history and a novel which that history inspired. In 1883, as already noted, there was a cowboy strike in west Texas. The cowboys walked out (or did they ride out?), demanding not shorter working hours, not safer working conditions, but wages of $50.00 a month. After a brief period of sometimes violent confrontation, they gave up their cause, winning as a consequence of their uncowboylike effort only bad reputations, possible blacklisting, at best a chance to work at the same old wages. As much as any single event, this frontier aberration of 1883 might perhaps have occasioned a proletarian range history or a proletarian cowboy novel.

That it did require some changes in the conception of the historical cowboy is evident in Robert Zeigler's comprehensive study of the strike. The historian seeks, as he says, "to put the cowhand in better prospective [*sic*] as a workingman." "A realistic examination of the various determinants leading to the outbreak of the Panhandle walkout creates serious doubts as to the validity of any romanticized picture of the cowboy."[27] What the historian means here by *romanticized picture* and *workingman* is not entirely clear. There are romantic cowboys who do no work, and there are cowboys who work romantically. Indeed, to the extent that they work according to some ideal pattern of freedom, loyalty, and skill, all cowboys may be said to work romantically. To the extent that they work full of the joy of living, singing and whistling over the flower spangled prairies, they may be said to work romantically.[28] The cowboy who works long and hard and finds little sustaining fulfillment in his assigned tasks, who feels the frustration of being caught in circumstances which he cannot control or alter, who sees the hiring company as faceless but powerful may be the socially real cowboy, but this cowboy may never have existed in history. We do not really know. At least, from the evidence available, Zeigler's workingman who was involved in the strike of 1883 need not be so radically defined.

A fictional account of the strike and its consequences came in 1971 with the publication of Elmer Kelton's novel *The Day the Cowboys Quit.* Kelton's title, however, is somewhat misleading, for the novel is not really about the day the cowboys went on strike. At least that event has not been used as the dramatic center of the book's theme and action. Certainly the novel is not a strike novel in the proletarian pattern of *The Land of Plenty* and *To Make My Bread.* Had it been, it would not have been dedicated to J. Evetts Haley, and certainly it would have been an unlikely winner of the Spur Award.

Insofar as there is a sociology explicit or implicit in *The Day the Cowboys Quit,* it is the classic sociology of frontier America. Mobility is its key. There are no proletarians. Using the jargon of the old left, one might rightly call even the poorest of cowboys the *petite bourgeoisie* of the range lands. The critical issue that leads to the strike is the right of the cowboys, while working for the big ranches, to own their own cattle, to start their own shirttail herds. Likewise there are no capitalists, at least none of easy economic definition. Big ranching power is represented by Prosper Selkirk, John Torrington, and Charlie Waide. Only Selkirk is clearly villainous, and he not because he owns many cattle and controls many acres and thus has vast economic power, but because he lacks all western values. He is an indoor man who sees the Figure 4 Ranch as a beef factory, the neighboring ranches as competitors, and his cowboys as names on a payroll book.[29] Torrington, on the other hand, is a tough old pioneer who has worked and fought his way up. Even though he is found legally wrong for helping to lynch a cow rustler, he is admired for his stubborn adherence to frontier ways. Waide is an old cowboy who in spite of the size of his herd maintains cowboy ways, keeping a personal, paternalistic relationship with his men. He joins Selkirk against the cowboys only because, as he puts it, Selkirk has him by the short hair:

Selkirk has influence with the Kansas City bankers from whom Waide has a substantial loan.

The novel is really the story of High Hitchcock, who, identifying with the cowboys when their right to ownership is challenged, becomes their strike leader. After losing his own small herd to the power of Selkirk and seeing a cowboy lynched by that same power, he is persuaded to run for sheriff. Winning that office, he can then ensure justice—at least the beginning of it. The novel can thus conclude happily, with Hitch, as he is called, seeing his own romantic good fortunes in the smiling face of Kate. Obviously the novel is only a slightly different sort of western. It is no more Marxian than is *The Virginian* or *Chip of the Flying U.*

Suppose, nevertheless, this radically different sort of novel. What would be its distinguishing features? What would be some of its special literary problems?

The writer of such a novel will start, one assumes, by accepting as valid a particular set of historical and social propositions. Central among these are two which will perhaps serve to illustrate basic conceptions and to introduce consequent literary problems. First, the cattle industry was an economic complex much larger than the vast ranges on which its cattle grazed and its cowboys rode. Its centers of power were not merely the ranch offices of Texas and Wyoming, the livestock commissions of Abilene and Kansas City, the railroad markets of Chicago, but also the brokerage houses of New York and London. In spite of distances, the economic lines were firm and tightly drawn. Although one might look out across the wind-swept oceans of grass and see nothing more hard and binding than the float of cloud and the whirl of dust, the impression was nonetheless deceiving. An economically unconditioned place and people was always more apparent than real. What finally mattered in the cattle industry was not the geography of Eden, but the price of beef and the inexorable conditions of producing it. Secondly, the cowboy was a worker in the full industrial sense. He not only performed the labor of roping, branding, herding, line-riding, and trail driving, but carried out these assigned tasks under economic circumstances which defined his cowboy nature and which gave him his social destiny. If to some observers he seemed free and playful, such boyish antics merely obscured his inescapable dependence on wages and found. Within limits he could change employers, but he could not remain unemployed. He could not live like a squirrel in the wilderness. An unemployed cowboy was finally as hungry as an unemployed miner or textile worker.

The novelistic problems following from these propositions are formidable to say the least. They can perhaps be summed up by saying that here we need a social novel when the traditional form of range fiction, the frontier novel, has been asocial, if not downrightly antisocial. It seems natural that Marx would admire Balzac—has a novelist ever given us a social world as thick and full?—but it may seem curious that Balzac admired Cooper. Yet the frontier novels of Cooper do not of course leave society out, though they may seem to leave it far behind. How to keep society active and relevant was, as Henry Nash Smith and others have pointed out, a problem. Cooper's awkward solution in *The Prairie* might thus be seen as a warning to subsequent novelists needing to use a range setting while at the same time recognizing that important decisions are being made not only offstage but also off-continent.

There is, so far as I am aware, no cowboy novel in which this broad economic context is attempted. There is, however, a Canadian range memoir which one might try out as a partial model. In 1882 John R. Craig assumed the heroically impossible position of managing the Oxley Ranch in southwestern Alberta. The virgin ranges were excellent; a stock of cattle could be driven north from Montana; cowboys, Canadian and American, were available for hire. The trouble lay in the fact that the capital and lordly power to misuse it remained in England. The cattle industry of the West had already come to depend on the machinery of high finance, but in this instance there was little smooth-running machinery, only the uncertain whims of the British owners. *Ranching with Lords and Commons or Twenty Years on the Range* recounts this curious story.[30]

The model is, however, at best suggestive. In the perspective of our radical conception, the larger economic world remains incompletely rendered. The social tissue proves inadequate for our purposes not so much because it is abstract as because it is loose and personally comic. Events take place not so much as they are conditioned by a close texture of economic forces as they are left to happen through the ignorance and blindness of the British owners. Thus to see the range development recounted in this book as a relentless imperialistic invasion of Alberta's grasslands would be indeed to read the evidence through red-colored glasses.

The second literary problem may be even more difficult to solve, that is, how to deal with the person of the cowboy as an industrial worker. At this point the Canadian memoir is not even suggestive, for in it the economic problems of ranch management are kept strictly at the management level. Thus we discover nothing about the concrete life of the cowboys in this whimsical system of transatlantic finance. We know that they worked and were paid somewhat irregularly, but about the differences the overall economic circumstances made in their thoughts and feelings we learn nothing.

The novelist who takes up the challenge, one should say in warning, must be prepared with both presumption and patience. The presumption will be required when he ventures imaginatively into the cowboys believing that he can establish a cowboy identity in terms of work and class. The patience will be required not only because the novelist's task is extremely difficult but also because his audience and his critics will be against him from the outset. To imagine the cowboy in this way is to work against two time-honored stereotypes, or, elevating the perspective a bit, it is to allow oneself to be caught with apparently subversive intentions between two mythic conceptions, at a time when mythic conceptions have achieved a metaphysical status which makes the Platonic forms seem vulgar indeed. The cowboy was a free spirit, independent, self-reliant, and individualistic. No matter that he worked twenty hours a day for $25.00 a month, that he had little choice on the ranch or on the trail, that what he perhaps wanted most of all was to be a type, a cowboy, to bear that distinct uniformity that came with hat and boots and spurs. The worker is an unfree spirit, dependent, only collectively reliant, and as unindividualistic as a machine bolt. No matter that these notions have arisen less out of a close concrete study of the worker as person than out of popular traditions of romantic agrarianism or an equally romantic (perhaps inversely so) proletarianism.

Whether the novelist can convincingly join cowboy and

worker will depend, in my judgment, wholly upon his power as novelist. If, caught between two myths, he subverts both, that will not matter. Certainly as novelist he is under no Olympian imperative to synthesize the two myths into a third and higher myth. He is, however, under the human imperative to create a fictive person who believably exists as a cowboy in a social context that defines the nature of his work and thus the nature of the cowboy-worker himself. It is not, I submit, an impossible task, but doing it may be, as a cowboy critic might say, harder than roping a dehorned rhinoceros.

But is the task worth the effort? the traditionalist may ask. Let us leave the cowboy alone. It is time, he may add, for all of the shorthorned critics and philosophers to realize that the cowboy is just the way we want him. I reply, nevertheless, that the literary venture is worth whatever creative sweat and anguish it may require. We are not after all trying to put Louis L'Amour out of the writing business. We are simply trying to add new literary dimensions to an old figure, supposing that in this lank figure costumed in Stetson and chaps we can embody many meanings, one of these being the meaning of isolated man, seemingly asocial man, whether cowboy, mountain man, prospector, even sheepherder, the meaning of this kind of man in society. The imaginative result may not be the proletarian cowboy the Avelings thought they had found, but it may nevertheless be a creation of some lasting interest and importance.

The Cowboy with a Sense of the Past

In the years before the First World War, two literary friends, then approaching the close of their distinguished writing careers, seemed moved in their special ways by a sense of the past. In a preface to *Members of the Family,* Owen Wister spoke of crossing the plains again twenty years after a youthful westering journey. As his train sped through the old cowboy country, his mind was stirred into reverie.

What was this magic that came in through the window? The smell of sagebrush. . . . All day long it breathes a welcome and a sigh, as if the desert whispered: Yes, I look as if I were here; but I am a ghost, too, there's no coming back. All day long the whiffs of sage-brush conjured old sights before me, till my heart ran over with homesickness for what was no more, and the desert seemed to whisper: It's not I you're seeking, you're straining your eyes to see yourself,—you as you were in your happy twenties, with the illusion that I, the happy hunting-ground of your young irresponsibility, was going to be permanent. You must shut your eyes to see yourself and me and the antelope as we all used to be.[1]

The remembered experience offered a theme Wister's friend Henry James might well have considered. Although the author of "The Real Right Thing" and "The Jolly Corner" seemed to prefer eastern and European ghosts to western ones, to Wister he had admitted that he envied him his wild West,[2] and had he taken Wister's earlier suggestion seriously, to do what may seem to us the unthinkable, turn from Europe to the American West,[3] he could perhaps have found a fully Jamesian fiction in an account of a cowboy writer meeting the cowboy he once was or might have been.

In those years, however, James was engaged in writing another sort of ghost story. In 1914, in the months before a stroke destroyed his creative powers, he had again taken up a novel put aside in 1900. But now there was too little time or perhaps too many literary problems, and *The Sense of the Past* remained unfinished, the complexity of its sense or its nightmare, as a recent critic has called it,[4] suggested rather than fully novelized. But it is a Jamesian simplicity rather than a Jamesian complexity that concerns us here.

In the opening chapter of the novel, Ralph Pendrel, a "yearning and budding historian," as James described him in his notebooks, is rejected by Aurora Coyne, a handsome young widow who has made a permanent rediscovery of America after years of European experience. For Pendrel, as James wrote in the novel, "experience had lagged . . . behind interpretation, and the worst that could have been said was that his gift for the latter might do well to pause awhile till an increase of the former could catch up. . . . . He knew too much for a man who had seen so little."[5] Aurora, on the other hand, has had a surfeit of experience; she has seen much, and what she has learned from all this does not make her happy. If what Ralph yearns for is an experience of the past, and thus a "going-back" to Europe, what Aurora seeks now is a sense of adventure unburdened by the past. She is rejecting Europe as she is looking to America. "What I'm dying to see," she says, "is the best we can turn out quite by ourselves." That, suggests Pendrel, is the cowboy. "You want a fellow only who shall have had adventures," he says to Aurora. "The cowboy of middle-age, say—" She interrupts, "I don't even know what a cowboy is!"[6]

Aurora perhaps here dissembles just a bit, but no matter. At this moment in the story the novelistic purpose is not to find a proper mate for a handsome widow but to define the position of Pendrel. James, we may be sure, knew what a cowboy is or at least what he meant a cowboy to be. He could at this moment have pictured someone like the Virginian, but all he really needed briefly was a popular antitype. For that rhetorical purpose the cowboy would serve him well.

Like the noble savage, the cowboy as antitype does not require authentication.[7] We do not need to prove that the cowboy was historically this or that. We are simply defining a cultural type by antithesis. What we mean in the antitype depends wholly on what we want to mean in the type. What James meant in the cowboy we can thus readily see if we invert what he says about Pendrel: the cowboy is experienced but is not given to interpretation of that experience. He has seen a lot but knows little. However, this does not mean that he is ignorant in the popular sense of that word; it means simply that he is innocent. If he needs a name, it might well be Christopher Newman.

That the cowboy has been one of the American Adams or one of the children of nature needs no further argument. From Charley and Nasho to young Martin and Tot Lohman, innocence has been as much a part of literary range life as prowess with the gun and rope. If the cowboy has had a past, that past has scarcely been revealed, and it has not usually mattered. Experience before entering the range has not really counted; it has had little bearing on what he has become as a cowboy.[8] It is indeed as if these ranges have been unfenced Edens. For in Eden there is no past, and of course there is no history.

Yet however useful it has been in literary and intellectual history to consider the cowboy in this image, the sometimes exclusive persistence of the focus has blinded us to other possibilities and problems. In the criticism of literature and historiography, the prevalence of the image, whatever its identifiable presence in many works, has sometimes been reductive rather than enlarging. To adapt the language of the other James, there are important concrete facts that cannot be strung together with this abstraction.

Let us consider, then, another sort of cowboy, the cowboy with a sense of the past. And let us consider this cowboy and this sense in two ways, novelistically and historiographically. Considered novelistically, the sense assumes a character dimension based on the shaping and defining force of past personal experience. Considered historiographically, the sense assumes a cultural dimension based on the value-giving force of ideological traditions. In the novel the past may be internalized in the sense that the character acts consciously or unconsciously out of an awareness or a blind grip of what he has been. He may have the sense that some things are over, finished, facts rather than possibilities. In history the past may be less individualized and personal, but no less subjective. Certainly, for this discussion, we need not assume that a sense of the past in history is a perception of objective states, things as they actually were. In history the sense of the past is internalized not within individual characters but within ideological traditions. These traditions are of course internal to the historians, who in turn may internalize them further as a means of explaining individual historical persons. Thus a cowboy may have a sense of the past not because he remembers, not because he bears the burden of what he has done or not done, but because the historian gives him a role in the pattern of past events.

I

A middle-aged cowboy, it happens, is readily at hand for our critical consideration. If the Virginian himself is perhaps too young, the gray-haired Paul Priest of *The Log of a Cowboy* wears the appropriate years and experiences. As closely as we can count, he is thirty-five—scarcely middle-aged as most of us add up our years—but already he has gone up the trail six times and back of the trail lie experiences enough for several men. "I've traveled some in my life," he says at one point. He may not be a suitable match for Aurora Coyne, but he does admirably focus our critical questions.[9]

What specifically do we know about him? How is his nature as cowboy defined? Does a sense of his past contribute to that nature?

Although Andy Adams does not give us a carefully sustained picture of Priest, we do nevertheless see a certain wholeness by way of features briefly mentioned in the novel. He always wears a black hat; he dresses with mature good sense; and he never wears spurs. He is a light sleeper and an early riser. He is reticent in his opinions of people, but sometimes he talks his bunkie to sleep, and he can be profane about the way government representatives count cattle. He is deeply superstitious, and when he feels his luck is with him he can become an obsessive gambler. The last note we hear of him in the novel is that he is itching for a monte game.

As a cowboy he possesses the basic skills and responsibilities of his chosen work. He reads cattle well, for example seeing in their stiffened movements the consequence of a stampede. He plays an important supporting role in the building of a bridge across the Boggy. He greases a wagon when asked to, scouts for crossings, and in a tragic episode arranges the purchase of a coffin for the drowned Wade Scholar. Above all he is a reliable counter. Furthermore, he takes an apparently willing part in the playful side of cowboy life. Although he will not waste cartridges in open-air shooting, he does rope a large buffalo calf, baits an angry steer that has been pulled from the quicksand, and occasionally draws upon his repertoire of comic folk tales.

However, the starkest, most memorable look of Paul Priest associates him not with the fun and freedom of innocent cowboys, but with the destiny of deadly violence. An iron-gray man, he waits and watches at the distant end of a frontier bar.

What sets Priest apart from the other cowboys is not his matured cowboy skills, his great know-how about cattle, but "his years and experience in the ways of the world," to use Tom Quirk's cliché for a knowledge he cannot possibly understand. In a number of vernacular ways, Priest attests to his experience. He alludes to his "checkered career"; he says he's "too old a girl" to let a "pullet" teach him when to discard; he observes that he has met "a good many innocent men" in his life. Early in the novel young Quirk perceives what might be called an outline of what Priest is: he was "a wonderfully complex nature, hardened into a character the gamut of whose moods ran from that of a good-natured fellow to a man of unrelenting severity in anger."

Unfortunately Adams does not show the relative importance of Priest's various experiences; he does not indicate what particularly has hardened him. But one guesses that more consequential than any event of cowboy life itself has been the great event signified through Priest's special nickname The Rebel. Indeed, insofar as Priest has a concrete past, that past issues out of the Civil War. If Adams's count is reliable, The Rebel rode in the Confederate cavalry while still in his teens. The notorious Ben Thompson was one of his comrades. It is this violent past upon which he draws whenever he bothers to explain himself. "I'm superstitious," he admits, "and I can't help it. . . . I never was afraid to go into battle but once, and just as we were ordered into action, a shell killed my horse under me and I was left behind. I've had lots of such warnings, good and bad, and I'm influenced by them." This superstitiousness explains his never wearing spurs. "I own a fine pair of silver-plated spurs that have a history," he tells young Quirk. "They were given to me by a mortally wounded Federal officer the day the battle of Lookout Mountain was fought." "Take them off," Priest remembers the dying officer saying. "Listen to their history: as you have taken them off me to-day, so I took them off a Mexican general the day the American army entered the capital of Mexico." Thus the spurs for Priest are never merely the tools of a cowboy trade; they are historical artifacts joining the destinies of doomed men. Finally, the Civil War provides the motivating background to the confrontation and shoot-out between Priest and the nameless northern stranger. The stranger proposes a toast to General Grant; The Rebel tauntingly proposes a counter-toast to Jeff Davis and the southern Confederacy. When the drama has run its course, the stranger is dead and Priest has started back over the trail.

These details have been given not to answer any final questions about Priest and the novel in which he appears, but to raise questions about the function of the past in defining the cowboy character. Clearly The Rebel has a past; clearly a sense of that past breaks forth from time to time in his consciousness of himself. But is that sense of the past truly integral to his nature as cowboy?

If the critic concludes that it is not—and that is the conclusion of this reader—he can give himself a variety of explanations. He can reason that after all Adams was not centrally interested in Priest; the narrative is the story of the herd and its outfit, not of individual characters. Yet why then point to Priest's "wonderfully complex nature," if that nature is not be explored concretely and made important to the novel? He can, of course, reason that Adams was not a sophisticated novelist, that his honest but primitive art of fiction could not novelize Priest completely, even if Adams had wanted to make more of him. Or finally he can conclude that the cowboy world of The Log seems to have no historical dimension in which a past may have its proper roots. To an important degree, Adams imagined that world, as young Quirk perceives the country beyond the Red River, "as primitive as in the first day of its creation." In a western Eden, what does a novelist do with a character like Priest?

Andy Adams, one senses, felt the tension between history and myth. Committed to a naïve kind of historical realism, he nevertheless sometimes gave way to a deeper impulse and saw the ranges in myth. Yet he did not seem to confront the resulting imaginative warp in his account of things. He did not seem able to use in his fiction that tension which he must sometimes have felt, the uneasable strain between the destiny of the past and the dream of beginning again. Following the popular image, he could after all settle for cowboys who, if not riders on the ranges of Eden, were seemingly, by their total preoccupation with the immediacy of trail experience, unburdened by a sense of the past. The myth for Adams would of course rarely be overtly dreamed. Thickly surrounded by the historical authenticity of their trail work, these cowboys would be no sun gods. But at the same time the myth would not be subverted. In an important way, no matter how many rivers they swam, no matter how many stampedes they experienced, these cowboys would remain innocents. Growing older, they could yet be James's antitype. The Rebel's complexity would in effect be put aside. The cowboy novel, one can argue, would consequently be that much the poorer.

II

To insist that the cowboy in history has no past is of course not only unhistorical; it is also anthropologically naïve. It is to insist on a fiction which, however related to myth it may be, takes little account of existence, disregarding the very ways men experience and remember. And yet in history as in the novel, one sometimes finds cowboys—even middle-aged cowboys—who seem to ride in a virginal freedom unconditioned by the burden of the past.

That the cowboy is history does have a past is succinctly illustrated by a grizzled old fellow who worked for Theodore Roosevelt in the 1880s. "Born in Maine," Roosevelt wrote of him, his "career had been varied to an extent only possible in America, he having successively followed the occupations of seaman, druggist, clerk, buffalo hunter, and cowboy."[10] But did the old cowboy have a sense of that past? Did he think of all that lay back of him and understand that his nature as cowboy was conditioned by experience as seaman and buffalo hunter, even as druggist and clerk? We do not know, for Roosevelt does not bother to tell us although he had the advantage, had he wanted to use it, of being able to ask the subject himself. In his ranch house in Dakota, when he wrote his biography of Benton, Roosevelt evolved the senator, as he said to Henry Cabot Lodge, "from my inner consciousness," adding, "I would prefer to have some foundation of fact, no matter how slender, on which to build the airy and arabesque superstructure of my fancy—especially as I am writing a history."[11] One suspects, however, that even if he had questioned the old cowboy from Maine Roosevelt would still have evolved the cowboy's past from his own (Roosevelt's) inner consciousness.

The literary ranchman did not need to ask the old cowboy about his sense of the past, for the historian already knew the meaningful past of a cowboy. He could already read the lines the years had printed on his grizzled face. Whatever personal ideas the old fellow may have kept in his head would not have mattered, for whether he thought of himself as typical or not, he was a type, a variety of the frontier species. It was his evolutionary past that gave him meaning.

Like others of his time, Roosevelt was a convert to social Darwinism, but true to his own highly individualistic—and American—nature, his version of social evolution was an adaptation to meet his own special intellectual and moral needs. He wrote of biological analogies in history, suggesting there might even be homologies.[12] He found the beginning of history in the acts of "beast-like man"[13] and saw its progress in the relentless march of peoples strong in race, ancestral stock, strains of blood. The past of the cowboy, Roosevelt's evolutionary ideology, can be summed up in a few propositions. "During the past three centuries," he began his major historical work, "the spread of the English-speaking peoples over the world's waste spaces has been not only the most striking feature in the world's history, but also the event of all others most far-reaching in its effects and its importance."[14] An important locus among these spaces has been the wilderness lands of the American coast and the wilderness mountains, woods, and plains of the American West. Dominant among these venturing peoples have been the westering pioneers. The mountaineers and woodsmen thronged through the gaps and passes of the Appalachians, and now it is their descendants, "in the saddle instead of afoot, and with rope and revolver instead of axe," who are "the reckless horsemen" "guarding the wandering cattle herds" of the great Far West.[15] Recklessness here, it should be noted, is not so much the mark of irresponsibility as of courage, self-reliance, and vitality, those character traits brought out by the frontier environment and indeed necessary for survival in that environment. "The men of the border," wrote Roosevelt, "reckon upon stern and unending struggles with their iron-bound surroundings; against the grim harshness of their existence they set the strength and abounding vitality that come with it."[16] In Roosevelt's social evolution, then, whatever the importance of raw biological power, pragmatic reason, and intellect, character came first.[17] It gave permanence to national types; it gave progressive direction to races. The ideal character-building environment was the frontier, and among the ideal characters evolved was the cowboy.

Thus when we talk about the Rooseveltian cowboy with a sense of the past we mean something quite different from a Paul Priest, who along with his rope and revolver may carry consciously or unconsciously a burden of unchangeable personal experiences. We mean that the cowboy as a type has meaning, has a coherent relationship to the past, because he continues a valued evolution claimed for him by his defender and historian. And we mean too in this instance that the cowboy with a conscious sense of that evolutionary past is the strenuous rancher from Dakota, Theodore Roosevelt.

Yet here the discussion must take an ironical turn. In the fall of 1884, from his Maltese Cross Ranch, Roosevelt wrote to Lodge, "The Statesman (?) of the past has merged, alas I fear for good, in the cowboy of the present."[18] Put into the context of the writer's frontier ideology, the statement becomes curious indeed. If Roosevelt meant merely that the statesman had become the cowboy, the political skills and insights being absorbed integrally into the ideal figure of the cowboy, then there would be no need for the verbal sigh of unhappiness and fear. The change would indeed be *for* the *good*. Obviously, however, Roosevelt did not mean this. The past of the statesman had not become an integral part of the cowboy present. While Roosevelt would occasionally suggest cowboy solutions to political problems,[19] there is no evidence, so far as I know, that he thought traditional political experience had anything to do with cowboying. When he said that the statesman had merged with the cowboy, he meant only that the person who had recently been trying to influence Republicans in Chicago was now running cattle in Dakota, that the person who had recently sported a chipper straw hat was now wearing a sombrero. However much he personally might assume the image of the frontiersman and thus seem to add to the historical evolution of the cowboy, biographically there was little continuity between eastern politics and western ranching. On the contrary, there was what seems to have been a psychological rupture. In June 1884, had Roosevelt stopped to order his immediate sense of the past, he would have remembered the deaths of his mother and his first wife Alice on the same day in February and he would have felt again the pain and frustration of many political battles. Would he take all of this into the cowboy of the present? His recent biographer gives an answer: "*Saturday June 7* Henry Cabot Lodge heads east to muse on the future; Theodore Roosevelt heads west to forget about the past."[20]

When "that matchless cowboy of the West," as John W. Springer characterized Roosevelt,[21] celebrated the life of the range he emphasized, as has already been noted, its freedom above everything else. "I heartily enjoy this life, with its perfect freedom," he wrote to Lodge.[22] In his first western book, he observed that "the charm of ranch life comes in its freedom."[23] But what did he mean by this freedom? He had, of course, the position and means to do pretty much what he wanted. He could help with the roundup, but he could also range as he pleased, hunt new varieties of game, indulge for days at a time in the pursuit of rare and difficult trophies. He had the freedom to do all of this. But is this what he meant? Was there perhaps a freedom *from* as well as a freedom *to*?

The matchless cowboy of the West galloping over the rolling

limitless prairies, rifle in hand, is of course a mythic figure, a mythic figure who rides in freedom from the past. And yet again what seems lyrically simple obscures a tangle of tensions and inconsistencies. Biographically and historiographically the idea of freedom becomes ironic. "The hunter is the arch-type of freedom," Roosevelt wrote in one of his books.[24] Perhaps the mythic hunter was free, but the human hunter whose past experiences weighed so heavily upon his mind could scarcely be free. Indeed, the compulsion to hunt might be the very opposite of freedom. This at least is a recent biographical interpretation. "I have had good sport," Roosevelt wrote to his sister, "and enough excitement and fatigue to prevent overmuch thought." The biographer adds an elaboration: "A list culled from the pages of this little book [the diary] indicates how much blood was needed to blot out 'thought.' (Since Alice's death his diaries had become a monotonous record of things slain.)"[25]

Furthermore, if the cowboy historian had stopped to consider himself a sort of cowboy manikin in history, he would have seen that the manikin is a figure of evolutionary destiny, not a bold, free spirit romantically creating his world around him. In Roosevelt's account of history the metaphors of destiny occur frequently. The wilderness "must pass away before the onward march of our peoples." "The tide of white settlement during the last few years has risen over the west like a flood; and the cattlemen are but the spray from the crest of the wave, thrown far in advance, but soon to be overtaken." He wrote of the "sinewy men of the border, fearless and self-reliant, who are forever driven restlessly onward through the wilderness by the half-formed desires that make their eyes haggard and eager."[26] History thus leaves its human marks on the men it sweeps along. In *Hunting Trips of a Ranchman*, Roosevelt observed of the cowboys that "the passing over their heads of a few years leaves printed on their faces certain lines which tell of dangers quietly fronted and uncomplainingly endured." In *Ranch Life in the Far West*, he noted that "years of long toil broken by weeks of brutal dissipation, draw haggard lines across their eager faces." And in *The Wilderness Hunter* he mentioned meeting a large horse-herd driven by "three travel-worn, hard-faced men, with broad hats, shaps, and long pistols in their belts."[27]

The radical incongruity of Roosevelt's images of the cowboy becomes evident if we try to bring them together in a self-portrait of the cowboy historian himself. Let us use as manikin the Dakota rancher of 1884. Let us start with the famous photograph in buckskins. It is, of course, the young Leatherstocking. Add the glasses and we only brighten the already eager and determined eyes. But where are the marks of history? Where are the signs of the past? One cannot convincingly add hardness and haggardness to this face. It would be like giving a limp to Hermes.

III

A similar though less biological past was provided the cowboy by Roosevelt's fellow western enthusiast, Owen Wister. Wister called his version "The Evolution of the Cow-Puncher," but in this genealogy of the cowboy there was little that was evolutionary in the Darwinian sense. Instead of slow modifications and adaptations of living forms, there was a long persistence of a racial type. And that persistence, by the calendar of most evolutionists, had been relatively short. Whatever lay back of the Age of Arthur, Wister was content to begin—and to end—his descent of man with the Knight of the Round Table. How the Saxon knight had acquired "the cardinal surviving fittest instinct," out of what obscure struggles he had emerged, Wister did not inquire. In Lancelot the racial type was fixed. What remained for the "evolutionist" was to close the gap of centuries, to run the historical line between "the tournament and the round-up."[28]

In claiming that the cowboy was no new type, no product of the frontier,[29] Wister seemed not only to deny the new frontier environmentalism, but also to eliminate the defining forces of history itself. If "the knight and the cowboy are nothing but the same Saxon of different environments,"[30] then environment is merely place and a racial type seems to have escaped altogether the reshaping weight of the centuries. Perhaps only in the 1890s could so much that we might call genealogy sink beneath the visible surface of human events. Like Roosevelt, Wister could trace the ancestry of the cowboy to the adventurous sons of Kentucky and Tennessee,[31] but the binding link with the Saxons was much less immediately evident in the traditional historical records. So what better intellectual notion for the times than atavism. It was the time of criminals as throwbacks. It was the decade of Norris and the brutes. Obviously Wister did not see cowboys as criminals or brutes, but cowboys could nevertheless be throwbacks to Saxon times. Thus again one notes the absence of any sort of biological history, any sense of the development one might assume in even a foreshortened evolutionary period of only a few centuries.

Wister illustrates that cowboying runs deeply in the blood by showing the transformation of a transplanted English nobleman. "Directly the English nobleman smelt Texas," Wister wrote, "the slumbering Saxon awoke in him, and mindful of the tournament, mindful of the hunting-field, galloped howling after wild cattle, a born horseman, a perfect athlete, and spite of the peerage and gules and argent, fundamentally kin with the drifting vagabonds who swore and galloped by his side."[32]

However, Wister, like Roosevelt, was caught in unresolved ambiguities by his commitment to this "evolutionary" past for the cowboy. To link the cowboy atavistically with the Saxon knight might seem to give him a usable past, but curiously Wister the novelist did not seem to use this past. The Virginian, even at twenty-four, has a past of sorts; he has "looked over the country" from Arkansas to Wyoming; he has taken care of himself and survived.[33] But nowhere does Wister suggest that he has survived because he carries "the surviving fittest instinct" of the Saxon. On the contrary, the Virginian, like his fellow cowboys, is rooted not so much in Saxon blood lines as in soil and sagebrush. In short he is a primitive, and primitives owe nothing to civilized pasts. In fact they have by their naturalness made a radical break with those pasts. "They know better" not because some Saxon wisdom has pushed to the moral surface but because "they live nearer nature."[34]

With Wister, then, as with Adams and Roosevelt, the cowboy was assumed to have a "history," a past. In the late nineteenth century it would have been as unthinkable for intellectuals like Roosevelt and Wister to grant the cowboy freedom from historicism as it would have been unthinkable for Henry Adams to define Jefferson as a Virginian Triptolemus. Nevertheless, when

Wister, like Roosevelt, moved from concept to image, from theory to creative identification, an ontological sea change took place. History gave way to myth. Knowledge and tradition gave way to a beautiful and powerful innocence. The Virginian might indeed be a Virginian. The novelist might revise carefully to keep the flavor of the cowboy's regional speech. But even less than The Rebel would that cowboy carry the burden of a southern past.

IV

That the cowboy could be further invested with a past is revealed in what might be called official "histories" and in autobiographies trailing what might be called the long root. *Prose and Poetry of the Live Stock Industry,* the largest of these histories, begins its account "In the Night-Time of Human History." "In some remote and dateless day," its first sentence reads, "a wild and savage being, walking erect," catches and takes into his cave a wild canine creature. The domestication of the dog leads to the acquiring of other animals, the goat, cow, and horse, and "this great revolution in his [savage] affairs" opens "to him the higher, more peaceful and plentiful pastoral life, in which so many of the changes in character, habits, manners, and customs that eventually made him a civilized being were wrought."[35] The first illustration in *Prose and Poetry* is a drawing of a European cave man. In the perspective of this history, with a touch of scholarly hyperbole, we can call this man the first cowboy.

Second in size among early cattle trade histories is James Cox's *The Cattle Industry of Texas and Adjacent Territory.* It too takes the long view, but its cowboy past begins in scriptural records rather than in paleoanthropology. "The Bible affords us," writes Cox,

the first records of cattle ranches and cattle raising. . . . Holy writ tells us of two patriarchs who, having decided they had better agree to differ, divided up their herds and flocks, and drove off in two different directions. From that day forward we have records in various forms and shapes about cattle and cattle raising, and while some people think it is a matter of pride to be able to trace back their ancestry for several generations and centuries, it is certain that the cattle raiser can prove that his calling was in good repute hundreds and even thousands of years ago.[36]

A combination of what might be called the sacred and the profane pasts of the cowboy can be found in J. L. Hill's *The End of the Cattle Trail*. A drover turned historian-autobiographer, Hill, as he said, turned back "the mystic pages of time to the Creation, searching for the first recorded mention of domesticated cattle." The "discoveries" he made and the interpretation he offered create an impressive, if curious, "historical" background to his life as a cowboy. "Of the great changes evolution is supposed to have wrought, from monkey to man, we have no record. We are forced," Hill concluded, "to believe that God created man in his own image, and that he created cattle for the use of man, leaving him in his primitive state, to make his own advancement in education and intelligence." In Hill's version of the cowboy past, Moses becomes one of the first great cattlemen. Records show, Hill observed, that there were cattle in the land of Canaan. "We can only infer that the Lord in His wisdom selected Moses for his knowledge of the country and his experience as a herder, to safely guide the children of Israel out of their bondage into Canaan, that land of freedom."[37]

It should be clear, from these examples and others like them, that the cowboy has indeed required a past. If for some writers and readers there could seem to be cowboy justification enough in the freedom and freshness, in the renewed Adamhood on the Edenic ranges, for others the value of the calling lay in its very oldness, in its having the sanction of tradition. As Joseph G. McCoy wrote, "The live stock industry has the seal of ancient and honorable record."[38] To fill out this record has thus been the task of more than a century of historians, biographers, and popular reconstructors of the old cattle trails, the unfenced ways, the happy young men of a time gone by. From this point of view, when we speak of the old-time cowboy, we refer not to a mythic figure like Hector or Achilles, but to the cowboy who experienced the years of danger and hard work, who was historical in the sense that everything about him was conditioned by his time and place and historical too in the sense that whatever continuity we may have with him today is an understanding running back through conditioning time. In short, his cowboyness was never transcendental.

It should also be clear, from these examples and others like them, that when we speak of this cowboy past we do not mean an objective history. It may well be that objective history of any kind is not only technically impossible to write but also epistemologically impossible to know. It may well be that the deep structures of all histories are ideological. It may well be that the deep structures of all histories are finally mythic. Yet short of enclosing ourselves in this final circle we can continue to make practical distinctions between history as a critical reconstruction of "things as they actually were" and the past as a "psychological reality" used to give ideological sanction or as a "dream time" used to provide romantic compensation.[39]

All of the versions of the cowboy past discussed above are perceptions of the past in this sense. Even when they use the name of history, even when they involve the assumptions of historicity, these versions do not mature intellectually into that fully critical account we call history. They are ideological creations, not critical reconstructions. Indeed they are fictions. This does not mean, however, that they are thus merely to be condemned as bad history. In fact, the nature of their fictiveness may be as interesting and important as their lack of rigor in historical method. Thus a further irony. While undoubtedly there have been cowboys with a sense of history, I believe, in spite of all that has been written in the name of history, that we have not yet had a genuine history of the cowboy. If perchance that history should yet be written, it will likely tell us some important things we need to know. But I am not at all certain that humanistically we shall learn more from that history than we can already learn from the long literary record of the cowboy past. The past as psychological reality may prove to be more important than the past as history.

We come again to James's Pendrel. The novelist does not allow us a chance to read any portion of the young man's historical essay. Our guess is that as professional history the essay is undistinguished. Had Pendrel been a tough and trained historian, he could scarcely have become so obsessed with the past. James knew this, and thus the novel is not so much a comment on the problems of historiography as a revelation of the human ambiguities so poignantly carried in one's sense of the past. The cowboy as primitivistic antitype could, of course, escape the burden of these ambiguities. But had Henry James, in one of the most unlikely taking of trails in American literary history, acted on Wister's suggestion, had he novelized a cowboy as a fully appreciated human being, he could not then have allowed that cowboy to be so lucky.

A Notice Left at the Gate Still Open

Historians, like philosophers, are engaged in a quest for certainty. Without being metaphysical, they like to believe that it is possible to establish a configuration of facts and thus re-create the truth of a past event. "The aim of *historia* is truth," wrote one of the Greeks. Herodotus subscribed to this principle; so, one assumes, does Fernand Braudel.

The trouble with certainty is that it proves to be uncertain. And the trouble with truth is that it proves to be our cautious commitment rather than a cornerstone of the universe. We nevertheless go about claiming new certainties for decaying old ones, and we find novel theories of truth as hopeful stays against the chaos of inaccuracy and error. We must ever roll the boulder back up the hill, hoping each time that it will rest like a monument untouched by time and change. But history is change. "History," observes Braudel, "is always being begun anew; it is always working itself out, striving to surpass itself. . . . No book is ever written once and for all, and we know it."[1]

All of this should be humbling; all of this should remind us that tentative answers are all we are ever likely to find. All of this, in our time, should indeed test our intellectual nerve. For however complicated historiography may have seemed in the past, whatever the problems of separating fact from opinion, history from myth, history from metahistory, in our time we have seemed to flounder in an epistemological sinkhole. Old structures have failed us. The time-honored chain of time no longer binds our meanings together. Configuration may be as much spatial as chronological. Re-creation may seem not so much the cementing together of old facts in "historical" patterns as the joining of these apparent facts to structures as much alive and present as the blood that warms the brain.

What, the stranger asks, does all of this have to do with cows and cowboys? My reader, I hope, can now give some sort of answer. But in the spirit of the gate left open we can remind ourselves for the last time, in this book at least, of what finally matters. Suppose a herd of cattle leaves a roundup ground in southern Texas. Suppose a cowboy outfit joins the northward march. It is a juncture of sorts, and now we can plot the interwoven destinies of cows and men, destinies that moving on will reach a special point in time and space. It is Abilene, 22 September 1869.

We can plot this bit of history because the sources give us numbers, lines, and stopping places and because the old chronology, made right by lives of kings and fall of nations, holds facts and words in form and meaning. It is a story still satisfying in its clean simplicity.

But is it all there is to history? Are cowboys linked to cows, temporally and spatially fixed, in Abilene or Laramie or the fenceless grass of the northern plains, the important subjects of history? They are the objects, some of them at least, but the subjects they have all too rarely been. Is it not ironical that we know more about the *life* of a sheepherder in the Pyrenees in the early fourteenth century than we know about the *life* of an American cowboy in the late nineteenth century?

This book does not provide that life for that cowboy, but it does, I hope sincerely, point to some of the ways by which we can begin to know it.

Notes

Introduction

1. This leaves open a number of possibilities: for example, that meaning in history is independent of the historian's forms, that he in effect hangs the meanings he discovers on the conventional structures of exposition and narration; or that historical meanings become meaningful only when structured by a fusion of subjective insight and objective evidence.

2. *44 Range Country Books Topped Out by J. Frank Dobie in 1941 & 44 More Range Country Books Topped Out by Jeff Dykes in 1971* (Austin, Texas: Encino Press, 1972), p. 8.

3. Ramon Adams, *Burs under the Saddle: A Second Look at Books and Histories of the West* (Norman: University of Oklahoma Press, 1961), p. 431.

4. William S. Reese, *Six Score: The 120 Best Books on the Range Cattle Industry* (Austin, Texas: Jenkins Publishing Co., 1976), p. 61.

5. Dobie, *44 Range Country Books*, p. 2. Dobie did not include Edward Everett Dale's *The Range Cattle Industry* among his forty-four books, perhaps because it lacks vitality. Some prefer Dale's *Cow Country*, perhaps for the very reason that it seems to have vitality. Still one can argue that *The Range Cattle Industry* is nevertheless better history.

6. Dobie, *44 Range Country Books*, p. 13.

7. Reese, *Six Score*, p. 75.

History through a Cow's Horn

1. As McCoy was identified on the title page. Joseph G. McCoy, *Historic Sketches of the Cattle Trade of the West and Southwest* (1874; reprint

ed., Columbus, Ohio: Long's College Book Co., 1951).

2. J. Frank Dobie, *Guide to Life and Literature of the Southwest* (Dallas: Southern Methodist University Press, 1943), p. 66.

3. "The most important work pertaining to this subject [cattle drives]" (Ralph P. Bieber, Introduction to *Historic Sketches of the Cattle Trade of the West and Southwest* [Glendale: Arthur H. Clark Co., 1940], p. 17). "The range cattle industry got its first lengthy treatment of enduring importance . . . in his [McCoy's] book *Historic Sketches of the Cattle Trade of the West and Southwest*" (Fred Shannon, *The Farmer's Last Frontier* [New York: Farrar & Rinehart, 1945], pp. 398–99). "This is one of the first and most important books on the cattle trade," Ramon Adams, *The Rampaging Herd* [Norman: University of Oklahoma Press, 1959], p. 224).

4. McCoy, *Historic Sketches;* James Cox, *Historical and Biographical Record of the Cattle Industry and the Cattlemen of Texas and Adjacent Territory* (1895); James W. Freeman, ed., *Prose and Poetry of the Live Stock Industry* (1905); and J. Marvin Hunter, ed., *The Trail Drivers of Texas,* 2 vols. (1920–1923).

5. Bieber, Preface to McCoy, *Historic Sketches,* p. 13.

6. Adams, *The Rampaging Herd,* p. 224.

7. Joe B. Frantz and Julian E. Choate, *The American Cowboy: The Myth and the Reality* (1955; reprint ed., London: Thames and Hudson, 1956), p. 198.

8. For a comic version of a different possibility, see Walker, "Barney Tullus and the Bosboy," *The Possible Sack* 5 (November 1973): 1–10.

9. Fred Shannon, *An Appraisal of Walter Prescott Webb's "The Great Plains": A Study in Institutions and Environment* (New York: Social Science Research Council, 1940), p. 79.

10. Ramon Adams, *The Best of the American Cowboy* (Norman: University of Oklahoma Press, 1957), p. 9 note.

11. Frantz and Choate, *American Cowboy,* pp. 197–98.

12. Bieber's note: "Probably between 30,000 and 45,000 Texas and Indian cattle were trailed north into Kansas during 1867, most of which reached Abilene. About 18,000 or 20,000 longhorns were shipped from Abilene by railroad in the same year" (in McCoy, *Historic Sketches,* p. 122). One of Bieber's sources here is the *Report of the Commissioner of Agriculture for the Year 1870.* In that report, on the page cited by Bieber, the number of cattle shipped from Abilene in 1867 is 30,000, the authority being A. Anderson, general superintendent for the Kansas Pacific Railroad. Obviously counting cows in the 1870s had not yet become an exact science. And obviously too counting cows in historiography is sometimes better than a guess and less than a science.

13. It may, of course, be a historical fact that McCoy and others like him believed in the innate moral sense of cattlemen.

14. *Proceedings of the National Live Stock Association* (Denver, 1899), p. 99.

15. See Ralph P. Bieber, Introduction to McCoy, *Historic Sketches of the Cattle Trade.* Joe B. Frantz calls this "an excellent essay on McCoy's life"

(The Reader's Encyclopedia of the American West, ed. Howard R. Lamar [New York: Thomas Y. Crowell, 1977], p. 695). However, it is excellent only in the sense that it has more biographical facts than the other sketches. See also "Joseph G. McCoy," *Proceedings of the National Live Stock Association* (1899), pp. 323–24; "Joseph G. McCoy," *The Kings and Queens of the Range* 2 (January 1898): 3; Joseph G. McCoy, "Historic and Biographic Sketch," *Kansas Magazine* 1 (December 1909): 45–55.

16. As far as I know, the only historian to call *Historic Sketches* an autobiography is Jimmy M. Skaggs's Introduction to J. L. Hill, *The End of the Cattle Trail* (1923; reprint ed., Austin and New York: Pemberton Press, 1969), p. vi. Skaggs's reasons for this classification are not clear.

17. One contemporary who apparently knew McCoy well was C. F. Gross. Writing to J. B. Edwards, he characterized McCoy's book as "valuable" and "true," then added some notes on the historian himself, notes that confirm one's impression of the writer revealed in the book. He was "a Kind of a Woodrow Wilson in that he never asked any ones opinion of any act of his or any project he started or had in view, his will & wishes *were law* [Gross's emphasis] both himself and the rest of us had to Conform to his plan [illegible word] we were an [a]thema. In consequence as a Historian he extolled or Eliminated in his details those who had fallen under the Ban of his displeasure or did not do as he wished" (Gross to Edwards, 4 May 1925, Edwards Papers, Kansas State Historical Society, Topeka).

18. McCoy, *Historic Sketches,* p. 38. The version in the later "Historic and Biographic Sketch" is even more dramatic: "And the blackness of a starless midnight settled over the Texas ranchman and his industry" *Kansas Magazine* 1 (December 1909): 49.

19. McCoy, *Historic Sketches,* p. 40. The phrase *man for the occasion* comes here from the later "Sketch": "But difficult situations have ever developed the man for the occasion, and so it was in this case" (p. 49). The idea is also more dramatically conceived in the "Sketch": "It came upon his mind as the shadow of a cloud on a clear day, the conviction that Abilene was the place to establish a cattle shipping depot, and locate a trail thence to Texas" (p. 50).

20. McCoy, *Historic Sketches,* p. 40. "To him it became a waking thought, a sleeping dream" ("Historic and Biographic Sketch," p. 49). It "became to McCoy as a life mission, a waking thought, a sleeping dream" *(Proceedings of the National Live Stock Association* [1899], p. 324).

21. Of Meyers, McCoy wrote, in the biblical style he sometimes adopted: "When he is given the title of 'A father in Israel' among the drovers, there will [be] found few, if any, who will dispute his right or his worthiness of the appellation" *(Historic Sketches,* p. 77).

22. This in spite of prefatory intentions "to convey in simple, unpretentious language, practical and correct information upon the opening, development, and present status of the Live Stock Trade of the great New West."

23. McCoy, *Historic Sketches,* pp. 74–75. Gross in his letters to Ed-

wards gave a quite different account of McCoy's "inspiration."
24. The undaunted man is McCoy's later characterization of himself; the sense of mission is evident in the biographical accounts. However, the characterization of the railroad executive here is my own, with
the conviction that it is true to McCoy's own perception.
25. McCoy, *Historic Sketches,* pp. 42–43.
26. Although obviously a well-read man, McCoy did not clearly
reveal his literary models—if he had any.
27. McCoy, *Historic Sketches,* p. 206.
28. Ibid., p. 207. Gross suggests that the trouble with the railroad
was largely McCoy's fault, the result of failing to get a proper contract
drawn up. When the McCoy lawyer was ill, McCoy insisted on preparing
the contract himself. "Thats the Wooddrow phase of Joes Character,"
wrote Gross, "Mr. Know it all & then some, I am the whole Cheese & you
are skim milk" (Gross to Edwards, 4 May 1925, Edwards Papers, Kansas
State Historical Society, Topeka).
29. McCoy, *Historic Sketches,* p. 209.
30. Ibid., p. 210.
31. Ibid., p. 211.
32. It would, however, be naïve to suppose that because a fact looks
like a fact it is indeed a fact. There are many tricks, intended and
unintended, that one must watch out for. When Dan DeQuille, writing
about hunting jack rabbits, says he "fired once, badly wounded
several—in the leg—the left," the seemingly factual precision is specious,
a touch of the tall tale manner he and his friend Mark Twain liked to use.
The practical distinction intended here can be illustrated in a brief entry
in McCoy's diary kept during his livestock census of 1880. "July 23 After
provoking delay, get ferried over Red River which is flooded and pull up
to Red R. Station a Small Seedy unenterprising burg of 150 orny souls"
(Ms., Kansas State Historical Society, Topeka). There seems no reason to
question the factualness of the observation that the Red River was
flooded, but the characterization of the station is another matter.
33. McCoy, *Historic Sketches,* pp. 24, 31, 57, 102, 151–52, 256.
34. Ibid., pp. 55, 56, 146. In his biographic sketches McCoy did
include details which, from some points of view, might be regarded as
signs of moral weakness. For example, the Texans consider the carrying
of firearms "imperative"; they prefer "the strongest liquors, and take
them 'straight.' " In the context of the *Sketches,* however, they seem details
of heroic praise, not moral weakness.
35. Ibid., pp. 36, 90, 121, 123, 128, 130, 178, 279, 300. A note of
contrast: in his recent study of the cattle-trailing industry, Jimmy M.
Skaggs calls R. D. Hunter "a cold, calculating example of Social Darwinistic entrepreneurship" (Skaggs, *The Cattle-Trailing Industry: Between
Supply and Demand, 1866–1890* [Lawrence, Kans.: University Press of
Kansas, 1973], p. 81). Although seemingly more realistic and therefore
more believable, Skaggs's abstraction does little more than McCoy's to
help us understand the motivation of Hunter as a person in history.
36. See "Prose and Poetry of the Cattle Industry" in this book.

37. McCoy, *Historic Sketches,* pp. 111, 123, 130, 178, 201, 224, 269, 287, 296, 371.
38. Ibid., p. 61.
39. Ibid., p. 386.
40. For McCoy's portrait of "the great merchant of Abilene," see ibid., pp. 46–49; the scientific experts, ibid., pp. 153–56. The original edition contained illustrations by Henry Worral of Topeka, Kansas. Bieber dropped all of these from his edition. Included in McCoy's gallery of scoundrels might also be the Indians and the New Mexicans, the latter receiving a sustained charge of the historian's racist contempt.
41. Ibid., pp, 229–32.
42. Ibid., pp. 20–21, 115, 175, 395, 268. In a related passage, McCoy observed that no one should delude himself into believing that cattle ranching is a business wherein "the poetic or sentimental aspects of life or labor abound to any alarming extent " (p. 341). However, the elevated style in which McCoy develops this thesis about camp life can only be called poetic, in the popular sense of that term.
43. Ibid., pp. 82, 97.
44. Ibid., p. 139.
45. Ibid., p. 253.
46. Ibid., p. 231; *Proceedings of the National Stock Growers' Association* (1898), p. 28.
47. In an unpublished article, "The Comic Oratory of Colonel McCoy," based on his speeches to the National Live Stock Association, I have examined McCoy's comic gift at greater length.
48. Not the least of its features is its vocabulary of terms current in the cattle trade. A dictionary of western American will undoubtedly cite *Historic Sketches* many times.
49. "It is the province and scope of this work to treat only such subjects, as have a connection, bearing, or adaptability to the live stock business, or using a phrase more expressive than elegant, 'Look at every thing through a cow's horn' " (McCoy, *Historic Sketches,* p. 410).
50. "To close this brief roundup of the truthtellers, no more appropriate book could here be branded than Joseph G. McCoy's *Historic Sketches of the Cattle Trade of the West and Southwest,* the first of the whole cow lot" (Frantz and Choate, *American Cowboy,* p. 197).
51. The sort of truth stuccoed onto the text by Bieber.
52. It was, to be sure, a naïve kind of fiction, depending less upon the creative imagination than upon what was really a historical synthesis of factual details. For further consideration of Adams's fiction, see "Theory of the Cowboy Novel" and "The Cowboy with a Sense of the Past."
53. McCoy, *Historic Sketches,* p. 144.

The Rancher as Writer

1. Theodore Roosevelt, *Hunting Trips of a Ranchman* 2 vols. (1885; reprint ed., New York: Scribner's, 1906), 1:35.

2. Ibid., 1:23. Many, if not most, cattlemen did not see their enterprise as doomed. "In the cattle business there was an implicit assumption
that these conditions [unfenced, unrestricted, and an almost unlimited
source of fodder] would continue indefinitely, or at least long enough for
all practical investment purposes." Carleton Putnam, *Theodore Roosevelt:
The Formative Years* (New York: Scribner's, 1958), p. 332.

3. In a modest bibliographical paragraph one should mention
Hermann Hagedorn, *Roosevelt in the Bad Lands* (Boston: Houghton
Mifflin, 1921); Lincoln Lang, *Ranching with Roosevelt* (Philadelphia: Lip-
pincott, 1926); Ray H. Mattison, "Ranching in the Dakota Bad Lands,"
pamphlet published by State Historical Society of North Dakota, re-
printing articles in *North Dakota History* 19 (April and July 1952); Matti-
son, "Roosevelt and the Stockmen's Association," pamphlet published by
State Historical Society of North Dakota, reprinting articles in *North
Dakota History* 17 (July 1950); selected chapters in Putnam, *Theodore
Roosevelt;* and finally selected chapters in Edmund Morris, *The Rise of
Theodore Roosevelt* (New York: Coward, McCann & Geoghegan, 1979).

4. Putnam, *Theodore Roosevelt,* pp. 333–34.

5. Ibid., p. 334.

6. *Theodore Roosevelt: An Autobiography* (New York: Macmillan,
1913), pp. 106–7.

7. "To James Brander Matthews," 7 December 1894, Letter 503,
The Letters of Theodore Roosevelt, ed. Elting E. Morrison, 8 vols. (Cambridge, Mass.: Harvard University Press, 1954), 1:411.

8. "To Henry Cabot Lodge," 15 May 1885, Letter 135, ibid., 1:91.

9. "To Henry Cabot Lodge," 23 June 1885, Letter 137, ibid., 1:91.

10. "To Anna Roosevelt," 28 June 1886, Letter 154, ibid., 1:104.

11. "Stockmen are learning more and more to act together; and
certainly the meetings of their associations are conducted with a dignity
and good sense that would do credit to any parliamentary body" Theodore Roosevelt, *Ranch Life in the Far West* [1888; reprint ed., Flagstaff,
Ariz.: Northland Press, 1968], p. 7).

12. Details here from Putnam, *Theodore Roosevelt,* pp. 534–35, 570.
In a note Putnam suggests that the editor was echoing Roosevelt's famous
order to his cowboy to "hasten forward quickly there."

13. "To Anna Roosevelt," 22 April 1886, Letter 148, *Letters of Theodore Roosevelt,* 1:99.

14. Putnam, *Theodore Roosevelt,* p. 595.

15. "To Henry Cabot Lodge," 20 May 1886, Letter 151, *Letters of
Theodore Roosevelt,* 1:101.

16. "To Corinne Roosevelt Robinson," 12 May 1886, Letter 149,
ibid., 1:99.

17. "To Frederick William Kruse," 6 April 1891, Letter 315, ibid.,
1:241.

18. The sketches or series which make up *Ranch Life in the Far West*
appeared originally in 1888 in *Century* with illustrations by Frederic
Remington. A rearrangement of this material, with the addition of a

section on the bighorn sheep, became *Ranch Life and the Hunting Trail.* As the title indicates, *Hunting Trips of a Ranchman* is primarily concerned with hunting, but since the hunter is a ranchman and since the hunt is conducted on and from the ranch, the ranching setting is given some attention. Chapter 1 is titled "Ranching in the Bad Lands." The same is true of *The Wilderness Hunter.* Chapter 2, "Hunting from the Ranch; the Blacktail Deer," includes sections on ranch life, the roundup, and branding a maverick. The letter to Hay is a version in letter form of a narrative Roosevelt gave orally at a Washington dinner. It appears in *Cowboy and Kings; Three Great Letters by Theodore Roosevelt,* with an introduction by Elting E. Morrison (Cambridge, Mass.: Harvard University Press, 1954).

19. *Great lonely plains* may seem a literal geographical naming rather than a metaphor. My point, developed more fully later, is that it is not a literal representation but an image whose form comes less from mirroring than from structuring according to personal and ideological needs.

20. "To Richard Watson Gilder," 19 July 1888, Letter 203, *Letters of Theodore Roosevelt,* 1:143–44.

21. "To Owen Wister," 13 December 1897, Letter 876, ibid., 2:742.

22. For my argument that Roosevelt had a sense of the past, not a sense of history, see "The Cowboy with a Sense of the Past" in this collection.

23. Howard and Alden Eaton joined with A. C. Huidekoper to form the Custer Trail Cattle Company in 1880. A. C. Huidekoper, *My Experience and Investment in the Bad Lands of Dakota and Some of the Men I Met There,* Introduction by Usher L. Burdick (Baltimore: Wirth Brothers, 1947), p. 23. Gregor Lang and his son Lincoln had started their independent ranch in 1883 at the juncture of William's Creek and the Little Missouri. Putnam, *Theodore Roosevelt,* p. 320.

24. "History as Literature," in *History as Literature, and Other Essays* (New York: Scribner's, 1913), p. 15.

25. Theodore Roosevelt, *The Winning of the West,* 6 vols. (1889, 1896; reprint edition, New York: Scribner's, 1906), 1:1; 6:193–94.

26. Ibid., 6:1.

27. The nature of the historian's self is a matter of considerable contemporary interest. There is the view that no matter how deeply he investigates, no matter how much he empathizes with his material, the historian's self remains a disciplined constant, passive to new information in the sense of being open to it, but not thereby altered as a structuring intelligence. And there is the view that a journey into the historical material fundamentally alters (expands, reduces, or perhaps both) the subjective center of the historian. See Siegfried Kracauer, *History: The Last Things Before the Last* (New York: Oxford University Press, 1969), particularly "The Historian's Journey."

28. Roosevelt, *Ranch Life,* p. 6.

29. Roosevelt, *The Winning of the West,* 6:194.

30. Roosevelt, *Ranch Life,* p. 16.

31. Ibid., p. 16.

32. Ibid., p. 6.

33. Ibid., p. 8.

34. "To James Brander Matthews," 7 December 1894, Letter 503, *Letters of Theodore Roosevelt,* 1:410–11.

35. Theodore Roosevelt, *Ranch Life,* p. 18.

36. Ibid., p. 21.

37. Ibid., p. 24.

38. Ibid., pp. 4, 5, 31.

39. *Hunting Trips,* 2:22–23.

40. Theodore Roosevelt, *The Wilderness Hunter* 2 vols. (1893; reprint ed., New York: Scribner's, 1906), 1:67.

41. Charles Neider, Introduction to *The Great West* (New York: Coward-McCann, 1958), p. 15.

42. Owen Wister, "The Young Roosevelt," *Hunting Trips of a Ranchman and Ranch Life and the Hunting Trail* (1885, 1888; reprint ed., New York: Scribner's, 1926), p. 265.

43. Wister speaks of "the lively vigor of its [*Ranch Life*] style" ("The Young Roosevelt," ibid., p. 265).

44. Henry Beers, "Roosevelt as Man of Letters," in *Four Americans: Roosevelt, Hawthorne, Emerson, Whitman* (New Haven: Yale University Press, 1919), p. 13.

45. Brander Matthews, "Theodore Roosevelt as a Man of Letters," in *Tocsin of Revolt and Other Essays* (New York: Scribner's, 1922), p. 241.

46. Wister, *Hunting Trips,* p. 258.

47. Beers, *Four Americans,* p. 13.

48. Roosevelt, *Hunting Trips,* 1:126.

49. Ibid., 2:155.

50. Ibid., 2:49; Roosevelt, *The Wilderness Hunter,* 1:27; 1:67; 1:84–85.

51. Roosevelt, *Ranch Life,* p. 49.

52. Roosevelt, *The Wilderness Hunter,* 1:28; 1:30; Roosevelt, *Ranch Life,* p. 45.

53. "To Owen Wister," 13 December 1897, Letter 876, *Letters of Theodore Roosevelt,* 2:742.

54. Wister, *Hunting Trips,* p. 258.

55. The standard source is Hagedorn, *Roosevelt in the Bad Lands,* p. 101.

56. "To Charles Anderson Dana," 3 August 1895, Letter 572, *Letters of Theodore Roosevelt,* 1:471.

57. "To Edwin Lawrence Godkin," 23 November 1897, Letter 859, ibid., 1:719.

58. "To Charles Fletcher Lummis," 14 December 1897, Letter 877, ibid., 1:742.

59. Morison's note, ibid., 1:742.

60. *Prose and Poetry of the Live Stock Industry* (1905; reprint ed., New York: Antiquarian Press, 1959), p. 570.

Prose and Poetry of the Cattle Industry

1. Ramon Adams, Introduction to *Prose and Poetry of the Live Stock Industry of the United States* (1905; reprint ed., New York: Antiquarian Press, 1959), p. 21A.
2. Ibid.; Walter Prescott Webb, *The Great Plains* (Boston: Ginn and Co., 1931), p. 218 note.
3. For the difference between a sense of the past and a sense of history, see "The Cowboy with a Sense of the Past" in this collection.
4. In his presidential address to the National Live Stock Association in January 1903, John W. Springer spoke with a mixture of nostalgia and pride: "A few pilgrim cattlemen remain, hallowed with whitened locks and dim eyes, looking out at the tremendous strides being made all up and down the old trails of the days agone" *(Proceedings of the Sixth Annual Convention of the National Live Stock Association* [Denver, 1903], p. 139).
5. Ibid., pp. 141–42. It should be evident in even these small passages that Springer was an orator in the grand style.
6. Ibid., p. 30.
7. Ibid., pp. 163, 164.
8. *Proceedings of the Seventh Annual Convention of the National Live Stock Association* (Denver, 1904), p. 118. Charles F. Martin, secretary of the association, noted that the men of the historical association have "prosecuted the work with considerable diligence." "I predict," he went on, "that it will be one of the most interesting and valuable works which have been published in this country for many a year, and I think it should have the hearty support of every stockman in the United States." Further, he added, the proceeds from publishing the work ought to put a considerable sum into the treasury of the association. Ibid., pp. 31–32.
9. *Proceedings of the Eighth Annual Convention of the National Live Stock Association* (Denver, 1905), pp. 72–73.
10. Adams, in *Prose and Poetry*, p. 21B. The title page says: "Volume I. Issued in Three Volumes, Prepared by Authority of the National Live Stock Association, Published by the National Live Stock Association, Denver and Kansas City." The copyright entry at the Library of Congress is dated 24 February 1905. Two copies were received by the library on 8 April 1905.
11. These are, of course, guesses, in part extrapolations from personal acquaintance with stockmen. The project included, it should be noted, some selling apparatus; a number of young men were delegated by the publishing company to "wait upon" the delegates to the convention of 1905 and to go to all conventions in the West to secure subscriptions. *Proceedings Eighth Annual Convention*, p. 72. Discussion on the floor in 1903 reveals what some delegates seemed to think the book should be. One unidentified stockman asked: "Mr. Chairman, would 'Bill' Skinner's picture be in that book?" Springer answered that it would, that the book would not be complete without it. One suspects that if the book had

become a sort of yearbook, with pictures of every stockman and every stockman's prize cattle, horses, sheep, and swine, it would have had a better sale, at least to the stockmen themselves. In spite of the convictions of Springer and others, a sense of the past was not widespread and deep among the stockmen. The wife of a cattleman once told me that the only past her husband was interested in was the genealogical past of his breeding bulls.

12. Adams, in *Prose and Poetry*, p. 21A.

13. Many literary critics and some experts on historiography will be troubled by this simple distinction, but the writer intends no definitive contribution to contemporary rhetorical theory. He hopes only for the acceptance of a pragmatic conceptual tool with which to make some useful observations about the work at hand.

14. No historian has ever written history without using imagination. This proposition is indeed a central thesis of this collections of studies. Nevertheless, in talking about *Prose and Poetry*, one can assume a kind of discourse which is relatively free of the overt signs of the literary imagination.

15. There may, of course, be a difference between geography and the images of geography. Historians like Walter Prescott Webb, as we shall see, have seemed to believe with a positivistic faith that it is possible to describe the world (in his case the Great Plains of the West) in an objective but coherent way. Recent geography has moved from a dominating assumption of a world "out there" possible of being mapped to a knowledge mediated, indeed structured, by ways of perception and conception. In discussing the images of geography in *Prose and Poetry*, I intend no judgment on their mirroring faithfulness. If the geography of *Prose and Poetry* is really a geography of the mind, so be it.

16. Or geography that purports to be objective. Whatever the poetry in Webb's rendering of the western ranges, his geography will serve comparatively as objective.

17. *Prose and Poetry*, p. 81.

18. Ibid., p. 550.

19. The transvaluation of nature that came with Darwinism made man's goodness in nature a sentimental dream. Either man accepted an amoral unity with nature, or he constructed a humanistic ethic independent of nature. However, as we have seen in the instance of Roosevelt, curious personal adjustments could be made to this philosophical predicament. Roosevelt accepted the remote ancestral animalness of man, but unlike the naturalists he found little contemporary relevance in that beginning. Although he enjoyed living close to nature, he did not suppose that closeness guaranteed goodness. Nature did provide the occasions for self-reliance, physical toughness, and courage, but these virtues were humanistically, not naturalistically, conceived.

20. I use the singular here for convenience, not supposing that the whole of *Prose and Poetry* was written by one man. In his "Introduction," James W. Freeman, president of the National Live Stock Historical

Association, said that Jerome C. Smiley wrote the historical sections, but the internal evidence of style indicates that others contributed, particularly in the biographical sections. The official reports usually referred to "leading writers" or a "corps" of writers.

21. *Prose and Poetry,* p. 84.

22. Ibid., p. 64.

23. Ibid., p. 423.

24. Ibid., p. 599.

25. *Proceedings of the National Stock Growers' Association* (Denver, 1898), p. 18.

26. *Proceedings of the Fourth Annual Convention of the National Live Stock Association* (Denver, 1901), p. 190.

27. Ibid., p. 304.

28. *Proceedings Seventh Annual Convention,* p. 224.

29. *Proceedings of the First Annual Convention of the American National Live Stock Association* (Denver, 1906), p. 18.

30. Wilber R. Jacobs, ed., *Frederick Jackson Turner's Legacy: Unpublished Writings in American History* (San Marino, Calif.: Huntington Library, 1965), pp. 171–72.

31. Emerson Hough, *The Story of the Cowboy* (New York: D. Appleton, 1897), p. 337. The writers of *Prose and Poetry* used Hough's book as one of their sources, calling its story "exquisitely told" and suggesting that every reader of *Prose and Poetry* might peruse it "with pleasure and profit" (*Prose and Poetry,* p. 563).

32. Hough, *Story of the Cowboy,* pp. 219, 220. Some of the observations Hough put into *The Story of the Cowboy* he later used in *The Passing of the Frontier* (New Haven: Yale University Press, 1918). Seemingly slight differences may indicate a toning down of the strong romantic primitivism of passages in the earlier book. In *Story of the Cowboy* he wrote that "the very blue of the sky . . . has reflected into his [the cowboy's] heart the instinct of justice." In *The Passing* the text reads: "The very blue of the sky . . . seemed to symbolize his instinct for justice." This instinct for justice may seem to be incompatible with rudeness, but Hough's sense of the rude is colored, I believe, by the usage in romantic primitivism, as, for example, in Wordsworth.

33. Theodore Roosevelt, *Ranch Life and the Hunting Trail* (1888; reprint ed., New York: Scribner's, 1906), pp. 154–55. The use of Roosevelt's work as a source for *Prose and Poetry* has been noted in a previous study.

34. Frederick L. Paxson, *The Last American Frontier* (New York: Macmillan, 1910), p. 3.

35. The reader perhaps needs to be reminded that history is used here in its neopositivist version. A pragmatic justification of this usage was given earlier, but a further point might be made that most western historians seem to proceed on neopositivist assumptions. Obviously criticism is most meaningful when it proceeds on the same philosophical ground as the history it considers. Some concepts of history, of course,

concede that historical truth can be nowhere else but in us, that we can talk sensibly of a poetic of history, and that mythic structures of the Edenic sort may be deeply constitutive of all history.

36. Some instances: the setting of Cooper's *The Deerslayer* (1841), with its solitudes that speak of "scenes and forests untouched by the hands of man"; a beautiful valley in Emerson Bennett's *Leni Leoti; or, Adventures in the Far West* (1851). In the latter novel the narrator remarks: "Take it all in all, to me the place seemed a second Eden." Cattle, in William MacLeod Raine's story "No Man's Ranch" (1901), having survived a plunge over a high bluff, pasture in an inaccessible meadow of timeless serenity: "The sun beats down on a scene more primeval than the Garden of Eden." This story reminds one of a charming legend reported in James Cox's *Historical and Biographical Record of the Cattle Industry* (1895). Utah rustlers chase a herd of cattle over a precipice into a rocky confine. Some of the cattle survive the fall to live on "within this cow-garden of Eden."

37. Andy Adams, *Reed Anthony, Cowman* (Boston: Houghton Mifflin, 1907), pp. 225–26.

38. Owen Wister, *The Virginian* (1902; reprint ed., Boston: Houghton Mifflin, 1968), p. 299.

39. Hough, *The Story of the Cowboy*, p. 33.

40. Ibid., pp. 2, 31, 221, 329.

41. Roosevelt, *Ranch Life and the Hunting Trail*, p. 37. "The sweet, fresh air, with a touch of sharpness thus early in the day, and the rapid motion of the fiery little horse combine to make a man's blood thrill and leap with sheer buoyant light-heartedness and eager, exultant pleasure in the boldness and freedom of the life he is leading" (p. 91).

42. Ibid., pp. 126, 154.

43. *Prose and Poetry*, p. 592.

44. Ibid., p. 592.

45. *Proceedings First Annual Convention*, pp. 18–19.

46. A philosophical difference here and elsewhere in these studies may be clarified and reinforced by a note on Emerson Hough's novel *The Girl at the Halfway House* (New York: D. Appleton, 1900). In this novel Hough delineates the development of the West centered in Ellisville, a fictional Abilene or Dodge City. The progress from virgin grassland to civilized society complete with town balls is inevitable. Hough uses the metaphor of "the iron game of destiny." But such progress is not without its human losses, primarily the loss of man's last absolute freedom. The romantic primitivism of the book is often explicit. "Having become slaves, we scoff at the thought of a primitive, grand, and happy world, where each man was a master." Even the riotous violence of the cowtown is seen as "a mutiny of physical man, the last outbreak of the innate savagery of primitive man against the day of shackles and subjugation." Thus for Hough freedom was natural, not societal.

47. *Prose and Poetry*, p. 560.

48. Ibid., p. 552.

49. Ibid., pp. 551–52.
50. Stewart Edward White, *Arizona Nights* (New York: McClure, 1907), p. 348.
51. By design I mean the structure of chapters starting with "In the Night-Time of Human History" and including "Origin and Descent of Our Live-Stock Animals," made up of paleontological findings.
52. *Prose and Poetry,* p. 24.
53. Ibid., p. 58.
54. Ibid., p. 754.

Classics of the Cattle Trade

1. In the interest of bibliographical fullness, two works should be mentioned here: Clara M. Love's "History of the Cattle Industry in the Southwest," *Southwestern Historical Quarterly* 19 (1916): 370–99; 20 (1916): 1–17, a seminar paper prepared under Herbert E. Bolton; James Westfall Thompson's "A History of Stock-Raising in America from Earliest Colonial Times to the Present, 1607–1916." Thompson's history remained in manuscript until 1942 when it was published by the Department of Agriculture as *A History of Livestock Raising in the United States, 1607–1860,* Agricultural History Series, no. 5. The eight chapters of the manuscript covering the period 1860–1916 were omitted.
2. Louis B. Schmidt and Earle D. Ross, eds., *Readings in the Economic History of American Agriculture* (New York: Macmillan, 1925).
3. Other histories have not been included here for a number of reasons. Although general in scope, neither *Cattle* (1930) by William MacLeod Raine and Will C. Barnes nor *The Trampling Herd* (1939) by Paul I. Wellman was professional history in the sense in which I have used the term above. J. Evetts Haley's *The XIT Ranch of Texas* (1929) and *Charles Goodnight* (1936), while professional, were special studies of a ranch and of a cowman. The same can be said of Harley True Burton's "A History of the JA Ranch" (M.A. thesis, 1927) and William Curry Holden's *The Spur Ranch* (1934). The thesis of this study starts from the assumption in cattle trade historiography that the "story" was economic and impersonal and that it should be told in a "scientific," unromantic manner. The books introduced above provide a solid, if not exhaustive, textual base from which to develop this thesis.
4. Ernest S. Osgood, *The Day of the Cattleman* (1929; reprint ed., Chicago: University of Chicago Press, n.d.), p. v.
5. *Story* was Osgood's term. The concept of history as story will have bearing on the thesis of this study.
6. Joe B. Frantz, review of *The Day of the Cattleman* by Ernest S. Osgood, *Southwestern Historical Quarterly* 59 (1955): 126.
7. Edward Everett Dale, *The Range Cattle Industry* (Norman: University of Oklahoma Press, 1930), p. 72.
8. J. Frank Dobie, *Guide to Life and Literature of the Southwest* (Dallas: Southern Methodist University Press, 1943), p. 63.

9. Walter Prescott Webb, *The Great Plains* (Boston: Ginn and Co., 1931), p. 226.

10. Louis Pelzer, *The Cattlemen's Frontier* (Glendale, Calif.: Arthur H. Clark Co., 1936), p. 15.

11. Walcott Watson, review of *The Cattlemen's Frontier* by Louis Pelzer, *American Historical Review* 42 (1937): 799, 800.

12. Edward Everett Dale, review of *The Cattlemen's Frontier* by Louis Pelzer, *Mississippi Valley Historical Review* 23 (1936): 427.

13. Dobie, *Guide to Life and Literature of the Southwest*, p. 66.

14. Douglas Branch, review of *The Day of the Cattleman* by Louis Pelzer, *Mississippi Valley Historical Review* 16 (1929): 429.

15. I assume that *day*, insofar as it has historical precision, signifies a period of power or influence. Osgood, however, was seemingly less interested in a period than in a development. And although he wrote of the range *cattleman* as a western type, his book was not really a historical biography or portrait.

16. Since it had become important in range historiography to deal with developments as economic developments, Dale needed to assume that he was dealing with a structure of phenomena which could be called an industry. Certainly some of his historical phenomena were economic, but I believe it remains true nevertheless that he did not organize these phenomena within a covering concept of industry.

17. Insofar as the range cattleman or rancher was sovereign, Webb might better have spoken of *the cattle kingdoms*.

18. The quoted terms here are from Joe Frantz's review of the reprint edition of 1954. I assume that Osgood would have found them appropriate.

19. Louis Pelzer, review of *The Day of the Cattleman* by Ernest S. Osgood, *American Historical Review* 35 (1930): 424–25.

20. Branch, review of *Day of the Cattleman*, p. 430.

21. J. Evetts Haley, review of *The Day of the Cattleman* by Ernest S. Osgood, *Southwestern Historical Quarterly* 34 (1930): 177.

22. Pelzer review of *The Day of the Cattleman*, p. 424. Italics mine.

23. By a traditional picturesqueness I mean the conventional features of certain landscapes in the writings of Brackenridge, Field, Bradbury, Hall, Irving, and others, not just the colorful but the picturelike by virtue of certain scenic elements and certain compositional relationships. For the purposes of this study, the popular synonym *colorful* is enough. By economic setting I assume a setting defined or described in terms of its economic factors. When the cattle country was described in *Prose and Poetry of the Live Stock Industry of the United States* as "the great, lonely, and grieving plains," the landscape became literary. Such a landscape would have no economic meaning.

24. Edward Everett Dale, "Memories of Frederick Jackson Turner," in *Frontier Historian*, ed. by Arrell M. Gibson (Norman: University of Oklahoma Press, 1975), p. 349. Gibson notes in the same volume: "Most of what Dale wrote was autobiographical in that he had lived a

prototype of virtually every incident, movement, and circumstance contained in his essays" (p. 4).
25. Frederic L. Paxson, "The Cow Country," *American Historical Review* 22 (1916): 71. I say *lyrical* here meaning that *great unfenced* and *free grass* go beyond denotative statement to a celebration of personal values.
26. See for example chapter 22 in Washington Irving's *Astoria*.
27. Osgood, *Day of the Cattleman*, pp. 2, 7, 9.
28. Dale, review of *The Cattlemen's Frontier*, p. 426. Reviewing Dale's book, Everett E. Edwards called the formation of the cow country "the most romantic and picturesque" phase of American agriculture *(Agricultural History* 4 [1930]: 153).
29. Dale, *The Range Cattle Industry*, pp. xiii–xiv.
30. Needless to say, Dale was here not so much observing the historical terrain itself as he was remembering something he had read.
31. Pelzer, *The Cattlemen's Frontier*, p. 202.
32. Ibid., p. 113.
33. Ibid., p. 115.
34. Webb, *The Great Plains*, p. 226.
35. Ibid., p. 244.
36. Ibid., p. 246.
37. Ibid., p. 248. Webb gives no documentation at this point, but one supposes that he was perhaps drawing from Dorothy Scarborough's novel *The Wind*, which he mentions in another connection. It seems a curious source for a scientific geographer.
38. William Cunningham: "Economic history is not so much the study of a special class of facts as the study of all the facts from a special point of view" (Quoted by Pei-kang Chang, *Agriculture and Industrialization* [New York: Greenwood Press, 1969], p. 18 note). One supposes that a special point of view necessitates a special form in the organization of the historical work. The form of *The Conquest of Mexico* or *The Winning of the West* may no more satisfy the economic historian's needs than will the form of *The Rise of Silas Lapham* satisfy the needs of a Henry James or a William Faulkner.
39. Osgood, *Day of the Cattleman*, p. 26.
40. Dale, *The Range Cattle Industry*, p. 167.
41. For many, if not most, conceptions of economic history, *reduced* seems the appropriate verb, for the effort at explaining economic events, if not the persons involved, has meant a drastic simplification of motives. The result may have been a cleanness of economic theory, but it may also have been a mutilation of an appropriate historical anthropology.
42. Dale, *The Range Cattle Industry*, p. 195.
43. Pelzer, *The Cattlemen's Frontier*, p. 150.
44. The newness lay perhaps less in the novelty of the facts used than in the concerted effort by professional historians to abandon the old romantic story of the cattle trade and present its economic reality. For well over half a century there had been a limited, special concern with the economics of the ranges. It began with the establishment in 1863 of a

Division of Statistics in the Department of Agriculture. That same year the commissioner of Agriculture, Isaac Newton, noted in his report that "there is no logic so irresistible as the logic of statistics, and [that], in this country, those relating to agriculture are of the highest importance" *(Report of the Commissioner of Agriculture for the Year 1863* [Washington, 1863], p. 15). Also that same year Silas L. Loomis offered one of the first economic "laws" relating to the cattle trade. "The great law of the movement of cattle," he wrote, "is here plainly developed. Cattle must be moved eastward and capital westward to supply the pressing demands of our people" *(Agricultural Report for 1863,* p. 259). Ironically, Loomis claimed, just before the flood of Texas cattle began, that Texas cattle were too wild to be driven east in great numbers. Down through the years there was a trickle of studies economic in their concern, for example, Robert M. Barker, "The Economics of Cattle-Ranching in the Southwest," *American Monthly Review of Reviews* 24 (1901): 305–13; and William Hill, "Conditions in the Cattle Industry," *Journal of Political Economy* 13 (December 1904): 1–12. The latter work echoed Newton's point about statistics: "The need for complete and unquestionable statistics of the cattle industry, constantly kept up to date, is probably greater, and felt by more people, than is the need for any other kind of agricultural statistics" (p. 6). However, the full swell of interest came in the twenties and thirties. The Bureau of Agricultural Economics was established in 1922. There was a striking increase in historical scholarship: the index of the *American Historical Review* for the decade 1895–1905 shows only three titles in economic history; the index for the decade 1925–1935 required fifteen and a half inches of column to list the contributions.

45. Webb, *The Great Plains,* p. 225.

46. Ibid., p. 223.

47. Ibid., p. 227.

48. At the close of "The Cattle Kingdom," Webb again sounded this stylistic note: "Cowboys at work, eighteen hours a day, for the herd left the bed ground at daybreak and kept it until dark; cowboys at work, riding, singing, nursing the cattle" (p. 268). If the prose here had been more observational and less lyrical, one supposes that Webb would have taken care of the referential obscurity in the pronoun *it.* It should perhaps be added that other historians did indeed use the term *epic* to characterize the story of the cattle industry. "The story of the American cattle industry," wrote Harry E. Maule, "is *per se* the epic of the cowboy" (Introduction to *Cattle, Cowboys and Rangers,* by William MacLeod Raine and Will C. Barnes [New York: Grosset and Dunlap, 1910; Dunlap, 1930] p. xi).

49. Dale, *The Range Cattle Industry,* p. xiii.

50. Ibid., p. xiii.

51. Thomas Jefferson, "To William Ludlow," 6 September 1824, *The Writings of Thomas Jefferson,* 20 vols. (Washington, D.C., 1903), 16:75–76.

52. Werner Sombart, "Economic Theory and Economic History,"

The Economic History Review 2 (1929): 10.

53. The historian could, of course, document the facts that in a certain part of the West there were first hunters, then herders, then farmers. He could perhaps denote the successive movements of these types of producers as a march, though *march* would certainly connote a relentless steadiness which the movements might very well lack. However, all of these facts would scarcely suggest a general theory of frontier social history.

54. Paxson, "Cow County," p. 81.

55. For example: "Thus the disintegrating forces of civilization entered the wilderness" *(The Frontier in American History* [New York: Henry Holt, 1920], p. 13).

56. Harry E. Maule, Introduction, *Cattle,* by Raine and Barnes, p. xii.

57. Ibid., pp. 4, 13. With the first of these images compare William Graham Sumner: "Everyone of us is a child of his age and cannot get out of it. He is in the stream and is swept along with it" *(War and Other Essays* [New Haven: Yale University Press, 1911], p. 209); Henry Adams: "They [Jefferson, Madison, and Monroe] appear like mere grasshoppers kicking and gesticulating on the middle of the Mississippi River" *(Henry Adams and His Friends,* comp. Harold Dean Cater [Boston: Houghton Mifflin, 1947], p. 126).

58. Dale, *The Range Cattle Industry,* p. 31.

59. Ibid., p. 46.

60. Ibid., p. 135.

61. Webb, *The Great Plains,* p. 223.

62. Pelzer, *The Cattlemen's Frontier,* p. 153.

63. Osgood, *Day of the Cattleman,* p. 120. Economic necessity, of course, need not mean economic determinism. It remains true nevertheless that social and economic circumstances have conditioned a particular historical effect. These circumstances were, of course, initiated by a random push of persons, but abstracted into the social state of the ranges, they have in a sense become impersonal.

64. Webb, *The Great Plains,* pp. 226, 227, 245.

65. Webb, "History as High Adventure," in *History as High Adventure,* ed. E. C. Barksdale (Austin: Pemberton Press, 1969), p. 13.

66. Osgood, *Day of the Cattleman,* pp. 199, 96–97.

67. Dale, *The Range Cattle Industry,* p. 195. The student of style can further note the literary effect of Dale's series of the difficulties met. It is one thing to say that men meet hardship, danger, and financial reverses, another to say that they meet hardship *and* danger *and* financial reverses.

68. Webb, *The Great Plains,* pp. 245, 246. I say *assertion* here meaning that Webb did not induce courage and self-reliance from his historical sources. Rather he added these historical "consequences" from his own frontier ideology.

69. Pelzer, *The Cattlemen's Frontier,* pp. 65, 73, 81, 108. No doubt

here and elsewhere some of the push of personality came from the sources. Pelzer cited McCoy, and McCoy, as we have already seen, was rarely given to understatement.
    70. This is probably true even of the Cliometricians. Quantitative history, as practiced, for example, by Emmanuel LeRoy Ladurie, may seem to put the burden of proof on the computer rather than upon the historian's imagination. "The Conscripts of 1868," using data about nearly twelve thousand young Frenchmen, may seem an instance of letting technology write history. However, the computer remains a humanistic tool; it is LeRoy Ladurie, not the computer, who determines which correlations are significant. See LeRoy Ladurie, *The Territory of the Historian,* trans. by Ben and Siân Reynolds (Chicago: University of Chicago Press, 1979).
    71. Some readers indeed missed the customary western flavor. Pelzer, reviewing *The Range Cattle Industry,* noted the consequence of "recording results and effects rather than processes. . . . And so the odors from branding, the trail dust, mutinous cowboys, the rollicking life . . . are lacking" (review of *The Range Cattle Industry, American Historical Review* 36 [1931]: 658). John D. Hicks observed of Dale's book: "From some of the photographs he reproduces there is a hint of the interesting and spectacular side of the subject, otherwise so unfortunately omitted" *(Mississippi Valley Historical Review* 27 [1931]: 647).
    72. Recent reflections on agricultural history have emphasized the importance of personal motivation. Reginald Lennard speaks of overlooking "the personal factors" which modify economic action "in individual cases." "We must remember," he says, "that at all times it is not geographical conditions which affect the use to which the land is put, but man's knowledge of the opportunities they present and his ability to take advantage of them" ("Agrarian History: Some Vistas and Pitfalls," *The Agricultural History Review* 12 [1964]: 85, 88–89). P. J. Perry writes that "economic emphasis within agricultural history often gives no place. . . to the role of perception or of the individual . . . . The farmer [here we might substitute the historical cattleman] is . . . of necessity a decision-maker acting in an uncertain and imperfectly perceived environment; he cannot be the economic or the customary automaton he has sometimes been assumed to be" ("Agricultural History: A Geographer's Critique," *Agricultural History* 46 [1972]: 265).
    73. Two additional works might be considered briefly, for they add further evidence of the historiographical problem I have been discussing. Rudolph A. Clemen's *The American Livestock and Meat Industry,* published in 1923, was, as the title indicates, an economic study. Yet Clemen, like the historians who came after him, held to a dramatic view of history. "The story of the origin and development of this vast and many-sided group of industries from colonial times to the present is," he wrote in his preface, "dramatic in the extreme" *(The American Livestock and Meat Industry* [New York: Ronald Press, 1923], p. v). In a chapter devoted to "The Western Range Cattle Industry," he noted that "it is well to consider

the economic relations of that institution [the open cattle range], about which there has been thrown great glamor and which has been the subject of much literary romance" (p. 181). Yet his own historical method sometimes provided more color than economic analysis. He suggested catching the spirit of the lives of the stockmen and cowboys in their songs: "Here again one may see the cowboy at work and at play: hear the jingle of his big bell spurs, the swish of his rope, the creaking of his saddle gear, the thud of thousands of hoofs on the long trail winding from Texas to Montana" (p. 183). And like other historians he saw some range events as unusual dramatic sights: "The round-up and the driving of cattle on the trail were two great spectacles of the range cattle industry" (p. 184). In 1926 Clemen contributed an article "Cattle Trails as a Factor in the Development of Livestock Marketing" to the *Journal of Farm Economics*. Again, while he ostensibly was concerned with the economic problems of the cowman, he easily fell to emphasizing colorful action and heroic personalities. The chapter covering the cattle trail period in the story of the cattleman "is," he noted, "romantic, colorful, a-thrill with high adventure and stirring experience" (*Journal of Farm Economics*, October 1926, p. 427). "The economic problems these men [the Texas cowmen] faced started them through a process of molding that left them with a craft, a vernacular, and a character distinctly their own" (p. 430). It was a promising sentence, but unfortunately Clemen did not really elaborate it. His considerations of "the noted cattleman" Goodnight and "one of the great drovers of those days" George W. Littlefield were no more economic than were the accounts of earlier historians. Additionally the section called "The Day of the Cattleman," in Joseph Schafer's *Social History of American Agriculture* (New York: Macmillan, 1936), begins as historical drama. "Thus, when 'the day of the cattleman,' as the last third of the nineteenth century has been called, opened up, the theater on which he was destined to play his dramatic role in American agriculture was already roughly defined" (p. 98).

Freedom and Individualism on the Range

1. One need not, perhaps cannot, find an absolute beginning here. Fascination with the cowboy figure may go back to Colonial times and the cowpen keepers of the back country in the Carolinas. According to James Westfall Thompson, "The cowpen struck the imagination of cultured Easterners in the middle of the eighteenth century much as the ranch life of the Far West has allured urbanites more recently" (*A History of Livestock Raising in the United States, 1607–1860*, Agricultural History Series, no. 5 [U.S. Department of Agriculture, 1942], p. 62 note). However, corroboration for this claim is difficult to find. Various scholars have traced the emergence of the fictive cowboy in the nineteenth century. Joseph Leach has examined the literary genealogy of the heroic Texan in *The Typical Texan: Biography of an American Myth* (Dallas: Southern Methodist University Press, 1952). Douglas Branch and Warren French have dealt with

the dime novel cowboy, Branch in "Alkali Ike in Belles-Lettres," *The Cowboy and His Interpreters* (1926; reprint ed., New York: Cooper Square Publishers, 1961), French in "The Cowboy in the Dime Novel," *Studies in English* 30 (1951); 219–34. As I indicate elsewhere, one of the first significant imaginative responses by a major American writer came in an excited prose note on Kansas cowboys written by Walt Whitman in the late 1870s.

2. McCoy, as we have seen, was committed to providing practical and correct information although one of the consequences of his method may have been to move the cowboy away from actuality.

3. Edward Everett Dale, *The Range Cattle Industry* (Norman: University of Oklahoma Press, 1930), p. 73. A similar statement appeared in Dale's introduction to Harry E. Chrisman's *Fifty Years on the Owl Hoot Trail* (Chicago: Sage Books, 1960), p. xvi: "It [the story of Jim Herron's life] gives to the reader a more authentic understanding of ranch life and the *social history* of the American frontier than he is likely ever to get from fiction or so-called 'Westerns.' "

4. Dale, *The Range Cattle Industry*, p. 195.

5. Ibid.

6. As Granville Stuart described the sons of eastern capitalists who invested in the western cattle business *(Forty Years on the Frontier,* 2 vols. [Glendale: Arthur Clark Co., 1957], 2:238).

7. One of Pelzer's sources was John Clay's *My Life on the Range,* published in 1922 and 1924. Describing the prospects for young Hubert Teschemacher, Clay wrote: "There was before him *the wild free life of the cowboy* [italics mine], the morning cup of coffee, the long rides to circle around the cattle . . . and at night sweet sleep under clear skies, breathing refreshing air" *(My Life on the Range* [1924; reprint ed., New York: Antiquarian Press, 1961], p. 77). In Pelzer's *The Cattlemen's Frontier,* p. 107, this becomes, "Before him was the life of the cowboy, the morning cup of coffee, the long rides to circle around the cattle . . . and then sleep under clear Wyoming skies." Describing the cowboy from Texas, Clay wrote in *My Life on the Range,* p. 108: "The Texan, like *a bird of the wilderness, accustomed to freedom* [italics mine], not trained to be interfered with, a child of the frontier handy with his gun." In Pelzer, *The Cattlemen's Frontier,* p. 69, this becomes, "The youth of Texas who had come to Dodge City in their saddles were, like birds of the plains, unaccustomed to the restraints of the invading grangers." Changing Clay's simile *like birds of the wilderness* to *like birds of the plains* may well have been a movement away from terms with the aura of romantic primitivism.

8. Theodore Roosevelt, *Hunting Trips of a Ranchman,* 1:17. The spring roundup provided "exultant pleasure in the boldness and freedom of the life" the riders were leading. Roosevelt, *Ranch Life and the Hunting Trail,* p. 91. It may be that Roosevelt was more cattleman than cowboy, yet there is no clear distinction in his writings between the man who owns the cows and the men who work them. When Roosevelt wrote

about his own ranch experiences and values, he clearly assumed that the ordinary cowboy shared them.

9. William MacLeod Raine and Will C. Barnes, *Cattle, Cowboys and Rangers*, p. 287. While Raine, in the judgment of some historians, may have seemed to add to the false conceptions of fiction, his novels should not be confused with his history. Even in a somewhat popular work like *Cattle*, one supposes that he is not working with novelistic conceptions. So far as I know, Will Barnes has seemed matter-of-fact enough to satisfy most historians.

10. Ramon F. Adams, Preface to *From the Pecos to the Powder: A Cowboy's Autobiography* (Norman: University of Oklahoma Press, 1965), p. vii.

11. But as any cowboy would know, one did not have the freedom to shoot at the moon. The shot might cause the cattle to stampede.

12. Ernest Osgood, *The Day of the Cattleman* (1929; reprint ed., Chicago: University of Chicago Press, n.d.), pp. 115, 117.

13. Some sociologists, Karl Kraenzel particularly, have sought to demonstrate the difficulty and the cost. The form of the sociological proposition would, of course, be *isolation makes*.

14. In an interesting speculation, Charles Neider speaks of the cowboy's "ego exhaustion." Psychologists, particularly existential psychologists, recognize that the psychic encounter with vast space will have very different consequences depending upon the psychic structures brought to the encounter. Even behaviorists, I suspect, must question the simplifications involved in Turner's notion of the plasticity of pioneer life.

15. Early in the chapter called "Organization" Osgood did cite the final essay in *The Frontier in American History*. The introduction to his course "History of the American Frontier" at the University of Minnesota was, as I personally remember it, pure Turner.

16. Frederick Jackson Turner, *The Frontier in American History* (1920; reprint ed., New York: Henry Holt, 1958), p. 37.

17. Ibid. p. 30. There are, of course, other references to individualism in *The Frontier*. See, for example, pp. 78, 107, 140, 153, 165, 183, and 203.

18. Ray Allen Billington, *The Genesis of the Frontier Thesis: A Study in Historical Creativity* (San Marino, Calif.: The Huntington Library, 1971), pp. 69–70, 71, 72, 122–23, 126, 139, 141.

19. For a brief discussion of the structure of the American ideology, see Yehoshua Arieli, *Individualism and Nationalism in American Ideology* (Cambridge, Mass.: Harvard University Press, 1964), pp. 22–30.

20. Lewis Atherton, *The Cattle Kings* (1961; reprint ed., Lincoln: University of Nebraska Press, 1972), p. 108.

21. McCoy, *Historic Sketches of the Cattle Trade of the West and Southwest* (1874; reprint ed., Columbus, Ohio: Long's College Book Co., 1951), pp. 145, 146.

22. Ibid., p. 146. McCoy repeated the idea on p. 254.
23. Walter Prescott Webb, *The Great Plains* (Boston: Ginn and Co., 1931), p. 245.
24. R. H. Williams, "The Live Stock Ranges of Texas," *The Cattleman* 17 (March 1931): 35.
25. Thus one tends to accept the testimonies in *The Trail Drivers of Texas,* ed. by J. Marvin Hunter (Nashville: Cokesbury Press, 1925). "Men have been solving problems that required courage, self-reliance, willingness to assume responsibility" (p. 208). "Men depended upon themselves" (p. 28). "John R. Blocker, being a hardy, self-reliant young man . . . was especially fitted for trail life" (p. 319).
26. "Jim [Redfern] was 'sufficient unto himself'" (John K. Rollinson, *Wyoming Cattle Trails* [Caldwell: Caxton Printers, 1948], p. 160).
27. J. Frank Dobie wrote a chapter in his *Cow People* (Boston: Little, Brown, and Co., 1964) called "Having His Own Way."
28. See Charles A. Burmeister, "Six Decades of Rugged Individualism: The American National Cattlemen's Association," *Agricultural History* 30 (1956): 143–50.
29. Some writers have played what seem to me ideological tricks at the point of this individualism. Philip Ashton Rollins, for example, asserted that "every Westerner was an intense individualist," letting other people "do as they liked, provided they neither improperly interfered with his rights nor contravened such of the tenets of the Cattle Country's code of ethics as the West deemed to be vital and fundamental both to the maintenance of life and liberty and to the pursuit of happiness" (*The Cowboy* [New York: Scribner's, 1922], p. 302). To imply that the cattleman's code of ethics continued the democratic ideals of the Declaration of Independence is a bit of Cow Country idealism, to say the least. The implication has no solid foundation in empirical history.
30. James C. Shaw, *North from Texas: Incidents in the Early Life of a Range Cowman in Texas, Dakota and Wyoming, 1852–1883* (Evanston, Ill.: Branding Iron Press, 1952), pp. vi, x.
31. It can be argued, of course, that the evidence of Shaw's individualism is to be found in other documents. Such an argument, however, would not make Brayer's claims relevant to Shaw's text. If there is other evidence, it certainly would be critically relevant to the introduction, for that introduction as a piece of history does not somehow float free of the need for substantiation.
32. Verne Lawson, "The Passing of the Range," reprinted in *Proceedings of the Seventh Annual Convention of the National Live Stock Association* (Denver, 1904), pp. 410–12.
33. *Proceedings of the First Annual Convention of the American National Live Stock Association* (Denver, 1906), p. 18.
34. Quoted in Cordia Sloan Duke and Joe B. Frantz, *6,000 Miles of Fence: Life on the XIT Ranch of Texas* (Austin: University of Texas Press, 1961), p. 179. There is irony here. The cowboys of the XIT say nothing

about the freedom of the frontier. That notion thus comes solely from a ranchman whose big interest was playing polo and whose wife cruised the Mediterranean on a yacht.

35. J. Evetts Haley, *George W. Littlefield, Texan* (Norman: University of Oklahoma Press, 1943), p. 91.

36. Stuart Edward White, "On Cowboys," *The Outlook* 78 (3 September 1904): 83.

37. William Timmons, *Twilight on the Range: Recollections of a Latter-day Cowboy* (Austin: University of Texas Press, 1962), p. 33. Even Billie's hopes were much more modest than those of the cowboy of traditional conception. Freedom meant the right to keep a horse even if it threw him several times. One suspects that Billie did not have the faintest notion that there might somewhere be a condition of spiritual openness.

38. Quoted in *Prose and Poetry*, p. 533.

39. Bob Kennon, *From the Pecos to the Powder* (Norman: University of Oklahoma Press, 1965), pp. 61–62. Italics mine. In the cow towns, the cowboys "were no longer the reserved, self-repressed men of the range, but threw off all restraint, and measured their 'enjoyment' of their few days of freedom and revelry by the degree of uproar with which they proclaimed their presence" *(Prose and Poetry*, pp. 551–52).

40. Elton Miles, Introduction to Will Carpenter, *Lucky 7: A Cowman's Autobiography* (Austin: University of Texas Press, 1957), p. ix.

41. J. Orin Oliphant and C. S. Kingston, eds., "William Emsley Jackson's Diary of a Cattle Drive from La Grande, Oregon, to Cheyenne, Wyoming, in 1876," *Agricultural History* 23 (1949): 273.

42. E. C. Abbott and Helena Huntington Smith, *We Pointed Them North: Recollections of a Cowpuncher* (1939; reprint ed., Norman: University of Oklahoma Press, 1954). "Texas cowpunchers, the most independent class of people on earth" (p. 13). "Another thing about cowpunchers, they were the most independent people on earth" (p. 212). It can, of course, be argued that independence is freedom. But without knowing concretely the nature of the Texan independence—the rhetorical quality of the assertions here and elsewhere makes one doubt the objective signification—we cannot easily substitute one term for the other. I once knew an old hermit miner who lived alone with his cats in a dirty dugout. He was independent, but I think one could say that he was a slave to his independence. Abbott's wildness and fun seemed to come almost entirely in the "cowboying" done in the saloons and whorehouses. There is, one can say, nothing primitivistic in *We Pointed Them North*. Note Abbott's attitude toward nature, pp. 28–29.

43. Edward and Eleanor Marx Aveling, *The Working-Class Movement in America* (1891; reprint ed., New York: Arno & the New York Times, 1969), p. 155.

44. I say *should have*, believing that, as a matter of fact, the full consequences of social Darwinism were not presented. As I have already indicated, there are Darwinistic assumptions in the structure and sub-

stance of *Prose and Poetry of the Live Stock Industry*, but there is also a philosophy of nature of a quite different kind. Theodore Roosevelt liked to use Darwinistic language, as for example, "the struggle for existence is very keen in the far West" *(Ranch Life and the Hunting Trail)*, but it cannot be argued that Roosevelt examined ranch life as a biological complex. Webb wrote in *The Great Plains*, p. 246, "a process of natural selection went on in the cattle country as it probably did nowhere else on the frontier," but he did not really validate the assertion. If the cowboy had been generally seen as a pawn of biological circumstances, we would perhaps have had a naturalistic novel with a cowboy hero (victim). While there are cowboys in the fiction of Frank Norris and Stephen Crane, at least one cowboy in the writings of Jack London, and naturalistic forces in Dorothy Scarborough's *The Wind*, there has never been, so far as I know, a thoroughly naturalistic cowboy novel.

45.   Abbott and Smith, *We Pointed them North*, p. 154.

46.   Ibid., p. 89.

47.   The nature and importance of the model will, of course, depend on our historical philosophy. We may believe that the model is a present model in the sense that it issues out of us now, that the only way we can know past man is to assume that he had (has) a human structure with which we in the present can identify. But in contrast to such neoidealism, our position may be that it is possible to derive the model empirically, that we can reconstruct a historical model, say of Puritan man in New England, solely from Puritan sources. Obviously the importance of any anthropological model will depend on how much historical explanation it provides. If we believe that historical explanation lies in geographical circumstances, economic processes, social institutions, not in historical persons, we may still need models but these models are not likely to be anthropological. In contemporary historiography, a good example of both the empirical approach using models and the deemphasis upon person is the work of Fernand Braudel.

48.   Some sociologists are, of course, reluctant to engage in historical sociology. The kinds of data they need are too often simply not available. Still there are those who are trying to develop valid social generalizations from historical records. See, for example, Roy Sylvan Dunn, "Drouth, History and Sociology," *West Texas Historical Association Year Book* 48 (1972): 154–64. See also Allan G. Bogue, "Social Theory and the Pioneer," *Turner and the Sociology of the Frontier*, ed. by Richard Hofstadter and Seymour Martin Lipset (New York: Basic Books, 1969), pp. 73–99. Two of Bogue's observations are particularly to the point here, one an assumption, the other a warning. "The individual finds primary and secondary relationships essential to satisfactory living. Few individuals are really content to be hermits. Taken from their accustomed web of social relationships they may suffer from what is termed *anomie* or normlessness" (p. 90). "Each westward settler was a unique individual and if many in a pioneer neighborhood reacted similarly and made similar decisions some did not. Knowing that this was so, we cannot be too

rigorously deterministic in explaining the behavior of the pioneers" (p. 92). A bad example of historical sociology, in my judgment, is Murray Melbin, "Night as Frontier," *American Sociological Review* 43 (1978): 3–22.

49. This may depend upon whether one considers ideology "a total system of interpretation of the historic-political world" or "the formulation of a historical attitude or scale of values." See Raymond Aron, *The Industrial Society: Three Essays on Ideology and Development* (New York: Simon and Schuster, 1967), p. 164. We may be able to escape such total systems as the Marxian or the liberal system which seems to support the so-called Whig interpretation of history. Scales of value, however, may be always with us, even in our most rigorous and objective historiography.

50. Whatever the complications in historical epistemology, we may still be motivated professionally by the notion that the past is past and not merely the present antiqued with old facts.

51. See the distinction made between *history* and the *past* in J. H. Plumb, *The Death of the Past* (1970; reprint ed., Boston: Houghton Mifflin, 1971). See also my use of this distinction in "The Cowboy with a Sense of the Past."

The Fence Line between Cowboy History and Cowboy Fiction

1. Glenn R. Vernam, *The Rawhide Years: A History of the Cattlemen and the Cattle Country* (New York: Doubleday, 1976), p. 64.

2. Robert R. Dykstra, *The Cattle Towns* (New York: Alfred A. Knopf, 1971), p. 123.

3. Jimmy M. Skaggs, *The Cattle-Trailing Industry: Between Supply and Demand, 1866–1890* (Lawrence, Kans.: University Press of Kansas, 1973), p. 123.

4. James Harvey Robinson, "The Newer Ways of Historians," *American Historical Review* 35 (1930): 255.

5. Skaggs, *Cattle-Trailing Industry,* p. 73. One might observe here that quite aside from its distance from fiction, such reduction to abstract economic drama may prove to be damaging to history. To borrow a metaphor from a well-known Canadian historian, such history tends to present us with a ghostly ballet of bloodless economic categories. Frank H. Underhill, "Some Reflections on the Liberal Tradition in Canada," in *Approaches to Canadian History,* ed. Ramsay Cook, Craig Brown, and Carl Berger (Toronto: University of Toronto Press, 1967), p. 41. While history need not, of course, be bloody, it would nevertheless seem to need the sense of blood moving in the living tissues of historical persons. "After all," writes Sir John Hicks, "the way the economist develops his hypothesis is by asking the question: 'What should I do if I were in that position?' It is a question that must always be qualified by adding: 'if I were that kind of person.' . . . It is only by getting a feel of what people were like that one can begin to guess" *(A Theory of Economic History* [Oxford: Clarendon House, 1969], p. 6). G. E. Fussell has recently made a similar point in the context of farming history: "It is . . . the human

person who makes changes" ("Farming History and Its Framework," *Agricultural History* 51 [1977]: 138).

6. David Gallenson, "The Profitability of the Long Drive," *Agricultural History* 51 (1977): 751, 750, 758.

7. Rudolph Bultmann, *The Presence of Eternity: History and Eschatology* (New York: Harper & Brothers, 1957), p. 43.

8. That is, outer representations of inner thoughts and feelings. A poem is clearly an objectification; however, a boot may represent nothing more than acceptance of peer practice and available product.

9. Marc Bloch, *The Historian's Craft*, intro. Joseph R. Strayer, trans. Peter Putnam (New York: Vintage Books, 1953), p. 151.

10. Wayne Gard, *The Chisholm Trail* (Norman: University of Oklahoma Press, 1954), p. 139.

11. Philip Ashton Rollins, *The Cowboy* (1922; reprint ed., New York: Ballantine Books, 1973), p. 251.

12. George C. Duffield, "Driving Cattle from Texas to Iowa, 1866," *Annals of Iowa* 14 (1924): 252.

13. "I must say," noted one trail driver, "that the trail drives appear now more like a dream than a reality" *(The Trail Drivers of Texas*, ed. by J. Marvin Hunter [Nashville, Tenn.: Cokesbury Press, 1925], p. 218).

14. Ibid., p. 218.

15. Ibid., p. 768.

16. Ibid., p. 665.

17. Ibid., p. 825. See also: "A kind and all-wise Providence guarded us through all the dangers and hardships of pioneer life and will be with us to the end" (p. 766).

18. E. C. Abbott ("Teddy Blue") and Helena Huntington Smith, *We Pointed Them North: Recollections of a Cowpuncher* (Norman: University of Oklahoma Press, 1954), p. 29.

19. This study, while it is somewhat philosophical, is not finally an essay in the philosophy of history. The continuing problems in historical epistemology are not here solved once and for all. It seems reasonable to suppose that as historians we start with models of man and that however enduring these models may seem to be they are not transcendental. They have their origin and modification in history.

20. In the practical act of writing history, the historian may take certain facts as given. They lie before him hard and certain; the risks of perceptual distortion seem minimal. Technically, however, historical facts are not given. A contemporary position is given by Murray G. Murphey, summarized here by Traian Stoianovich in *French Historical Method: The Annales Paradigm* (Ithaca: Cornell University Press, 1976), p. 36: "Historical facts are thus not given. They are rather postulates designed to explain the characteristics of contemporary data relating to the past or future."

21. The historian's configurations may indeed be called fictions. There remains, however, at least a methodological difference between the fictions of the historian and the fictions of the novelist.

22. This model of the historian may itself be open to argument. Does the historian approach his task with a tightly disciplined set of attitudes and skills, remaining firmly himself no matter how far he ventures in time and historical space? Or is his historian's self profoundly altered by his journey into the past? See p. 173, note 27. Is it possible that only as he opens himself, and relaxes his discipline that he understands?

23. Robert Jay Lifton, "On Psychohistory," *Explorations in Psychohistory: The Wellfleet Papers,* ed. by Robert Jay Lifton and Eric Olsen (New York: Simon and Schuster, 1974), p. 32. "Recognizing that subjective distortion can render the advantage [of beginning from concrete information that is the product of his own direct perception] a mixed one, so can it be said that exaggerated concerns with detached objectivity have too often caused us to undervalue what can be learned of history from our direct perceptions."

24. Abbott and Smith, *We Pointed them North,* p. 38.

25. J. Frank Dobie, *The Longhorns* (Boston: Little, Brown, 1941), p. 130.

26. Charles M. Russell, "Longrope's Last Guard," in Dobie, *The Longhorns,* p. 138.

27. For an account of the writing of the play, see Vance Palmer, *Louis Esson and the Australian Theatre* (Melbourne: University of Melbourne Press, 1948), pp. 16–19.

28. Louis Esson, "The Drovers," in *Six One-Act Plays* (Sydney: Mulga Press, 1944), p. 7.

29. Ibid., p. 15.

30. Ibid.

31. W. Dilthey, *Selected Writings,* ed., trans., and intro. H. P. Rickman (Cambridge: At the University Press, 1976), p. 84.

Theory of the Cowboy Novel

1. William W. Savage, Jr., *Cowboy Life: Reconstructing an American Myth* (Norman: University of Oklahoma Press, 1975), p. 13.

2. We too easily suppose that some subjects are worthwhile to one writer but valueless to another. Thus we tend to conclude that a cowboy could be interesting to Wister while his friend Henry James needed another kind of subject, say an aristocratic American living in Europe. We need to be reminded of James's interest in what Wister was writing: his going over *Red Man and White* with Wister, "minutely pointing out many things"; a letter to Wister admiring Wister's subject, in this instance the Virginian himself. *The Virginian* rewritten by James would not be as radically different a novel as some readers might suppose. Devout westerners will, of course, bridle at the thought of James's presuming to know how to write a western novel. Douglas Branch took a fierce western pride in the fact that "no Henry James had ever spent a night bluepenciling a manuscript of . . . [Andy Adams]" *(The Cowboy and His Interpreters* [1926; reprint ed., New York: Cooper Square Publishers, 1961], p.

255. For further discussion of Wister and James, see "The Cowboy with a Sense of the Past" in this series. Whatever the need of the West for cultural independence, whatever the arrogance of eastern literary critics, the stubborn rejection of literary ways Eastern or European is not only silly, it is artistically impoverishing. The writer, whether writing about cowboys or captains of whalers, needs a world of literature from which to learn his own appropriate way.

3. Savage, *Cowboy Life*, pp. 12–13.

4. I should like to hold my position on high ground here. If the reader supposes that a cowboy novel cannot under any circumstances be a form of imaginative art, he had better turn aside from the critical trail I am attempting to mark.

5. In what might be called the mythology of cowboy criticism, one can conjure up a scene in which a real "working" cowboy picks up a cowboy dime novel, reads a bit, then throws it down, exclaiming, "Hell, that isn't the way it is at all." I say *mythology* here believing that most of the throwing down has occurred in the minds of would-be critics who need this act to dramatize the special horse sense of their "literary" arguments. Most of the cowboys I know enjoy popular westerns. Of course, neither their enjoyment nor the supposed throwing down constitutes serious literary criticism.

6. Quite aside from the immense popularity of *The Virginian* and its influence on later westerns (an influence in my judgment exaggerated by western scholars), it was a serious and sophisticated novel. Taken with *Lin McLean,* published four years earlier in 1898, it made Wister the first major novelist of the American cowboy. One should remember, however, that Wister was not heroically alone in his interest in the cowboy. In that same year (1902) appeared Henry Wallace Phillips's *Red Saunders* and Alfred Henry Lewis's *Wolfville Days,* works to be taken with perhaps a different degree of seriousness. Also that year Eugene Manlove Rhodes made a number of appearances in *Out West Magazine.* Finally one should add that Andy Adams's *The Log of a Cowboy* was to come out the following year.

7. Nye does not of course mean all that I mean by *invent.*

8. Critics of a similar point of view have been predicting the end of the literary cowboy ever since. One would think after three-quarters of a century that they would have become discouraged enough to stop making the same prediction or, better still, to start wondering why the cowboy that ought to go away keeps on riding in the literary imagination. Sophisticated movie pundits have the same trouble. From his tower of wisdom in the *New York Magazine,* John Simon just a few years ago announced in oracular tones: "The western is in trouble." Quoted in the *Salt Lake Tribune,* 27 September 1976.

9. Arthur Chapman, "The New West and the Old Fiction," *Independent* 54 (1902): 100.

10. Technically no observed and known cowboy is wholly out there.

The very act of perception, as well as conception, brings him at least partially in from the world.

11. Philip Ashton Rollins, *The Cowboy* (1922; reprint ed., New York: Ballantine Books, 1973), p. xiii.

12. Terms here from preface to Philip Ashton Rollins, *Jinglebob* (New York: Grosset & Dunlap, 1927), p. ix.

13. Ibid.

14. Rollins, *The Cowboy,* pp. 38, 43.

15. Rollins wrote in the preface to *Jinglebob:* "May the synthetic puncher forever continue!" Rollins obviously liked entertainment, even the melodramatic kind.

16. The text cited here is "The Cowboy: His Cause and Cure," as Rhodes originally and whimsically titled his article. Reprinted in *The Sunny Slopes of Long Ago,* ed. Wilson Hudson and Allen Maxwell (Dallas: Southern Methodist University Press, 1966), passages cited, pp. 26, 31.

17. Adams's biographer, Wilson Hudson, observes: "In no novel of Andy's is the final solution reached by means of gunfire." *(Andy Adams: His Life and Writings* [Dallas: Southern Methodist University Press, 1964], p. 219). This statement is, however, somewhat misleading. In *The Log of a Cowboy,* the solution of the Rebel's problem may not be the solution of the novel's central problem, but his use of gunfire is nevertheless dramatically important. See "The Cowboy with a Sense of the Past" in this series.

18. An old ranchhand I once interviewed reported spending most of his time during the summer months haying (cutting, raking, hauling), most of his time in the winter feeding the hay to cattle. Here is a subject to satisfy many critics: a cowboy who works and who is closely involved with cows. The historian of the cattle trade may find this actuality significant, but the novelist will probably have to look elsewhere, to the West of his imagination.

19. E. C. Abbott ("Teddy Blue") and Helena Huntington Smith, *We Pointed Them North: Recollections of a Cowpuncher* (1939; reprint ed., Norman: University of Oklahoma Press, 1954), p. 214.

20. There are, of course, what seem to be special exceptions to this observation. In a short story like Galsworthy's "Quality," the handicrafting of fine shoes is the thematic representation of a man's commitment to quality. In a novel like Anderson's *Dark Laughter,* the painting of buggy wheels shows a man's discovery of the satisfactions in manual expression. But in neither of these examples is the work detailed for its own sake. In the so-called proletarian novel, much attention may be paid to work, for it is in oppressive work that the class is exploited. Still what is important here is not that a man works but that he is oppressed by that work or alienated from a share in the worth of the product. For a discussion of the cowboy as proletarian, see "The Left Side of the American Ranges: A Marxist View of the Cowboy," following in this series of studies.

21. Branch's main discussion of Wister can be found on pp. 192–200 in his *Cowboy and His Interpreters.*

22. Ibid., pp. 200–9.
23. Ibid., pp. 254–65.
24. But as I hope this series of studies makes clear, they have only a limited appropriateness for the historian.
25. Harry Sinclair Drago, in his introduction to the 1961 reprinting of Branch's book, gives Branch credit for first pointing this out. See p. iv. Drago's emphasis would be no greater if he had discovered that Branch had discovered there are no whales in *Moby Dick*.
26. For a comic treatment of this position, see my "The Love Song of Barney Tullus," *The Possible Sack* 3 (November 1971): 1–10.
27. *Cows* used here in the western generic sense. Old Sancho is, of course, all steer. In a radical revision of his critical estimate of Hough's *North of 36*, Dobie praised Old Alamo, the lead steer in the trail herd, as the best character in the book.
28. But rarely if ever the important work of castration. An interesting study could be made of the evasion of this bit of authentic cowboy work.
29. Some working skills of this kind have been removed from their working context and made rodeo sports. The rodeo novel, of course, has almost nothing to do with what the older critics called the "real" range.
30. The horse may be another matter. A writer noted a few years ago, "As every movie script writer knows the popular cowboy image thrives lustily in total absence of the cow, but would fall flat without the horse" (Lloyd J. Linford, "Hoofprints Across the Early West," *Utah Farmer-Stockman* 95 [7 August, 1975]: 7). From the point of view of authenticity in work situations, the horse perhaps has no more essential rightness then does the cow. It remains true, nevertheless, that the horse has additional functions. The horse is in important ways an extension of the cowboy's personality, giving him mobility, an intensified capacity for action, even the aura of myth.
31. A cow has been attacked by roundworms. A cowboy armed with a medigun loaded with thiabendazole paste must shoot her in an unmentionable part of her anatomy. This is what I would call a cowboy problem. In a carefully imagined dramatic situation, a cowboy armed with a six-gun loaded with cartridges must kill or be killed. This is what I would call a human problem.
32. In a number of unpublished works, Adams did try to fit a woman into his cowboy world. The titular heroine of *Tom* was one earnest try, but she is a novelistic failure. Adams never seemed to understand how he needed to go about his literary task. He attached to his character all of the appropriate trappings, as if he were dressing her for the stage. Tom likes cows and sweaty horses. She can roll cigarettes although she does not smoke. Cowboy profanity is music to her ears. But all of this does not make a character. None of it provides a conception of a person who can hold these trappings in a living coherence.
33. No reader should suppose that I prefer schoolrooms to trail

herds. The problem is to define the character as fully as possible. There are, I suppose, some advantages to the schoolroom since some important human responses are perhaps more likely there. But in my judgment a good novelist can solve his problem on the trail drive too. The old notion that historically there were few women along on the drive is novelistically beside the point.

34. Branch, *Cowboy and His Interpreters*, p. 268.

35. But at most one of his functions. Through his researches, he in a sense makes the past available; he gathers within some usable limits the evidence by which a particular time, event, or person may be known. In effect, he says to other historians, go back and take a look for yourselves.

36. The historian may aspire to explain as many particulars as possible by the simplest possible principle. If he can tidy up the existential messiness of a decade or a century by discovering the inevitable progress of freedom or the acceleration of changes in historical energies, he may seem to have brought clarity, the same sort of clarity that came in physics with Newton's law. Yet there may be a paradox here. It may be that the clearer history becomes, the less historical it becomes. See Herbert Butterfield, *The Whig Interpretation of History* (London: G. Bell and Sons, 1963), pp. 24–26.

37. Clarity, of course, comes in a variety of kinds. There is the visual clarity of a pageant or a travel film. *The Log of a Cowboy* has something of this. There is the logical clarity of a good how-to-do-it book, say a work entitled *How to Drive Five Thousand Cows from Texas to Kansas. The Log* has this clarity too. Scholars and professors—particularly the latter— presume to make clear for their readers or students such complexities as the philosophy of Kierkegaard or the novels of Faulkner. A horde of clarifiers armed with maps, charts, etc. have "clarified" *The Sound and the Fury*—and left it the dead skeleton of the novel it once was.

38. Why not carry the thesis to a final absurdity by arguing that he ought to write his novels on the clean side of an old pair of chaps, using a piece of charcoal taken from a branding fire?

39. J. B. Frantz and J. E. Choate, *The American Cowboy: The Myth and the Reality* (1955; reprint ed., London: Thames and Hudson, 1956), pp. 162, 163, 169.

40. One unfortunate feature, among others, of *The American Cowboy* is the curious diction and imagery which sometimes seems to distort critical perception. Good stories do not capture cowboys; on the contrary, they free them. Capturing, like preserving, is all right for scientific specimens, say black flies, rattlesnakes, and carrion beetles. Rhodes, the writers say, wrote "from atop a literary mesa" while Zane Grey wrote from a "valley wasteland." I can think of no novel by Grey which sees the cowboy from the circumstances of a wasteland. At one point, the critics note that "if the cowboy is accepted as a major folk hero of the American people, then Adams's chronicle [*The Log*] deserves to stand as a cornerstone of that heroic erection." At an earlier point, they note that range

fiction after 1915 had "a flirtation with Freud." Have the critics also flirted? Perhaps they need to.

41. Frantz and Choate, *American Cowboy*, pp. 146, 149, 159, 160, 154, 155. As an instance of action well handled, I would suggest the death of Anderson in the shoot-out with Sheriff Watson. "The whole body of Ike Anderson, shot low through the trunk, as was the sheriff's invariable custom, melted down and sank into a sitting posture, leaning against the edge of the stoop." *Melted down* seems to me accurate and vivid; the reader sees. If a thousand later writers have made a cliché out of this action, one can hardly blame Hough writing in 1900.

42. Ibid., p. 164.

43. Ibid., pp. 165, 166. How important is understanding here? Does the novelist use them because they are accepted, or does he use them because they illuminate, bring self-knowledge to the reader?

44. Ibid., p. 14. When the historian begins talking about capturing an essence, he stirs up more epistemological dust than the craft of history can easily handle. Some scholars will begin running for the corral fence.

45. Another instance of the writers' seemingly naïve notions about the art of fiction. Archetypal myths, if they are to have imaginative vitality, must be organic to the whole central vision of the novel. They cannot be added, braided into the larger story, as one might braid a red string into a hackamore rope.

46. But they do point to a large body of critical theory which ought to be considered for its possible relationship to mythic features of the cowboy novel. With some exceptions, western critics have kept their safe distance from works like Northrop Frye's *The Anatomy of Criticism.*

47. W. H. Hutchinson, Introduction to *The Rhodes Reader* (Norman: University of Oklahoma Press, 1957), p. xx, note.

48. Elsewhere I have discussed DeVoto's criticism at some length under the general title "The Dogmas of DeVoto." See *The Possible Sack* 2 (July 1971): 1–7; (August 1971): 6–8; 3 (November 1971): 1–7; (February 1972): 1–4; (March 1972): 14–18.

49. Bernard DeVoto, "Phaethon on Gunsmoke Trail," *Harper's* 209 (December 1954): 10–11, 14, 16.

50. The narrow dogmatism of this judgment is almost incredible. Wister, in my opinion a far better artist, failed of course in historical authenticity. See my discussion of DeVoto on Wister, *The Possible Sack*, 3 (November 1971): 1–7.

51. "The whole archeology of the cattle kingdom can be recovered from Rhodes' books" (Bernard DeVoto, "The Novelist of the Cattle Kingdom," Introduction to May Davison Rhodes, *The Hired Man on Horseback* [Boston: Houghton Mifflin, 1938], p. xxvii).

52. Ibid., p. xxvi.

53. Ibid., pp. xxviii, xxix.

54. The trouble with history is that we really never know what we may find. Suppose we turn up a cowboy with what seems a compulsion to

take baths. See J. Evetts Haley, ed., James G. Bell, "A Log of the Texas-California Cattle Trail, 1854," *Southwestern Historical Quarterly* 35 (1932): 208–37, 290–316.

55. Novelists will seem to disagree at this point. "The term 'creation of character' (or characters)," said Elizabeth Bowen, "is misleading. Characters pre-exist. They are *found*. They reveal themselves to the novelist's preception—as might fellow-travellers seated opposite one in a very dimly-lit railway carriage" ("Notes on Writing a Novel," *Pictures and Conversations* [New York: Alfred A. Knopf, 1975], p. 172). Finding in this sense is, nevertheless, different from historical discovery. It involves, one supposes, a good bit more *creative* perception than goes into the historical reconstruction of a historical personality.

56. Or if a distortion, a distortion intended to enhance his reality or to be truer to our ways of perceiving his reality. The distortions common to modernism have so far had little impact on the cowboy novel.

57. Yet another novelist of considerable imaginative gift has seen "the day of the cowboy" "now well into its evening." "Commitment to the myth [of the cowboy]," writes Larry McMurtry, "carries with it a terrible emotional price—very often the cowboy becomes a victim of his own ritual" (*In a Narrow Grave: Essays on Texas* [New York: Simon and Schuster, 1971], p. 148). One accepts this note as a valid piece of social or cultural observation, but what it augers for the literary cowboy is another matter. If the novelist must accept what social change offers him, he has at least the cowboy in his evening, a victim of his own ritual. This seems a predicament fraught with interesting novelistic possibilities. But if the novelist makes not only his fictive cowboys but also the worlds in which they ride, he creates other possibilities. Indeed, on this artistic frontier, he is limited only by the power of his imagination.

58. And little on the art of history.

The Left Side of the American Ranges

1. Edward Aveling, *An American Journey* (New York: John W. Lovell Co., 1887), p. 155.

2. Edward and Eleanor Marx Aveling, *The Working-Class Movement in America* (1891; reprint ed., New York: Arno & The New York Times, 1969), p. 16.

3. "There is one aspect under which this class of men seem little known to their fellow-countrymen, and are almost wholly unknown to other people's [*sic*],—that is, in their capacity as proletarians" (ibid., p. 154).

4. So far as I know, this pamphlet is not extant.

5. Edward and Eleanor Aveling, *Working–Class Movement*, pp. 158, 159.

6. Ibid., p. 18.

7. Edward Aveling, *An American Journey*, pp. 146–47.

8. Henry Irving, the English actor.
9. Edward Aveling, *An American Journey*, p. 154.
10. V. F. Calverton, *The Liberation of American Literature* (New York: Charles Scribner's, 1932), p. xi.
11. Ibid., pp. 435, 438, note p. 438.
12. Quoted by H. M. Kallen, Introduction to Frank Harris, *My Reminiscences as a Cowboy* (New York: Charles Boni, 1930), p. 10.
13. For a discussion of Gropper as a cartoonist and painter, see my "American Art on the Left, 1910–1950," *Western Humanities Review* 8 (1950): 323–46.
14. Walt Whitman, *The Complete Poetry and Prose of Walt Whitman*, 2 vols. (New York: Pellegrini & Cudahy, 1948), 2:148.
15. Joseph Nimmo, Jr., "The American Cow-boy," *Harper's* 73 (1886): 880.
16. See "Classics of the Cattle Trade: A New Look at Some Old Standards."
17. Peter F. Drucker, *The Future of Industrial Man* (1942; reprint ed., New York: Mentor Books, 1965), pp. 46–47.
18. See "The Fence Line between Cowboy History and Cowboy Fiction: Frontier in Dispute or Meeting Ground of Human Understanding?"
19. Marvin Farber, "Descriptive Philosophy and the Nature of Human Existence," in *Philosophic Thought in France and the United States*, ed. Marvin Farber (1950; reprint ed., Albany: State University of New York Press, 1968), pp. 425–26.
20. Georg Lukács, *Realism in Our Time* (New York: Harper Torchbooks, 1971), p. 20.
21. The hero of Arthur Paterson's *A Son of the Plains* (1895) is clearly a son of Leatherstocking. This novel, in my judgment, is a good text in which to see the transmutation of the hunter-trapper hero into the cowboy hero. In revising the manuscript of *The Virginian* at the point of defining his hero, Owen Wister very carefully changed *this rough ungrammatical man in overalls* to *this handsome, ungrammatical son of the soil*. A few pages later the hero is identified as one of the sons of the sagebrush. However, while he is primitivistic in important ways, Wister's cowboy, like Cooper's Leatherstocking, has deep roots in civilization. Morally he is not really a son of the sagebrush.
22. John Clay, *My Life on the Range* (1924; reprint ed., New York: Antiquarian Press, 1961), p. 108.
23. Stewart Edward White, "On Cowboys," *The Outlook* 78 (3 September 1904): 83.
24. See "Freedom and Individualism on the Range: Ideological Images of the Cowboy and Cattleman."
25. Even most forms of existentialism, a philosophy which is sometimes radically individualistic, would insist on this. See John Macquarrie, *Existentialism* (1972; reprint ed., Pelican Books, 1973), p. 103.

26. For example, Webb, Dobie, and Haley, to name just three.

27. Robert Zeigler, "The Cowboy Strike of 1883: Its Causes and Meaning," *West Texas Historical Association Year Book* 47 (1971): 33.

28. See Edward Everett Dale's version of the working cowboy in "The Romance of the Range," *West Texas Historical Association Year Book* 5 (June 1929): 17.

29. Elmer Kelton, *The Day the Cowboys Quit* (1971; reprint ed., New York: Ace Books, n.d.), p. 21.

30. John R. Craig, *Ranching with Lords and Commons or Twenty Years on the Range* (1903; reprint ed., New York: AMS Press, 1971).

The Cowboy with a Sense of the Past

1. Owen Wister, *Members of the Family* (New York: Macmillan, 1911), pp. 8–9.

2. Letter to Wister, quoted in Carl Bode, "Henry James and Owen Wister," *American Literature* 26 (1954): 251–52.

3. In the preface to *Members of the Family,* Wister speaks of returning with a "tenderfoot's enthusiasm" for the artistic use of the West and besieging "the ears of our great painter and our great novelist." He adds, however, that "both painter and novelist were wiser than to leave what they knew to be their own for unknown fields." In a postscript to a letter to Wister, Theodore Roosevelt exclaimed, "Heavens! Think of you daring to wish Henry James to write of the West!" ("To Owen Wister," 23 May 1911, *Letters of Theodore Roosevelt,* ed. Elting E. Morison, 8 vols. [Cambridge, Mass.: Harvard University Press, 1954], 7:269). The editor adds a comment from Wister: "No wonder he said Heavens! In the eighties, I had begged Henry James to drop Europe and do this. My preface mentioned it, and caused Roosevelt's postscript."

4. Sergio Perosa, "The Sense and Nightmare of the Past," *Henry James and the Experimental Novel* (Charlottesville: University Press of Virginia, 1978), pp. 131–60.

5. Henry James, *The Sense of the Past* (New York: Scribner's, 1917), pp. 53–54.

6. Ibid., pp. 28–29.

7. The concept of the cowboy as antitype follows an analysis by Hayden White in "The Forms of Wildness: Archaeology of an Idea," in *Tropics of Discourse: Essays in Cultural Criticism* (Baltimore: Johns Hopkins University Press, 1978), pp. 150–82.

8. Critically considered the innocence might, of course, be more apparent than real. The cowboy might bring all sorts of experience with him when he entered the range—he might even be an outlaw. The point is that he was accepted for what he was and could be, not for what he had been. He was in effect defining himself as cowboy from scratch. If this is not innocence, it at least seems to open up an almost limitless range of human possibility.

9. The following account of Paul Priest derives closely from Adams's text, *The Log of a Cowboy: A Narrative of the Old Trail Days* (1903; reprint ed., Lincoln: University of Nebraska Press, 1964). I have chosen to follow Adams himself in calling the work a novel.

10. Theodore Roosevelt, *Hunting Trips of a Ranchman: Sketches of Sport on the Northern Cattle Plains,* 2 vols. (1885; reprint ed., New York: Scribner's, 1906), 1:96. Although Roosevelt does not identify the cowboy, he was probably Captain Robins, the "grumpy old sea captain" described in a letter to Roosevelt's sister as having had "a rather diversified life, trying his hand as sailor, buffalo hunter, butcher, apothecary *(mirabile dictu),* and cowboy." Quoted in Hermann Hagedorn, *Roosevelt in the Bad Lands* (1921; reprint ed., Boston: Houghton Mifflin, 1930), p. 167. Carleton Putnam says of Robins: "He had come to the Bad Lands originally as a trapper, then had gone to work for the Langs as a cook" *(Theodore Roosevelt: The Formative Years* [New York: Scribner's, 1958], p. 471 note). Add trapping and cooking, and the variety of experiences before cowboying becomes diversified indeed.

11. "To Henry Cabot Lodge," 7 June 1886, Letter 152, *The Letters of Theodore Roosevelt,* 1:102.

12. Theodore Roosevelt, "Biological Analogies in History," in *History as Literature and Other Essays* (New York: Scribner's, 1913), p. 45.

13. Roosevelt, "History as Literature," in ibid., p. 15.

14. Roosevelt, *The Winning of the West,* 6 vols. (1889; reprint ed., New York: Scribner's, 1906), 1:1. Almost exactly the same sentence would appear in Roosevelt's Romanes Lecture for 1910, "Biological Analogies in History," *History as Literature,* p. 78.

15. Roosevelt, *Thomas Hart Benton* (1886; reprint ed., New York: Scribner's, 1906), p. 4.

16. Theodore Roosevelt, *Ranch Life in the Far West* (1888; reprint ed., Flagstaff, Ariz.: Northland Press, 1968), p. 50.

17. "We shall find that the permanent national types will more and more tend to become those in which, though intellect stands high, character stands higher" *(History as Literature,* p. 86). At the close of a review of Benjamin Kidd's *Social Evolution,* Roosevelt emphasized the same point: "In other words, character is far more important than intellect to the race as to the individual" ("Social Evolution," in *American Ideals and Other Essays* [1897; reprint ed., New York: Scribner's, 1906], p. 156).

18. Quoted in Edmund Morris, *The Rise of Theodore Roosevelt* (New York: Coward, McCann & Geoghegan, 1979), p. 292.

19. For example, he wrote from Medora: "My men here are hardworking, labouring men, who work longer hours for no greater wages than many of the strikers; but they are Americans through and through; I believe nothing would give them greater pleasure than a chance with their rifles at one of the mobs" ("To Anna Roosevelt," 15 May 1886, Letter 150, *The Letters of Theodore Roosevelt,* 1:100).

20. Morris, *Rise of Theodore Roosevelt,* p. 268.
21. At the first annual convention of the American National Live Stock Association in 1906, Gifford Pinchot presented a message from the president. In his response Springer characterized Roosevelt in this elevated way. *Proceedings of the First Annual Convention of the American National Live Stock Association* (Denver, 1906), p. 20.
22. "To Henry Cabot Lodge," 24 August 1884, Letter 125, *The Letters of Theodore Roosevelt,* 1:80.
23. Roosevelt, *Hunting Trips,* 1:17.
24. Roosevelt, *Ranch Life,* p. 78.
25. Morris, *Rise of Theodore Roosevelt,* p. 285.
26. Roosevelt, *Ranch Life,* p. 16; *Hunting Trips,* 1:23; *Ranch Life,* p. 68.
27. Roosevelt, *Hunting Trips,* 1:8; *Ranch Life,* p. 8; *The Wilderness Hunter,* 2 vols. (1893; reprint ed., New York: Scribner's, 1906), 1:116.
28. Owen Wister, "The Evolution of the Cow-Puncher," *Harper's* 91 (1895): 604, 606.
29. "It was no new type, no product of the frontier, but just the original kernel of the nut with the shell broken" (ibid., p. 610).
30. Ibid., p. 606.
31. Ibid., p. 608.
32. Ibid., p. 603.
33. Owen Wister, *The Virginian* (1902; reprint ed., Boston: Houghton Mifflin, 1968), p. 37.
34. Ibid., p. 20.
35. *Prose and Poetry of the Live Stock Industry* (1905; reprint ed., New York: Antiquarian Press, 1959), pp. 25–26.
36. James Cox, *Historical and Biographical Record of the Cattle Industry and the Cattlemen of Texas* (1895; reprint ed., New York: Antiquarian Press, 1959), p. 31.
37. J. L. Hill, *The End of the Cattle Trail* (1923; reprint ed., Austin, Texas: Pemberton Press, 1969), pp. 5–7.
38. Long Horn [Joseph G. McCoy], "Sketches, Historic and Otherwise," *The Kings and Queens of the Range* 2 (January 1898): 15.
39. Terms and distinctions are adapted here from J. H. Plumb, *The Death of the Past* (1970; reprint ed., Boston: Houghton Mifflin, 1971).

A Notice Left at the Gate Still Open

1. Fernand Braudel, *Afterthoughts on Material Civilization and Capitalism,* trans. by Patricia M. Ranum (Baltimore: Johns Hopkins University Press, 1977), p. 115.

Index

Abbott, E. C. ("Teddy Blue"): on cowboy freedom, 88–89; on cowboy death and burial, 104; on cowboy work, 116

Abstractions: use of in history, xix–xx

Adams, Andy, xii; use of Edenic landscape, 54; favored by historians, 95; praised by Rhodes, 115; *The Outlet,* 119; Taisie as fifth wheel, 120; *Tom,* 196 n. 32. See also *Log of a Cowboy*

Adams, Henry: compared with McCoy, 8; compared with Roosevelt, 33; and scientism, 71

Adams, Ramon: *The Rampaging Herd,* xi; on the cowboy in McCoy, 4; on *Prose and Poetry,* 46; on Sam Riding's *The Chisholm Trail,* xvi; on freedom in Bob Kennon's life as cowboy, 77

American National Live Stock Association: McCoy's address to, 22; sponsor of *Prose and Poetry,* 47–48; speeches to, 52

Anthropology: need for, 91; Marxist, 139

Aron, Raymond: on ideology, 191 n. 49

Atavism: Wister's use of, 159

Atherton, Lewis: *The Cattle Kings,* 78; use of McCoy as source, 80–81

Aveling, Edward: view of the cowboy as economic slave, 131–32; on Cody's Wild West show, 133

Aveling, Eleanor Marx: view of the cowboy as proletarian, 131–32

Barker, Robert M. ("The Economics of Cattle Ranching in the Southwest"), 182 n. 44

Barnes, Will C.: on cowboy freedom, 77; as historian, 179 n. 3, 187 n. 9

Beers, Henry (*Four Americans*): on Roosevelt, 39

Bennett, Emerson (*Leni Leoti*): Edenic landscape in, 178 n. 36

Bieber, Ralph P.: edition of *Historic Sketches,* xii, 1, 2

Billington, Ray Allen: on the genesis of Turner's idea of frontier individualism, 79–80

Bloch, Marc (*The Historian's Craft*): cited, 99

Bogue, Allan G. ("Social Theory and the Frontier"): quoted, 190–91 n. 48

Branch, Douglas: On Osgood's book, 63; criticism in *The Cowboy and His Interpreters,* 117–22

Braudel, Fernand: quoted, 164

Brayer, Herbert O.: on the cattleman as an individualist, 84

Brisbin, General James S. (*The Beef Bonanza*): influence of on Roosevelt, 26

Bultmann, Rudolph (*The Presence of Eternity*): quoted, 99

Bureau of Agricultural Economics: importance of in the development of economic history, 182 n. 44

Burton, Harley True ("A History of the JA Ranch"), 179 n. 3

Calverton, V. F.: on cowboys, 134

Carpenter, Will Tom (*Lucky 7*): frontier ideological freedom in, 87–88

"Cattle Kingdom" (Webb): classic of cattle trade historiography, xi, 61; economic approach in, 62; setting in, 65–66; historical symbolism and lyrical style in, 69; deterministic imagery